ECCENTRICS, HEROES, AND CUTTHROATS
OF OLD BERKELEY

A PEN AND INK IMAGE TAKEN FROM A STOCK CERTIFICATE OF THE BERKELEY DEVELOPMENT COMPANY OF THE 1890S. IT FEATURES AN IDEALIZED VIEW OF THE INTERSECTION OF SHATTUCK AND UNIVERSITY AVENUES, WITH A STEAM TRAIN APPROACHING FROM THE SOUTH ON SHATTUCK AVENUE. STREET CARS AND PEOPLE FILL UNIVERSITY AVENUE.

ECCENTRICS, HEROES, AND CUTTHROATS
OF OLD BERKELEY

RICHARD SCHWARTZ

RSB BOOKS
BERKELEY, CALIFORNIA

RSB Books
Telephone and fax: 510-524-1683
Email: richard@richardschwartz.info

Cover and text design: Lisa Elliot/Elysium
Editor: Lila LaHood
Developmental Editor: Tara Weaver
Copyeditors: Pamela Joy Edelstein and Steven Hiatt

Cover painting: Carl von Perbandt, "San Francisco Bay," ca. 1896, oil on canvas, 12 x 60. Courtesy of the California Historical Society.

ISBN-13: 978-0-9678204-2-2 (paper)
ISBN-13: 978-0-9678204-3-9 (cloth)
First printing, 2007
Printed in Canada on recycled paper.

10 9 8 7 6 5 4 3 2 1

Contents

A PEN AND INK DRAWING REPRESENTING THE UNKNOWN ARTIST'S
IMPRESSION OF A HUCHIUN OHLONE WOMAN WITNESSING THE
ARRIVAL THROUGH THE GOLDEN GATE OF THE SPANISH IN 1769
OR ADVENTURERS DURING THE GOLD RUSH OF 1848.

Human salvation lies in the hands
of the creatively maladjusted.

—Martin Luther King, Jr.

THE PIONEER TEAGUE FAMILY. PHIL TEAGUE, ON THE UPPER RIGHT WITH THE STRAW HAT, WAS A VOLUNTEER FIREMAN IN BERKELEY AND SON OF ONE OF THE EARLIEST SETTLERS, WILLIAM TEAGUE OF THE CLAREMONT AREA AND LATER WEST BERKELEY. PHIL'S WIFE, LIZZIE, IS SEATED IS FRONT OF PHIL, HOLDING THEIR FIRST-BORN, DAUGHTER CORA. LIZZIE'S SISTER, MAGGIE, IS TO THE LEFT OF PHIL AND HER HUSBAND, WILL, IS SEATED IN FRONT OF HER. THE OTHER FIGURES IN THE PHOTOGRAPH ARE NOT IDENTIFIED. IN 1879, PHIL TEAGUE'S BROTHER, WILLIAM TEAGUE, JR., CAUGHT A NINE-POUND SALMON IN CODORNICES CREEK NEAR FIFTH STREET.

TOO OFTEN HISTORY IS PRESENTED AS AN ABSTRACT FORCE OUTSIDE of human control that has happened to others sometime in the past. Humans did not shape history but were shaped by it. Worse yet, those same humans never really become people, especially people like you and me or, for that matter, anyone who you and I know. In truth, however, history is created by people very much like us. In the end (to paraphrase Tip O'Neill) all history is local. All history is personal. And all history is a story—or the undetermined sum of many stories. All modesty aside, we common sort can be pretty fascinating.

If you want proof of this simple truth, all you have to do is pick up Richard Schwartz's collection of stories on Berkeley, California, and the East Bay in the last half of the nineteenth and first quarter of the twentieth centuries. In this small book of stories on a single community, Schwartz touches all of the abstract themes that you will find in grand histories: class struggle, ethnic conflicts, economic greed, and political intrigue. To be sure, you will meet the full cast of outlandish characters that you would expect to find in Berkeley: a national-caliber humorist known locally as "the Boss Baggage Buster of Beautiful Berkeley," a lone widow washerwoman who maintained a 20-year fight against the power of both the city government and the railroad, and a hotdog maven who advertised with a sign that read, "Eat Here; Die at Home."

At the same time, however, all of these dead, historical people come dressed in clothes, wearing the faces and speaking the voices of people we will recognize. By the time Richard Schwartz is through with each portrait, we don't just know the story, we know the person. Wait, doesn't she live next door? The past, as Richard Schwartz tells it, comprises a lot of people who look, act, and sound a lot like us. For me, at least, that is comforting news.

—David Crosson
Executive Director, California Historical Society

—A gentleman (spiritualist) visited Berkeley a few days ago for the purpose of buying a homestead lot. He sighted one pointed out by that clever real estate agent, N. C. Carnall, who with much persuasiveness descanted on the grand scenery and educational advantages of Berkeley. The spiritualist was almost persuaded, but begged the favor of an hour's time in which to consult with the spirits. Mr. Carnall was almost exhausted, but being alive for a trade awaited patiently for his customer, who, when he put in an appearance, stated that the spirits did not approve of the lot. As Mr. C. was clearly under the influence of his own active spirit he quickly pointed to another lot near by. Again the customer wanted another hour to consult with the spirits, and this time with a better result, at least to Mr. Carnall, as they approved of the purchase, which was duly made. It is said that the bad spirits were in the ascendancy at the second conference, as the lot chosen is worth about $250 less than the first sighted.

BERKELEY ADVOCATE, AUGUST 13, 1881.

AN OLD-TIMER READS HIS NEWSPAPER WITH HIS WINE GLASS AT HAND. NINETEENTH-CENTURY AMERICANS OFTEN WORKED ELEVEN HOURS A DAY, AND READING THE NEWSPAPER AFTER WORK WAS FOR MANY A CHERISHED RITUAL, FREQUENTLY ACCOMPANIED BY AN ALCOHOLIC BEVERAGE.

BERKELEY'S ENDURING REPUTATION AS A HAVEN FOR ECCENTRICS— the magical, the magnificent, and the malevolent—has contributed greatly to the community's rich cultural history. Though most of today's residents and visitors are unfamiliar with Berkeley's earliest roster of offbeat characters, their legacy became part of the foundation for one of the country's most vibrant intellectual communities.

In the mid-twentieth century, Berkeley grabbed the national spotlight as a bastion of freethinkers and rabble-rousers. But the area had been long established as a home for visionaries and individualists in the 1870s and 1880s, and even as far back as the gold rush era.

Early Berkeley was a true frontier town embodying all the excitement, potential, and danger of America's Wild West. From the outset, it was a place where new ideas were tested, and where people who didn't feel quite at home in other locales seemed to find comfort and camaraderie.

Of course, most of the town's population consisted of stalwart men and women—from ranchers, road builders, and business owners to maids, saloon keepers, and farmhands—who worked hard following their careers and visions of their lives. And among them lived innovators, artists, and campaigners whose head-turning discoveries and endearing antics were preserved in local newspaper accounts. These publications also captured the more sordid events of the day. In a place where urban areas hardly encroached on endless acres, disputes over land led to sad cases of murder; early attempts to mete out justice were often inconsistent and accounts of them are often baffling. Some of the events and sentiments of that era are still quietly influencing our culture today.

A century or more ago, anyone on the street would have easily identified these famous local characters. Over the years their stories sadly faded from common memory. But any community will benefit from reexamining its forgotten social and cultural roots. To that end, I present this book about early Berkeley's eccentrics, heroes, and cutthroats as a tribute to all those who have ever dreamed here or called this place home.

—Richard Schwartz

MAN OF MYSTERY MARRIES

Thorrington Chase, detective, Government scout, astrologist, mental telepathist, violinist, ad solicitor and for a brief time U. C. student, is married. At least, it is presumed he is from the following dispatch received by the Gazette: "Neosho, Mo., Aug. 7, 10 words paid, Gazette, Berkeley, Cal.— Thorrington Chase married here today Aida Louise Snively father's ward. T. C."

The "man of mystery" left here some three months ago, and his friends were in doubt as to whether he had received a message from Mars or was simply going to do some ranch work and attend to the live stock on his father's farm at Neosho in the "Show Me" state.

Chase while here went by the name of Thorrington Clarke Qhase and frequently regaled his friends with weird tales of his adventures by land and sea and his communications even with the stars.

His first advent at the University was marked by the now famous "Crocodile" advertising which was the freakiest ever seen in the State. Many business men who know him by no other name will remember him as the "Crocodile man." He was a fine violinist and organized a class at one of the U. C. cottages.

Several months ago he left Berkeley with the announcement that he was going to South America, called by some great detective mission from the Government. It subsequently developed that he had gone to Mare Island and was in some employment in the naval department.

Chase made a number of friends here who will be pleased to know that he has married and hope he will settle down and cut out the mythical and mysterious.

BERKELEY DAILY GAZETTE, AUGUST 8, 1905.

A PHOTO BELIEVED TO BE OF THE DUNN HOUSE AT THE BASE OF THE BERKELEY HILLS; 1882 WAS A YEAR WHEN A HEAVY SNOWFALL STRUCK BERKELEY AND THIS IS QUITE POSSIBLY A PHOTO TAKEN IN THE AFTERMATH OF THAT STORM.

1

MARTIN MURREY DUNN
AND DAVE THE FIRE HORSE

MARTIN MURREY DUNN BECAME A SAILOR AT THE AGE OF EIGHTEEN and within a few years had seen much more of the world than most men. Many of his fellow sailors immediately turned their pay into liquid refreshment, but Martin saved his money and made plans. In 1851, when he was in his mid twenties, Martin emigrated from Kilkenny, Ireland, to New York, and two years later set out for California. Upon landing in San Francisco, he met the lovely Miss Matilda Hampston, herself fresh from Ireland. When she saw the handsome and responsible young sailor with the kind face, she could not hold back a smile; this captured Martin's attention. Her familiar lilting voice, bright face, and loving glances drew the young sailor to her. Finding each other comfortably compatible, the two soon married. They didn't want to start a family in a crowded place like San Francisco and, seeing the possibilities for a country home and a peaceful life across the bay, Martin and Matilda made their crossing in the fall of 1856.

The Dunns first resided in the little town of Oakland for about three years and then purchased a remote place called the Claremont Ranch. When they arrived near the mouth of the quiet canyon below the grass-covered Berkeley hills, there were only a handful of settlers—every one a recent immigrant—living among five ranches. These East Bay pioneers raised cattle and horses, farmed barley and oats, and planted sprawling orchards. From the quiet remoteness of these open hillsides and bountiful orchards, the ranchers would look back at the smoky, crowded city of San Francisco.

The population was sparse, but plans were already under way to build the campus of the University of California at Berkeley. In 1866, the famous landscape architect Frederick Law Olmsted wrote about the local landscape in a report pertaining to the layout of the future university grounds: "The vicinity is nevertheless as yet not merely in a rural but a completely rustic and almost uninhabited condition, two small families of farmers only having established homes within a mile of

AN EAST BAY FIREMAN AND FIRE HORSES AT THE READY WITH A HOSE RIG. NOTE THE MUDFLAPS ON THE BOTTOM OF THE RIG, LANTERNS ON EACH SIDE FOR NIGHT FIRES, THE METAL-RIMMED WOODEN WHEELS FOR DURABILITY, AND THE HOSE REEL IN THE REAR OF THE RIG AS WELL AS ON THE SIDES.

Dunn's property as noted in 1878. His house sat in the area which is today the southeast corner of Tunnel Road and Domingo Avenue, right below the Claremont Hotel.

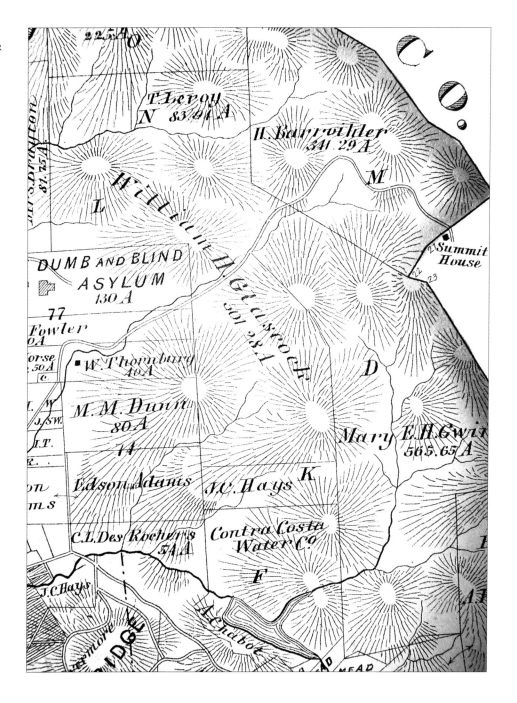

it."[1] The Dunn family, which is included in this report, had settled there ten years earlier when it was truly an isolated region where grizzly bears foraged in berry patches and mountain lions called to each other in the darkness with human-like voices.

Dunn purchased his 160-acre hillside tract on March 23, 1859, from Dr. L. A. Birdsall, a physician who had just purchased it himself in November of the previous year from a banker who speculated in land. The banker A. L. Pioche (who later became a UC Berkeley regent) had acquired the land from the group of investors who had bought the land of Domingo Peralta, son of Luis Maria Peralta, the original Spanish land grantee of 1821.[2] Dunn acquired land that today is bounded by Russell Street and Domingo Avenue and stretching east to the ridge of the hills. The southern boundary of the ranch would conform to the current southern boundary of the city of Berkeley. Dunn's house was situated just southwest of the current Claremont Hotel, which was built in 1912 on land that was also part of Dunn's holdings. Dunn's house would be found at today's southeast corner of

Domingo Avenue and Tunnel Road. The 1860 Census records show that Dunn,
a thirty-three-year-old farmer with a wife and two children, lived near Vicente
Peralta, Domingo's brother. Vicente's house and chapel were located at what is
now the northeast corner of Fifty-fifth Street and Telegraph Avenue in Oakland.
Dunn decided to raise cattle, since the sloping land on much of the property was
not conducive to farming. Dunn did farm some cereal crops on the better sections
of his land and found more success in agriculture than most of his neighbors.

Dunn also became a leading expert at raising a certain type of horse—the
offspring of Percheron workhorses bred with racing stallions. The resulting breed
was stocky, intelligent, and long-winded. By 1863, Dunn had started breeding the
horses for use by the early fire departments of nearby cities such as San Francisco
and Oakland. The fire departments typically bought unbroken colts between two
and four years of age from California ranches. The practice began with the use of
steam boiler wagons, which were much heavier than earlier equipment that the
men could pull on their own. These horse-drawn boilers gave the firemen water
under pressure, which meant that they could aim their hoses up into burning

buildings. By 1866, every fire station in San Francisco had been altered to accommodate horses. At their peak, many thousands of fire horses worked in the wood-built towns and cities that were sprouting around the Bay Area—and which were continually catching fire.

By the end of the 1860s, a great many of the local fire departments like San Francisco and Oakland came to Dunn for their station horses. Dunn's reputation as a breeder had spread far. The best breeders could train a horse to want to cooperate with a man's commands, which worked far better than trying to dominate the sensitive and intelligent animals. Dunn put a lot of time into training each horse, learning every nuance of each animal's personality.

City dwellers marveled at the thrilling sight of three huge horses running at full gallop to a fire with a 10,000-pound boiler careening behind them. The horses' dedication and intuition were inspiring. And these horses couldn't be fooled. They knew the difference between a fire drill and the real thing and would only come to their feet when they heard the official alarm. Photographs and stories from that era depict the close relationship between man and horse, working

AN OAKLAND FIREHOUSE TENDING ITS HORSES. NOTE THE HARNESS SYSTEM IN PLACE FROM THE CORNERS OF THE ROOM. THE SYSTEM WAS INVENTED BY A SAN FRANCISCO FIREMAN.

together in the vital job of fire fighting in a world of timber towns and cities.

The fire departments thoroughly tested new horse recruits before they could be approved to become working fire horses.[3] If a horse passed the veterinary exam and showed an ability to haul a heavy boiler up a hill with two experienced horses, its next challenge was gradual acclimation to the sounds of the fire—station-bells, stall gates slamming open, hooves on wooden floors, and fire rigs rumbling across the planks. The horses were further subjected to shouting followed by long periods of silence.

After the trial period, a horse would enter a serious training program. First, the horse's bit would be clipped to the stall while the stall doors were swung open repeatedly. Then, the horse's bit was released. When the doors sprang open again, a fireman whacked the horse's rear with a shingle and the horse typically bolted out of the stall. This was repeated until the horse ran out spontaneously whenever the stall doors swung open. Once out of the stall, the horse was guided between the raised poles of the fire rig. A device invented by San Francisco fireman Ed O'Sullivan in 1875 enabled a harness to be lowered from the four corners of the ceiling and clipped around the horse's neck automatically. This exercise was repeated until the horse no longer needed to be led through the steps; instead, the sounds of the fire bell and the stall gates opening triggered a dash to the harness station.

The drill was repeated alongside other experienced horses, who would nudge the newcomer into place with their shoulders or heads. The stalls of all three horses now opened simultaneously and they began working as a team.

The harnesses were cleaned daily with castile soap and water; sometimes they were treated with oil as well. The scent of the soap combined with the smell of horses, hay, lubricating grease, and kerosene lanterns was the signature smell of a firehouse.

The bonds between the firemen and their horses were strong, and the men enjoyed sharing their stories about the horses. One horse would open his stall and sneak up on the night watchman every time the watchman fell asleep in his chair. The horse would silently cross the wooden floor and rub its nose all over the watchman, waking the embarrassed fireman.[4] Another horse could not stand to be out of sight of its assigned fireman, and one night when the men were playing cards upstairs, the horse opened the stable door with its mouth, walked up the steps, and neighed loudly. The men had to remove a window and lower the horse to street level by ropes and harness the next day.[5]

While many of the stories are humorous, others are stunning examples of equine devotion and discipline. Once, the driver of a San Francisco Fire Department boiler rig on the way to a fire noticed a person in the road just as he swung around a corner at full speed. In a very long second, the driver realized he must drive his horses hard right—through a large plate glass window—to avoid slamming into the pedestrian. The horses did their job, smashing right through the large window, one of them severing an artery. A doctor who happened to be at the scene stitched up the horse's wounds and saved its life.[6]

Perhaps the most touching story of loyalty is that of Charlie, a carriage horse that belonged to a San Francisco fire chief.[7] Charlie, said to be the fastest carriage horse ever to wear a harness, was retired about eleven years before the chief. On the chief's retirement, a ceremony and a surprise were planned in his honor. The firemen found old Charlie. Charlie was an ungroomed mess and much time was spent brushing and cleaning him to the old firehouse standards. The firemen had intended to surprise the chief with his favorite horse, whom the chief had not seen in all those eleven years. Charlie would pull the chief on his last tour. The chief was brought to the appointed location and his buggy was prepared, shafts up and harness ready. A gong was sounded, and old Charlie had not forgotten his

duties. He sprang right into the shafts and the ready firemen clipped the harness
and looked at their chief, who was to climb in and drive one last round. But the
chief was totally overcome by the depth of his feelings and the surprise of it all.
He could do nothing but lurch forward to Charlie, wrap his arms around the big
horse, and bury his head in Charlie's neck. Tears streamed down the chief's face
and fell noticeably onto the floor. The chief remained locked in this embrace for
quite some time. No one moved or intruded on this most personal and universal
fireman's moment.

When a fire horse became too old to perform the most strenuous firehouse
duties, he was first moved to a station where calls were less frequent. It seemed to
the firemen that the horses wanted to serve for as long as they possibly could. But
at some point, the sad reality was that the horses had to retire. Most were sold to
perform menial jobs. These magnificently trained horses actually fetched less at
auction in retirement than horses that had never been in the fire department
because they had an unfortunate tendency to run away from their new jobs to
help fight fires, even if they were hauling a milk wagon or a wagon filled with
hay or sausage.

In Berkeley, horses retired from the fire department were sent to work
pulling the wagons of the street department. When the noble animals grew too
old to perform that task, they were simply sold at auction to the highest bidder.

Mary Dunn, the last living daughter of Martin and Matilda, reminisced in the 1950s about her father, who by then had been dead for almost fifty years. She told of one horse named Dave who was born on their ranch and trained by her father before being sold to the San Francisco Fire Department.[8] Dave served San Francisco for many years, running up and down the hills at breakneck speed. When he had reached a ripe old age, Dave was retired and sold to a Sacramento rancher. An express coach was hired to transport him from San Francisco to Sacramento, and Dave was tied to the back of the rig. Dave trotted along behind the coach until it crossed the bay, probably by an early morning ferry, and began heading up to The Narrowlands (later known as Thornburg Canyon for the man who built a house where the Claremont Hotel now stands; today the area is called Claremont Canyon). The coach turned toward Fish Ranch Road at the top of the canyon, the usual route to Sacramento. When the coach passed the Dunn Ranch right before entering the canyon, Dave reared up snorting and neighing and threw a fit until he broke loose. The driver of the stage couldn't wait. "The driver chewed curses into his chaw of tobacco, then drove on."[9]

A few minutes later, the Dunn family heard neighing outside their house. Coming out to investigate, Martin Dunn recognized the old boy and began

TOP: THE OLD STEEP AND DANGEROUS ROAD UP CLAREMONT CANYON, KNOWN VARIOUSLY AS THE NARROWLANDS AND, LATER, THORNBURG CANYON, IN ITS EARLY DAYS IN THE SECOND HALF OF THE NINE-TEENTH CENTURY. THE ROAD SPROUTED NEXT TO THE TELEGRAPH LINE, WHICH WAS STRUNG ON POLES UP THE CANYON IN 1858. THE LINES REACHED FROM OAKLAND TO WASHINGTON, D.C. TO CONNECT MANY WESTERN CITIES TO THE NATION'S CAPITAL. SETTLERS COULD BE DRAWN EASTWARD MORE EASILY BECAUSE OF THIS NEW ROAD. PIONEERS WOULD BUILD RANCHES BY THE ROAD IN CONTRA COSTA COUNTY SO AS TO BE ABLE TO TRANSPORT THEIR CROPS. THE ROAD PASSED RIGHT BY DUNN'S RANCH, WHICH SAT AT THE MOUTH OF THE CANYON.

BOTTOM: TWO MEN STAND BY THE OLD ROAD UP CLAREMONT CANYON WITH THE CREEK SHOULDERING THE DIRT ROAD.

stroking his mane as Dave nuzzled his "father" with his head. Dunn was moved by the horse's memory and sense of loyalty, and when he figured out what must have happened, he contacted the Sacramento rancher and offered to buy back old Dave, who spent the rest of his life in the Berkeley pastures of his youth.

Martin continued to maintain his ranch until 1890, when he moved his brood to 536 Twenty-fourth Street in Oakland. He had invested in real estate in Oakland as early as 1878, thinking it would evolve into a big city, and had done quite well. Dunn sold half of his ranch—the Claremont area property—in the 1870s for $100,000, fifty times what he paid for it. He improved the remaining portion, adding buildings and turning it into a dairy ranch.

Because of his deep belief in education for all, Dunn served as a school trustee and made sure his children understood the value of education. Martin Murrey Dunn passed away in 1904 after watching the century change and seeing dirigibles in the skies above the bay and motor cars occasionally rumbling down the streets of Berkeley. His three daughters became teachers and his four sons doctors and dentists. After his death, his wife, Matilda Dunn, moved to 380 Bellevue Street in Oakland.

It seems fitting to imagine Martin Murrey Dunn and Dave the fire horse in an ethereal pasture rubbing faces in celebration of their good lives lived in the peaceful and magical land of southeast Berkeley.

BERKELEY'S LAST FIRE HORSE

The last San Francisco fire horse left its station on December 31, 1921. The last Berkeley fire horse was retired from Station No. 2 of the Berkeley Fire Department on May 30, 1914. That horse, Kitty Kelly, was a large coal-black "American fire horse" with a white diamond on her forehead. She had come to Berkeley after serving in San Francisco for several years. In her ten years of service to Berkeley, she never missed a fire nor did she ever miss a day. Chief Kenney announced that the old horse would never be sold to perform menial labor, as had happened with many of the other retired fire horses. Instead, Kitty would remain an official member of the Berkeley Fire Department until her death. A Berkeley fireman interviewed upon the announcement of Kitty Kelly's retirement said this about his experience working with horses: "Autos are all right but an auto can never find the place in the 'heart of man' that a horse can. I used to enjoy feeding my team every night and morning and when we went to a fire, I knew that they would pull until they dropped. Faithful? There was never an animal more faithful than a fire horse. I used to enjoy currying and brushing my team, but now I polish brass every morning, and clean engines, and pour gasoline, and I grow sad when I think the horses are gone forever."

A 1907 PHOTO OF THE BERKELEY FIRE DEPARTMENT REGENT STREET FIREHOUSE TWO YEARS AFTER THE DEPARTMENT WAS FORMED. DAN HAFEY, LAURENCE BURCHENARY, CUNNINGHAM, DAN MIKLEY, TOM BEGLEY, AND HENRY ANDERSON ARE SHOWN IN THEIR HORSE-DRAWN RIGS, STILL IN OPERATION.

THE EARLY MECHANIZED OAKLAND FIRE DEPARTMENT, ENDING THE ERA OF THE FIRE HORSE.

Boys of Berkeley look for adventure near the Deaf and Dumb Aslyum, just outside of Berkeley circa 1888. This institution, built in 1868, was just north of Dunn's ranch.

THE HANGING OAK IS THE LARGE OAK IN FRONT OF THE BUILDING ON THE MID-RIGHT OF THIS 1888 PHOTO OF THE AREA JUST EAST OF SHATTUCK AVENUE AND ALLSTON WAY. STRAWBERRY CREEK GURGLES TOWARD THE BAY ON THE LEFT SIDE OF THE PHOTO.

2

THE HANGMAN'S TREE

IN THE LATE NINETEENTH AND EARLY TWENTIETH CENTURIES, A HUGE oak tree stood east of Shattuck Avenue near Strawberry Creek in old Berkeley. It was variously known as Gibbet Oak, Vigilante Oak, and Hanging Oak. A rumor persisted that in the 1850s a horse thief had been captured by ranchers who, wishing to return to their work and tired of waiting for the judge, tried the man themselves and hanged him from that tree.

There was certainly a huge oak on that spot, probably hundreds of years old, but no one could confirm the hanging. William Waste, an early Berkeley resident who was the first member of the State Bar of California, a graduate of Hastings Law School, and a member of the state legislature who would become Chief Justice of the California Supreme Court, had never heard of the incident—and he was known as a local history buff. Clarence Merrill, son of Berkeley's first druggist, Berkeley postmaster, and operator of the city's first telegraph service for thirty years, said he had heard the story, but, from what he gathered as a boy, no one was ever hanged there. William Warren Ferrier, premier Berkeley historian and author, agreed with that conclusion.[1]

This slate of early Berkeley luminaries clearly disbelieved the story of the hanging. So where did it come from? While the origin of the story is unknown, it appears to have been recounted by one of the great editorialists and working-class heroes of early Berkeley—the expressman known in town as the "Boss Baggage Buster of Beautiful Berkeley," John E. Boyd. In 1902, the *Berkeley Daily Gazette* published a story written by Boyd in which Cloromeda Mendoza was hanged on this tree. The *Gazette* reprinted this story on January 14, 1908.

Interestingly, Boyd had perpetuated quite another myth about the tree many years earlier. This version of the story appeared on April 2, 1887, in the *Berkeley Advocate* in a letter to the editor:

> *Talking to an old timer on the occasion of the recent trials in East*
> *Berkeley he gave me an account of the first trial ever held in what is now*

NATIVE SONS WILL PRESERVE HISTORIC TREE

The members of Berkeley Parlor No. 5, N. S. G. W., have under consideration plans to preserve the oak tree on Allston Way between Shattuck avenue and Fulton street, which is known as the "vigilante tree." Pioneer residents recall the time when an outlaw was hanged upon the tree.

The plan was brought before the lodge last night by Third Vice-President Lloyd C. Hawley. It is proposed to surround the tree by an ornamental fence and to properly inscribe it.

BERKELEY DAILY GAZETTE, MAY 8, 1902.

the town of Berkeley, and thinking that the story would be interesting to your readers I jotted down the particulars which are as follows: It appears that early in the year '51 a warrant was issued by Judge Blake against a man named William Harding who resided on San Pablo avenue about where Duffy's saloon now is [San Pablo Avenue near Folger Street], charging him with stealing hogs. The accused was arrested by a constable named Kellogg, and brought before Judge Blake at his residence in what is now known as the Poinsett house on Shattuck avenue, near Strawberry creek. A jury was quickly found and the court sat under the old oak tree which is still standing on the left of the railroad track. After the court was called to order, the prisoner pleaded "not guilty" and the jury impaneled. One of the jurymen announced that he was as dry as Strawberry creek and the prisoner at once offered to pay for the liquor if any person would go after it. The nearest gin and sugar establishment was at Temescal kept by Smith Bros. and a man known as "Whiskey Jack" volunteered to be the messenger if any one would lend him a "bronco." The horse was soon ready two demijohns were hung in grain sacks, one on each side and the rider started with "Temescal and whiskey only 3 miles away." Eager eyes watched for his return and soon a cloud of dust announced the looked for messenger.

The demijohns were quickly brought forth and all hands took a hearty drink which was soon followed by another. The judge then proposed to proceed when one of the hilarious jurymen proposed that all the liquor be drank up and then they would not be "hankerin" after it. All hands agreed to the suggestion, the liquor was soon disposed of and the court started to resume business when one of the jurymen said that he be hanged if he ever sat on a jury without whiskey and he was not going to begin now. Another adjournment took place and the prisoner handed over seven Mexican dollars and Whiskey Jack was soon riding away for more "juice." He quickly returned, another drink was taken and the business of the day resumed. Before the evidence was all in Whiskey Jack had made two more trips for supplies and about two o'clock in the afternoon the judge charged the jury who soon retired to deliberate. The jury room was under the other oak tree near the creek, each juryman first rolled his coat up for a pillow and after lighting his pipe lay down to deliberate. The prisoner, constable and spectators all picked out a soft place under the other tree and soon the majority were snoring. At this juncture Mr. Clark

By the time this photo was taken in 1898, everything in this area had changed. Strawberry Creek is culverted and the hanging oak is standing on Allston Way, just beyond the curb on the right side of the street.

PRESERVE FAMOUS OLD TREE

EDITOR GAZETTE: There is a report around town, which I hope is not true, that the old Vigilante Tree on Allston way, a relic of the early days, is in the road of improvements and must fall beneath the ax.

Some time ago I wrote the history of this tree and I gathered it from old pioneers, and which you were kind enough to publish in your paper. Still, it may not be amiss to remind your readers that a horse thief was hanged on the long limb which projects over the street, by the Vigilantes of Ocean View (as Berkeley was then designated).

Now, Mr. Editor, this tree stands partly on the sidewalk and partly in the street, and it looks to me as if the Town Trustees had some say in this matter. If so, I hope they will put a veto on destroying this interesting relic of "'49."

I understand that the order of Native Sons of the Golden West was preparing to place a sign on the tree to read, "Vigilante Tree. Upon this limb a Horse Thief was hanged, May, 1851."

Now, Mr. Editor I hope the Improvement Clubs, the ladies of the Town and Gown, the Native Sons and other kindred organizations, will take some steps to prevent this sacrilege. They will have the support of all good citizens and the hearty thanks of

JOHN E. BOYD.

Berkeley Daily Gazette, March 29, 1905.

(who now and for many years past has been in the employ of Capt. Bowen) gave the prisoner a wink and pointed to the foothills. The prisoner took the hint and not waiting to take a formal adieu, or not liking to disturb the sleeping multitude, quickly crept away through the tall grass. He remained hidden in the hills for about two weeks, his hiding place being near the pile of rocks situated on what is now known as Capt. Boswell's ranch, and being supplied with provisions by his friend Clark. After remaining in hiding a short time, a boat was procured for him and he made his escape to San Francisco. Many years have passed since the above occurrence but I never pass the old oak trees without thinking of the story of the first court in Berkeley as told to me by an old pioneer.

—JOHN E. BOYD

One possible explanation for the two differing stories told by the same John E. Boyd is that the later story was published at a time when many residents were attempting to save the tree from developers who planned to chop it down. In 1896, the city culverted Strawberry Creek, which had run down Allston Way, to make Allston Way a real street. The Berkeley chapter of the Native Sons of the Golden West offered to save the tree by donating an ornamental iron fence around it where it stood in the street by the south curb, near where Eddy's ice cream parlor later stood. It seems probable the second story was manufactured simply to save the tree. In the end, the developers won the fight. The tree was felled in 1908:

Acting upon the order of Superintendent of Streets Turner two laborers were at work today cutting down the historic oak tree which has been standing since time immemorial on Allston way, a short distance from Shattuck avenue. This gnarled old tree was standing long before Allston way or even Berkeley was thought of and is the one oak in the uptown district which unites the past with the present.

Out of a spirit of sentiment the tree has been left standing while all the other trees in the neighborhood have been destroyed. When Allston way was graded care was taken not to injure this tree and it stood unmolested until this morning. Then Turner gave his orders and the tree is now a thing of the past, not even a relic. Improvements are to be made on this street and it was found necessary to destroy this old landmark.[2]

Editor Gazette: The old Vigilante tree on Allston way, above Shattuck on which the horse-thief, Jesus Mendoza, was hung by the enraged rancheros who in "the days of '49" cultivated the land now known as the city of Berkeley, is passing away and dying with old age. A tree expert who at my request examined the venerable relic, assured me that sewer gas from the bed of Strawberry creek had much to do with sapping the vitality of the old tree. Years ago my old friend Professor Joe LeConte assured me that in all probability the old tree was a twig about the time Columbus discovered the Western world. I am sorry to see it decay and if there were any way to preserve this relic of pioneer days I would willingly assist and pay the cost, but I fear there is no help. But I do hope that some photographer of our town will make a picture of the old tree and present me with a copy.

Well, farewell, old relic of pioneer days. I shall hate to see you pass away, and I shouldn't wonder if when you leave us, some crank about my size will be begging money of our citizens to purchase and place a marble slab to mark the spot where stood the Vigilante trees of historic days.   JOHN E. BOYD.

Berkeley Daily Gazette, June 25, 1907.

Aye, cut it down, this old landmark
Tis but a relic of the past;
Though for ages it has stood
The storm king's wintery blast.
What though it sprang from mother-earth
Ere the white man reached this land,
Before kind earth did yield its gold
To the grasping Gringo's hand.
No matter if an outlaw met his death
By Judge Lynch's stern decree—
No matter if the court was held
Beneath the old oak tree.
No matter of the statement made
By one of Berkeley's sages,
No matter if the wise Le Conte
Said, 'tis a relic of past ages.
Aye, cut it down, ye ruthless sons
Of Berkeley's lovely clime;
Aye, cut it down and burn it up—
It has outlived its time.

    — Boyd, the Boss Crank of Berkeley
        Berkeley Daily Gazette, January 14, 1908.

A YOUNG SAMUEL HOPKINS WILLEY.

3

SAMUEL HOPKINS WILLEY AND THE FIRST UNIVERSITY WATERWORKS, 1867

IN 1849, AS NEWS OF THE GOLD RUSH FLUSHED CALIFORNIA AND THE world, Samuel Hopkins Willey stepped off a ship in Monterey.[1] He was filled with dreams of furthering the cause of education in a land swarming with wild men who were consumed with passion for gold and adventure.

Willey, a graduate of the renowned Kimball Union Academy in Meridian, New Hampshire, was a classmate of Frederick Billings, the man who would later propose the name of the city of Berkeley. Willey graduated from Dartmouth College and then the Union Theological Seminary of New York, intending to pursue a life of preaching and educating. In 1848, Willey experienced the first of several life-changing ruminations.[2] He sat on a hill overlooking Boston meditating on his future. Unable to shake thoughts of the unmet religious needs on the new frontier of California—then still a territory—his future suddenly crystallized before him. Once he heard this call to service, the comforts and familiarity of New England released their grip on him. He would go to California as a missionary.

He joined the American Home Missionary Society (AHMS) as its first representative to California and sailed from New York to California by way of Panama. During this voyage, news of the discovery of gold at Sutter's Mill in 1848 finally reached the East Coast. Willey's steamer, the *California*, was the first vessel to enter San Francisco Bay following the announcement of this discovery. The *California* was also the first steamship to arrive at a California port. When Willey reached Monterey on February 23, 1849, almost all the men of the town had already run to the gold fields, and the few who remained were preparing to join them. Willey nevertheless delivered the first sermon for the AHMS in California in Monterey, but determined to find a more stable community to serve. When he learned that San Francisco had suffered the same fate, Willey wondered how he would find a congregation to preach to, since, as he noted in his diary, "Men seem to forget their souls in their interest for gold."[3]

FREDERICK BILLINGS.

Maybe the men forgot their souls, but there was one woman in Monterey, Martha N. Jeffers, who kept hers well tended. Samuel was first smitten by this Philadelphia woman back in New York when he spotted her while he was standing on the dock on the day her government transport ship was leaving New York for Monterey. Unable to forget her face, Willey, whose ship arrived in Monterey ahead of Martha's, met her when she disembarked in California. Soon he was courting her while riding horses over the beautiful Monterey peninsula. After four months of such idyllic interludes, Samuel and Martha were married on September 19, 1849.

For Willey, finding love was easy; his work as a missionary proved much more challenging. Unable to gather support for a church, Willey taught school and served as one of two chaplains for the first state constitutional convention in 1849.

Later that year, the American Home Missionary Society sent Willey to assess the spiritual and educational needs in San Francisco, Sacramento, and the gold fields. Willey traveled first to Sacramento, where a chance conversation with a stranger about a man in San Jose who was offering funding for a school convinced Willey to disobey his employer's instructions. He instead traveled to San Jose to track down this lead. He acted wholeheartedly with absolute certainty about the correctness of his pursuit. His personal mission had become increasingly clear: he would found a university in California.

Many fine men were drawn into the endeavor to start a university in California, including Sherman Day, son of a Yale University president, who would become Berkeley's first town engineer and an original College of California trustee; and Thomas O. Larkin, the American consul in Mexican California before 1848. Together, Willey, Day, and Larkin signed a charter application and submitted it to the state. But the California state legislature did not grant their 1850 application to establish a school because the California Supreme Court ruled that their "unsettled" property titles to the land did not fulfill the legal requirements for a grant.[4]

While his prime goal was to start a university, Willey was also one of the state's strongest advocates of primary education. With a flair for drama and the dream of a school still focused in his mind, Willey led a parade of one hundred children through the streets of San Francisco in the early 1850s, hoping to inspire the city council to support education. The parade had the desired effect, and the city soon initiated a public school system.[5]

At the same time, fate was working on another member of the cast in the birth of a university; a minister in New England was forced to give up preaching because of a throat problem and decided to serve as a missionary in California. His name was Henry Durant, and he described himself as having "college on the brain."[6]

Soon, Durant would emigrate to California and meet Willey at a joint meeting of the Presbytery of San Francisco and the Congregational Association of California in Nevada City. After five minutes of conversation, Willey once again made an instinctive decision. He was convinced that the time had arrived to again pursue the founding of a college, and he believed that Durant was the right man to lead this new school. In June of 1853, with just three students, Willey and Durant founded the Contra Costa Academy in Oakland. In 1855, the College of California was incorporated and Willey became its first president. Day and Durant were among the trustees.

As the college and downtown Oakland expanded—and all the majestic oak trees that gave the city its name were cut down to make way for development—it became apparent that the school needed a new and larger campus in a place not surrounded by speculators and squatters. The administrators' first choice was a site in east Oakland, but the property was sold to another buyer before they could close the deal. Willey and his group then considered a location in the Napa area, but again they did not move fast enough and the property was sold to someone else. At this point, they decided to reconsider a site at the base of the hills in the remote northeast part of Oakland Township. They had originally rejected this site fearing an inadequate water supply. Ultimately though, they decided that this sparsely populated area dotted with a handful of ranches and cabins would be the perfect place to establish the new university. They purchased the grounds on April 16, 1860. Willey wrote about the site with great enthusiasm:

> *There is not another such college site in America, if indeed anywhere at all in the world. It is the spot above all others we have seen or heard of where a man may look in the face of the nineteenth century and realize the glories that are coming on.*[7]

To ensure an adequate water supply for their site, they purchased additional land from neighbor Captain Orrin Simmons, a retired sea captain turned rancher. Simmons' land, including the present sites of both the Greek Theatre and Memorial Stadium, stretched from Strawberry Creek to where Dwight Way is today. Negotiations between Simmons and the College of California went on for some years and, on August 14, 1864, Willey finally signed the contract for the purchase of Simmons' land. He wrote about the transaction in his journal:

AN ETHEREAL PAINTING OF THE FUTURE UC BERKELEY
CAMPUS BY R. D. YELLAND THAT SEEMS TO CAPTURE
WILLEY'S SPIRITUAL SENSE OF THIS PLACE.

*When the thing was decided by the execution of the papers in San
Francisco at four o'clock today, I left to come home on the boat—relieved
of one burden of suspense. While crossing the bay, although the sky was
overclouded elsewhere, the evening sun shone down clear and bright on
the spot we had just been purchasing, the site and its surroundings which
we had consecrated to the purpose of Christian learning. From my heart
went up the prayer to God to accept the transaction as a means of building the College for his own glory, the good of the country and the world—
to make it safe and successful by his gracious benediction upon all who
may in coming time resort to that spot to acquire learning.*[8]

Simmons was happy as well, having made almost nine times his investment in about four months. In September 1864, Willey and his associates purchased another 320 acres adjoining the college site. They had plans to subdivide the land into housing lots and sell them in order to raise money for the institution, and they formed a corporation to sell the land. Though many lots were sold, only one family actually moved onto this "College Homestead" tract—the Willeys. At that time, the site could only be accessed by a dirt trail that followed the south side of Strawberry Creek as it wove its way through the flatlands to the bay. The area was open and expansive and one could see the flatlands spread out for miles to the north and south with no obstructions. Grasslands carpeted the landscape, and the many creek channels could be traced by the oak, bay, and sycamore trees that lined their banks.

As the fog rolled in during the summer of 1865, Willey built his family home

THE CORNER OF DWIGHT WAY AND COLLEGE AVENUE. DWIGHT WAY RUNS AT THE BOTTOM OF THE IMAGE. THE FAMILY HOME OF THE WILLEYS APPEARS IN THE MID-LEFT OF THE PHOTO.

A NEWSPAPER STORY IN THE *SAN FRANCISCO CHRONICLE* ON APRIL 29, 1928, DISPLAYS THE WILLEY DAUGHTERS, MARIA AND ANNE, IN THEIR OLDER AGE AND THE WILLEY HOME. AS YOUNG GIRLS THEY HAD SHOWN PEOPLE WHERE THE STREETS WOULD BE WHEN BERKELEY WAS STILL JUST A DREAM.

FOUNDERS' ROCK, UC BERKELEY CAMPUS, JUST SOUTH OF THE TOP OF HEARST STREET AND WEST OF GAYLEY ROAD.

at the end of a muddy country road originating in Oakland at what is now Dwight Way and College Avenue (then called Audubon Street), with the entrance facing Audubon. From there, a crooked dirt trail led west to another dirt trail (possibly used by the Peralta brothers to go between their ranchos) later called Guyat Street (named thus only on the developmental maps; it was never actually called Guyat Street) and years later renamed Shattuck Avenue. The Willey girls, in their bonnets, would take visitors out and show them where the streets of the College Homestead tract would eventually be constructed.

Willey wrote of the endeavor on May 10, 1865:

> *I entered upon this Homestead enterprise last September. It was a piece of engineering I was not used to, and it had about it so much uncertainty that I did not take hold of it without apprehension. But I gained assurance as I went on and have lost none of it at this time."*[9]

The land sales came but never fast enough to obviate the need for borrowing money. People had been reluctant to invest in the east side of the bay, fearing dangerous boat crossings and isolation, but that was changing. The college later advertised that a man could sit down on a ferry leaving Ocean View (west Berkeley), begin reading his newspaper, and upon completing the task he would find himself in San Francisco with his peers at his workplace. Just as things seemed to be improving for Willey and Northern California's rainy season doldrums were coming to an end, the country—just emerging from the Civil War—was thrust into mourning at the death of President Abraham Lincoln.

By 1866, the state legislature had appropriated funds for an Agriculture, Mining, and Mechanical Arts College and even selected the Byrne Ranch as the site of the future institution. This site is in the vicinity of Live Oak Park. It has been suggested that Durant played a role in the selection of this location, thinking that the proximity of the two colleges would help them both.[10]

In May 1866, a number of trustees and friends of the college gathered around the base of a large rock (Founders' Rock) near what would years later become the top of Hearst Street. Six years earlier, these men had dedicated the college on this site. On this day, they looked out over the bay and Golden Gate and discussed college matters. Fredrick Law Olmsted had suggested "Peralta" as a possible name for the town they would found. A few lines were recited from a poem by Bishop Berkeley, a famous British theologian and educator. "Westward the course of empire" began one line. Frederick Billings, Willey's childhood friend, cried out that he believed they had just found the perfect name for the town: Berkeley. The group retired to Willey's house nearby to celebrate over lunch. Willey would later write, "It was a place too choice for any common name. Young parents never pondered so long over the name of their first baby."[11] Others were worried that with a name like Berkeley, future poets might have trouble writing of its glory and rhyming the name with any other word.

In 1867, the College of California completed construction of its first waterworks—a series of reservoirs and flumes in and around Strawberry Creek that would provide potable water to the future campus and the residents it hoped to attract. Water was the most valuable resource of the university and the fledgling town. Pioneer William Hillegass had given his Strawberry Creek water rights to the college and in return was granted three hundred gallons of water a day for life, which he used mostly for his orchards. The water from this first reservoir came from the area today known as Panoramic Way, then a gorgeous wooded canyon with springs, now near the site of the university's stadium. The reservoir had a capacity of three hundred thousand gallons. The *Alta California* reported that completion of the waterworks proved that the location was destined to grow into the greatest educational institution in the state.[12]

On August 24, 1867, the founders held a picnic at the base of the hills to officially open the College Waterworks at the future college site by Strawberry Creek:

> *Friends of the college were invited to the celebration marking the first time the water was turned on. The crowd gathered on the new college grounds, Mrs. Willey was sharing her husband's hour of triumph. She was dressed in her best.*
>
> *Down from a small reservoir in the hills through pipes poured the water. Dr. Willey turned on a nozzle. The gravity pressure sent the water high in the air. So thrilled was the college head that he suddenly drenched his wife before he realized it.*[13]

Twenty years later, Willey described the event's significance:

> *Early in the month of August, the waterworks were so far completed that they were ready for use. But few residences besides my own had at that time been built in all that region though the owners of many lots proposed to improve them by the use of water and have them in readiness for future building. But when the water was first turned from the pipes, and went*

ABOVE: THE FEEL OF THE OLD UC CAMPUS.

RIGHT: AN 1875 MAP OF STRAWBERRY CREEK, ITS
FORKS, FEEDER CREEKS, SPRINGS, AND TRIBUTARIES. IT
WAS DRAWN BY UC BERKELEY ENGINEERING PROFESSOR
FRANK SOULE, JR. TWO YEARS AFTER THE UNIVERSITY
MOVED TO THE REMOTE BERKELEY CAMPUS.

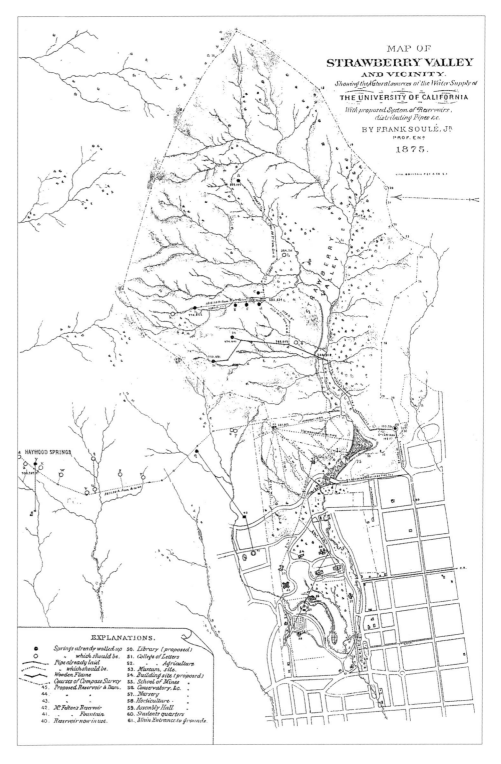

up in spray under a hundred and fifty feet of pressure at various points on the homestead tract and College site, playing jets fifty or seventy-five feet in the air. It was a sight novel and animating.[15]

Mrs. Willey's soggier description of the event went unrecorded.

Willey had big plans for his college water company, intending to tap both Wildcat and San Pablo creeks for profit to support the institution. However, when college officials met with continuing financial hardship, they decided in October of 1867 that in the interest of the institution's survival they must turn control of the college and its new site over to the state in exchange for funding. Part of the negotiations included incorporating a College of Arts and Letters into the plans for the Agriculture, Mining, and Mechanical Arts College. There had been public frustration with the state's plan for a mining and technical training college when the 1850 state constitution had mandated a "University of California." The College of California trustees all came from a tradition of liberal arts education and wanted to see this kind of education flourish in California. All of Willey's water plans ended with the state assuming authority over the old college, thereby forming the University of California. After the transfer of the college to the state, the new regents allowed the water rights that Willey had so carefully crafted and acquired to lapse and terminate.

After the college passed into the hands of the state, Willey moved to Santa Cruz and became pastor of the Congregational Church there. He subsequently moved to Benicia and San Francisco, where he held other church and educational positions. In 1896, Samuel Willey retired so that he could devote his time to writing.

By the turn of the century, the Willeys had spent a number of years in New Jersey, Mrs. Willey's home state. Because Martha yearned to return to lovely Berkeley, the Willeys moved west again in 1904 and took up residence at 2250 Telegraph Avenue near the university. In 1906, University President Benjamin Ide Wheeler asked Willey to return to UC Berkeley after a thirty-seven-year absence. Willey accepted the invitation and was given an honorary professorship, which allowed him to continue his writing. Wheeler considered Willey to be one of the most composed souls he had ever met, in spite of his living through a very rough and wild period of California's history. He remarked how Willey spent his life tending to spiritual matters while most others pursued gold and riches.[16]

On June 2, 1906, about a month and a half after the exodus of San Francisco earthquake refugees to Berkeley, Martha Willey, who had been ailing for about a

A WOMAN STANDS BY ONE OF THE HUGE ANCIENT OAKS, PROBABLY TENDED BY LOCAL INDIANS FOR HUNDREDS OF YEARS, ON THE RECENTLY ESTABLISHED UC CAMPUS.

The Rev. S. H. Willey, the Vice-President of the College of California, has been ill since October 22d with typhoid fever. He is at times delirious, and is dangerously sick, at his home in Berkeley.

OAKLAND DAILY NEWS, 1868.

ABOVE: TWO ADMIRERS OF THE UC CAMPUS STAND NEAR THE VICINITY OF BANCROFT WAY AND COLLEGE AVENUE.

RIGHT: A VERY EARLY PANORAMA OF BERKELEY AND THE FIRST TWO UNIVERSITY BUILDINGS, NORTH AND SOUTH HALLS, ON THE UC BERKELEY CAMPUS. UC OPENED ITS DOORS IN BERKELEY IN 1873.

A MAN LOOKING UP WHAT WOULD BECOME HEARST STREET FROM SOMEWHERE NEAR OXFORD STREET.

year, passed away following a four-day struggle with pneumonia.

In 1911, Wheeler again honored Samuel Hopkins Willey with the degree of Doctor of Laws at UC Berkeley's golden jubilee celebration. At Willey's funeral on January 21, 1914, Wheeler gave a sermon describing how the ninety-three-year-old Willey had for the past several months stopped by on his daily walks and sat on a bench on the campus near Wheeler's office. Somehow, Wheeler always sensed when Willey was there and "felt in his presence on the bench a blessing and a benediction. . . . He would come in silence, would sit in silence, and would depart in silence."[17]

TOP: A MIDDLE-AGED SAMUEL H. WILLEY.

BOTTOM: AN EIGHTY-NINE-YEAR-OLD SAMUEL HOPKINS WILLEY AT A UC BERKELEY CHARTER DAY EXERCISE IN 1910. DR. WILLEY IS ON THE FAR LEFT, ACCOMPANIED BY UC PRESIDENT BENJAMIN IDE WHEELER, REV. J. K. MCLEAN, PASTOR OF THE FIRST CHURCH IN OAKLAND, AND WARRING WILKENSON, PRESIDENT OF THE CALIFORNIA SCHOOL FOR THE DEAF FOR FORTY-FOUR YEARS, BEGINNING IN 1865.

An artist's portrayal of Wildcat Creek, circa 1888, in an area then named Wildcat Cascades. The author believes that this location is where the trails from the Meadow and Lone Oak meet in Wildcat Gorge.

4

PAT CURRAN'S RANCH, WILDCAT CANYON

IN THE SUMMER OF 1863, PAT CURRAN, AN IRISH CANADIAN, FLED Canada following a failed revolution for independence from British rule. He came to the ranch, dairy, and farming country at the northern extreme of Oakland Township.[1] In those days, Oakland Township encompassed the entire northern end of Alameda County from Oakland north to Cerrito Creek, since Berkeley was not incorporated until 1878. Upon his arrival, Curran began asking around for work. The locals told him to see James McGee, who had settled there about ten years earlier and was the first American farmer in the area. As it turned out, McGee did not need full-time help but was able to provide Curran with a part-time job.

There was a general store in Oakland where all the ranchers would congregate, especially after church on Sunday. It was called Kranhagen's and was located at Sixth and Clay streets. One day while McGee was at Kranhagen's he ran into Napoleon Byrne, another of Berkeley's pioneer ranchers, and told him about Curran. Byrne had arrived in 1859 and was an early settler in the area around Live Oak Park. He had come there from Missouri with his family and two freed slaves and owned land all the way into Wildcat Canyon. Byrne took a liking to Pat Curran and offered to make him a partner in his ranching business.

Although these men were pioneers, there was already much history under their feet. The dirt trail they rode through the hills to get to Wildcat Canyon was the same one used by Spanish *vaqueros* in the early nineteenth century. The *vaqueros* inherited this existing trail from the Huchiun Ohlone Indians, who had undoubtedly used it for centuries. The Ohlone, in turn, had most likely inherited the path from the deer, bear, and elk that had trampled the trail out over innumerable seasons. This sloping, winding path went right past Cragmont Rock and up what in the twentieth century would become Regal Road before dropping down the eastern slope of the Berkeley Hills into Wildcat Canyon. As the men rode into the canyon, they passed by the tallest waterfall in the East Bay, then known as Wildcat Falls.

JAMES MCGEE AND HIS WIFE. MCGEE WAS POSSIBLY THE FIRST NON-NATIVE OR CALIFORNIO (SPANISH/ MEXICAN) FARMER IN WHAT WOULD BECOME BERKELEY. HE ACQUIRED 160 ACRES OF LAND FROM DOMINGO PERALTA BY LEASE OR SALE IN THE EARLY 1850S. HIS LAND EXTENDED FROM WHAT IS NOW MARTIN LUTHER KING JR. WAY TO SACRAMENTO STREET AND FROM DWIGHT WAY TO ADDISON STREET.

NAPOLEON BONAPARTE BYRNE.

TOP AND RIGHT: TYPICAL LANDSCAPE IN THE UNDEVEL-
OPED CRAGMONT AREA. COWBOYS WOULD PASS THESE
FORMATIONS WHILE DRIVING CATTLE OUT OF THE
CANYON.

This waterfall, the highest in Alameda County, was in Wildcat Canyon and was located at the southern end of where Lake Anza sits today. The waterfall sat where the deep canyon cradled Wildcat Creek. The canyon in this spot is now filled by man-made Lake Anza, formed in 1937 when recreational needs were considered a very high priority, even at the expense of natural beauty.

On this trail, the men would encounter elk pushing through the foliage with their massive horns, a remnant of past elk populations displaced by the Spanish and their longhorn cattle. The trail started near what would have been an extension of what is now Rose Street, but after the spring of 1888 a new, better-graded County Road, now known as Spruce Street, was constructed over the Berkeley hills. Ranchers used the road to drive their steers out of the canyon to the slaughterhouses of Butchertown (now Emeryville) and west Berkeley, which arose in the later decades of the 1800s as the local populations grew.

Eventually, Pat Curran bought 320 acres of Wildcat Canyon from Byrne and returned to Montreal to fetch his family. His son James was born as their ship docked in Panama. Curran's land ran from Grizzly Peak down Wildcat Canyon over to Cape Horn, a grassy summit to the east on San Pablo Ridge. The area was open grassland ribboned by the oaks, bays, and sycamores that shouldered the creek. In the right seasons, dense covers of flowers blazed across the hillsides. Curran's land also included the famous caves of Wildcat Canyon. Byrne even provided Curran with some of his stock. The Curran Ranch raised steers and milk cows and grew feed for the livestock on the ranch. Many ranch hands were needed to milk and feed the cows, harvest the crops, bale the hay, store the feed, and

handle countless other chores such as fence mending and squirrel and raptor control. The sun was intense in the canyon; the men all wore wide-brimmed hats and everyone appreciated the trees for shade.

Pat and Mary Curran reared five boys and five girls on the ranch. They grew up scampering through the wilds of Wildcat Canyon, playing cowboys and Indians and picking wild berries. Pat had a genial, soulful nature, and was a kind husband and father. He also earned the respect of most of his neighbors and associates. Berkeley's original Californio settler, Domingo Peralta, was said to have sold Pat some pasture land around Spruce and Rose streets. Pat had learned the art of raising mules back in Canada and he took up this business on his new property, selling many mules to the U.S. Army at the Presidio in San Francisco.

Down in Wildcat Canyon north of the current Lake Anza (a man-made lake created in 1937), the Curran fruit orchard contained more than sixty apple, pear, and cherry trees. The Currans harvested the fruit, and what they did not preserve in glass jars they loaded onto a wagon and made the slow trip to Oakland, going north through Wildcat Canyon to a low point in the hills near San Pablo. They most likely turned west to the bay side of the hills and then began their trip south to the markets of Oakland Township and the city of Oakland. It was a long and

—A serious accident occurred on last Wednesday at Adeline station. P. Curran, who has a farm back upon the hills near Berkeley, was driving a mule team with a load of hay, and attempted to cross the track just as the local train came along. The wagon and hay were completely demolished and Mr. Curran thrown violently from his seat. His leg was badly injured. He was taken to Berkeley and the fracture attended to by Dr. Payne, and is in a good way of recovery. No blame can attach to the train hands. At last accounts he was improving.

BERKELEY ADVOCATE, OCTOBER 27, 1883.

—Patrick Mahony caused the arrest of Patrick Curran on a charge of disturbing the peace and disorderly conduct. The parties are neighbors, residing in the hills north of town, and appear not to have been on good terms. The accusations are varied and amusing and will be investigated to-day before Judge Lord.

CONTRA COSTA GAZETTE, SEPTEMBER 9, 1882.

A PICNIC ON THE CURRAN RANCH WAS A POPULAR OUTING FOR A SUNDAY. THE LONG RIDES TO AND FROM THE RANCH MADE FOR A FULL AND TIRING DAY IN THE SPLENDID, WILD, AND REMOTE LUXURY OF NATURE. NOTE THE CUSTOM OF MEN AND WOMEN DRESSING UP IN THEIR FANCIEST CLOTHES FOR A SUNDAY PICNIC. IN SUCH PHOTOGRAPHS IT IS VERY RARE TO SEE A MAN OR BOY WITHOUT A HAT ON.

rattling ride—the round trip took a full day. The old cattle trail over the hills was much too steep to chance with a wagon loaded with fruit. The journey became much easier with the opening of County Road (Spruce Street) in the spring of 1888.

In its day, Wildcat Canyon's Curran Ranch employed a host of colorful characters. Ramon Chavez was one of the ranch hands.[2] Ramon was known as a "Digger Indian," a derogatory and generalized term of the times for any Central Californian Indian. Many local Indians found that employment on the ranches was the only way they could survive after their lands, homes, and food sources were destroyed, first by the Spanish, and then by the American invaders. Many were skilled at ranching, having learned the trade in the mission years, beginning around 1776. These Indians were most often marginalized and given room and board and little else. Sometimes they were not given what they were promised by

their employers after a harvest.

Ramon made a living on the Curran Ranch and had a reputation as a horse wrangler who could tame the wildest bronco. Chavez also possessed a rare gift for healing ailing animals and for this he was renowned locally. East Bay horse owners would pasture their horses on Curran's ranch for recuperation knowing that Chavez could nurse them back to health.

When Ramon Chavez wanted to get away from his responsibilities and hard work on the ranch, he liked to go down to the town of San Pablo to his favorite saloon and dance hall, where he had a reputation as quite a dancer.

According to local legend, one night in 1879 Chavez danced with a Mexican girl, which made the saloon's proprietor jealous. As Chavez was leaving the saloon, he was shot in the back of the head. The local constable solved the killing after patrons of the saloon recalled that some nights before the owner of the saloon and dance hall had threatened to kill "Pat Curran's Indian" for cutting in on the queen of the dance hall. The constable declared that it was a case of self-defense and the shooter never stood trial.[3]

This story is contradicted in an 1882 newspaper account of the incident.[4] August 23, 1874, was an overcast Sunday. Constable John Wilcox, who also ran a bar, went to bed a little early that night. He was fatigued, since that day he had broken up several fights involving an intoxicated Ramon Chavez. Just as the tired

CONTRA COSTA GAZETTE, AUGUST 29, 1874.

HINDU WORKERS ON SHATTUCK AVENUE. *BERKELEY INDEPENDENT,* 1910.

constable drifted off to sleep, someone pounded frantically on his door and screamed that Chavez and his friend were killing a man. Wilcox jumped up and grabbed his gun. He was only partially dressed as he flew out the door. Upon reaching the street, he found Chavez and his companion both drunk on the road in front of the bar. They were wheeling their horses around and riding them over a man they had thrown to the ground. The injured man boarded at Wilcox's place and was known to be mentally ill. Wilcox commanded the men to stop their assault. Instead, Chavez rode off about ten feet, wheeled his horse around, and charged Wilcox at full speed. When Chavez was within a few feet of Wilcox, Wilcox fired his gun. Chavez fell dead with a bullet below his eye socket. A coroner's jury found Wilcox's actions justifiable.

Another employee of the Curran Ranch, known as "Old James," was employed as a milker.[5] Old James was a Hindu and had a name that the locals could not remember, let alone pronounce, and so he was known by this nickname. It was a rare thing for an East Indian man to be working on a ranch in the East Bay in the 1870s and '80s, since there were few immigrants from India then in the United States.

Old James wore a turban and chanted unusual songs that had never been heard before in these parts. On his days off, he read palms down in Oakland and Berkeley. He was well known for his trances, the sources of which were both mystical inspiration and his use of opium. He consumed an ounce of opium a week, rolling it into tiny balls and taking two each day. When his opium ran out, his eyes would roll back in his head. At this sign, young Jim Curran would be sent by his father to procure opium for Old James at an Oakland drugstore. In those days, opium was a common remedy sold over the counter.

In the interim, Old James would work around his addiction by making a concoction of soap and tobacco juice. The effect of drinking this was to make him so ill that he didn't care about not having his opium. Though Old James was clearly an addict, he lived to be nearly eighty years old. He had always predicted he would die on the first day of a month with two moons. In the late 1880s, when a month with two moons arrived, Old James began to wrap himself in rope from his feet to his waist. Sensing that something was wrong, his friends tried to unwrap him, but before they could free him from this entanglement he had departed this life.

The Currans' oldest son, Jim, was born in 1863. After he reached school age, Jim Curran attended Mt. Pleasant School for about two and a half years. The location of the former school is now under water in the San Pablo Dam Reservoir.

In its day, the school operated from April through September or until the rains made access to the little schoolhouse impossible. Jim studied by the light of an oil lamp at night and was able to graduate despite his ranch work and family responsibilities. These responsibilities would increase dramatically with the deaths of his mother in 1884 at the age of fifty-two and his father just two years later at the age of fifty. At that point, Jim was in charge of the ranch and the welfare of his eight surviving younger siblings. Even with these responsibilities, Jim went on to become a school trustee for Contra Costa County at the age of twenty-five.

In 1903, Jim Curran married Katherine "Katie" O'Toole at Berkeley's St. Joseph's Church and moved to 1931 University Avenue, near the Davis coal and wood yard. The couple met at a party in the area now called The Claremont. Even after moving to town, Jim got up at 5 a.m. every morning and went to the ranch in Wildcat Canyon to supervise operations. By then the ranch had begun operating as a dairy farm, selling butter and milk to Berkeley residents. The Currans ranched until 1915, when the water company condemned most of their land for watershed use. After that, James would plow the experimental fields of UC Berkeley at Oxford and Virginia streets and also worked in the school's botanical gardens. One winter Sunday in February 1934 a fire broke out at Davis's yard and

A WAGON FILLED WITH PICNICKERS IN THE CURRAN RANCH AREA, A POPULAR SUNDAY DESTINATION. PEOPLE USUALLY WORKED FOR TEN OR MORE HOURS A DAY, SIX DAYS A WEEK

spread with great speed.[6] The three-alarm blaze consumed the Curran home, including many mementos from the old Wildcat Ranch.

Jim and Katie had two daughters, Genevieve and Bernice; the latter became Sister Agnes and taught in San Francisco parochial schools. At the time of the Currans' forty-fifth wedding anniversary in 1948 they were living at 1928 Berkeley Way in Berkeley with Genevieve, who was the supervisor of the Berkeley office of the Pacific Telephone and Telegraph Company. Katie was then seventy years old and Jim was eighty-five; he still worked at the University Botanical Gardens when they were shorthanded. Jim agreed to be interviewed by the university and that interview is on file at the Bancroft Library.

Katie died in Alameda County on January 13, 1953. Jim died on April 23, 1954, having lived to the ripe old age of ninety-one.

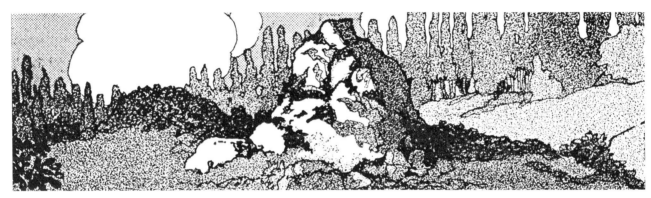

A pen and ink drawing of the rocks of Cragmont before development.

A FAMOUS 1861 PHOTO BY CARLETON WATKINS SHOT FOR THE LAND CASE OF DOMINGO PERALTA, STILL BEING DECIDED BY THE US DISTRICT COURT FOR NORTHERN CALIFORNIA. NOTE THE HILLS OF FLEMING POINT ON THE FAR LEFT AND ALBANY HILL ON THE FAR RIGHT. THE LARGE STRUCTURE BENEATH THE LEFT SIDE OF ALBANY HILL IS THE WILSON ROAD HOUSE, USED BY GOLD MINERS AND RANCH HANDS AS A HOTEL, SALOON, AND HORSE WATERING STATION. IT WAS ALSO KNOWN AS THE SEVEN MILE HOUSE, BEING SEVEN MILES FROM DOWNTOWN OAKLAND. HOTELS ON THIS ROUTE WERE NAMED IN THIS FASHION SINCE THE FERRY WHARF IN OAKLAND WAS WHERE MANY MINERS BEGAN THEIR TREK TO THE SIERRAS AND THE GOLD MINES. CAPTAIN BOWEN'S ROAD HOUSE, ONE OF THE EARLIEST AMERICAN STRUCTURES IN WEST BERKELEY, ESTABLISHED IN 1853 AT THE NORTHWEST CORNER OF SAN PABLO AVENUE AND DELAWARE STREET, WAS KNOWN AS THE SIX MILE HOUSE.

5

THE TRAGIC SAGA OF
SQUATTER ZELOTUS REED

IN THE EARLY 1850S, NORTH OF THE NEWLY SETTLED CITY OF OAKLAND and along the courses of Codornices, Marin, Middle, Blackberry, and Cerrito creeks, was a place known as Oakland Township. It was a squatter's haven for men returning empty-handed from the gold rush. Discouraged and broken, they resented the Californios—the Spanish and Mexican settlers who claimed ownership of huge stretches of land in the East Bay. One Californio, Domingo Peralta, owned all the land from Cerrito Creek south to Claremont Canyon. By way of comparison, Americans in the newly settled West typically owned 160 acres of farming land, which they acquired through land grants from the U.S. government. That the Californios' land was ranched rather than farmed also grated on some Yankee sensibilities. They considered anything but intensive farming to be mismanagement of natural resources.

Land was sold many times over in those early days, and often the sellers did not have clear title to the properties. This created havoc for pioneers; court battles over land lasted decades, as did anger and frustration.

The wild area on a rise above Blackberry Creek was prize land for these squatters, as it had been for the Native Americans who lived there before the Spanish arrived and claimed the territory. It was an area of rocky outcrops and vistas amid groves of ancient coast live oaks, caves, and sweeping grasslands teeming with wildflowers, rabbits, deer, and mountain lions. The creeks nourished the terrain all the way down to the bay and the marshes south of Albany Hill. But much as the elk and grizzly bear populations had declined through hunting and loss of habitat, the sycamore trees and other native flora were fast losing ground to the settlers.

Long-standing disputes and numerous court cases challenged the land titles

Ejected.

For years past a legal controversy has been progressing between Carpentier, Williamson and others, affecting the title to a large tract of land, about midway between this city and San Pablo. The matter has at last come to a final determination, and yesterday the Sheriff proceeded to execute the writ of restitution that had been issued. Seventeen families were affected, but in the case of all but one of them they acknowledged the title that had been established, and were granted leases on nominal terms.

FROM AN OAKLAND PAPER, CIRCA 1871.

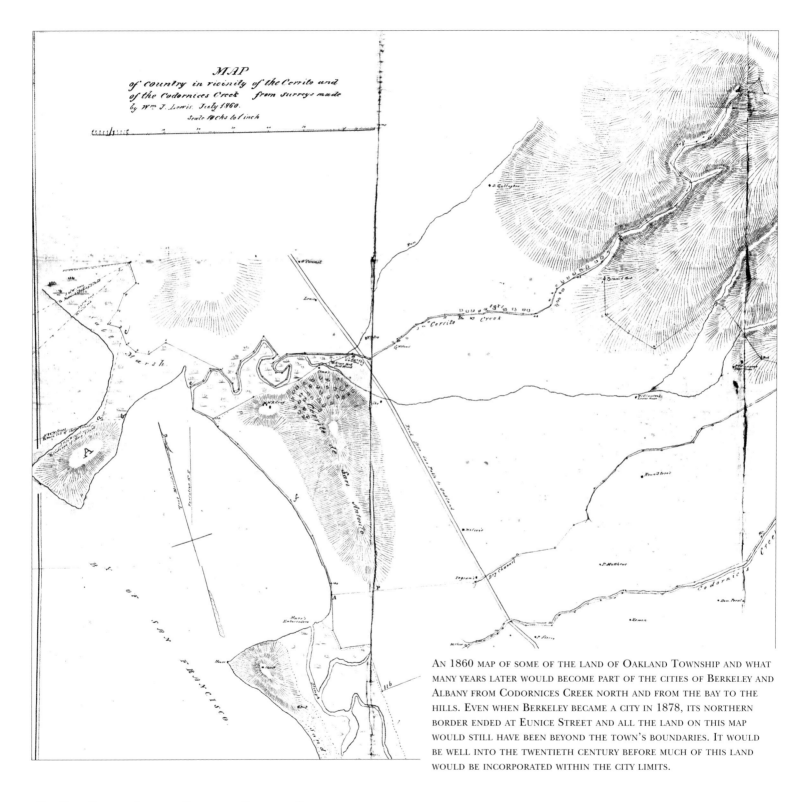

An 1860 map of some of the land of Oakland Township and what many years later would become part of the cities of Berkeley and Albany from Codornices Creek north and from the bay to the hills. Even when Berkeley became a city in 1878, its northern border ended at Eunice Street and all the land on this map would still have been beyond the town's boundaries. It would be well into the twentieth century before much of this land would be incorporated within the city limits.

of about eighteen settlers on Domingo Peralta's property near Codornices Creek. Peralta died in 1865, having lost almost all of his land to squatters, attorneys, taxes, sales, and an unpaid mortgage. Californios were wealthy in land and family but not in cash, a necessity in the new state of California, which had entered the Union in 1850.

The Williamson property—identified, like most, by the name of one of the families who lived there—comprised a large ranch with two clusters of houses and ranch buildings. The U.S. Census of 1870 listed one of the residents as Henry Williamson, who was born in New York in 1818. He had a wife named Amelia who was born in Michigan in 1839, and three children who were all born in California: Garritt (born in 1865), Mabell (1866), and Abbee (1869). He was a farmer and owned a stock ranch, listing his assets at $100,000 in real estate and $50,000 in personal property.

The upper site of the Williamson property was located near what is today the ball field of Thousand Oaks School; the lower site was situated near Neilson and Washington streets. The property was just east of the Wilson Road House, a large split-level gabled structure that was painted yellow and stood prominently on Contra Costa Road (now San Pablo Avenue), between Marin and Middle creeks. Men on their way from San Francisco to the gold fields used it as a road house, providing lodging and liquor. Carleton Watkins, a famous California landscape photographer, immortalized the building in an 1861 photograph.

The land title litigation on the Williamson property was finally decided in 1871 against the settlers and in favor of H. K. W. Clarke. Clarke, a partner in the law firm of Clarke and Carpentier, had purchased the mortgage on which Henry Williamson had defaulted, and now Clarke wanted to take control of the property. Some of the settlers purchased leases from the new legal owner and went on with their lives. But others rejected the ruling and refused to lease land they believed they already owned. Williamson evacuated his own family members, who had all been fighting illnesses, to the Castro Ranch just north of Cerrito Creek, and then to Alameda.

Among those who refused to leave was a disgruntled forty-seven-year-old man named Zelotus Reed.[1] For several years Reed had worked when he pleased, doing a variety of odd jobs in exchange for board at the Williamson Ranch. His coworkers considered him a quiet, calm man, but he was angered by the new ruling and refused to either lease or leave the land, despite the fact that he owned land out in the Moraga Valley.

Clarke, with his court ruling in hand, called on Sheriff Harry Morse of

AN ADVERTISEMENT BY THE WILLIAMSON BROTHERS IN *THE CALIFORNIA FARMER*, MARCH 1861.

THE CALIFORNIA FARMER, MARCH 1861.

This close-up shows the two compounds, upper and lower, of the Williamson Ranch.

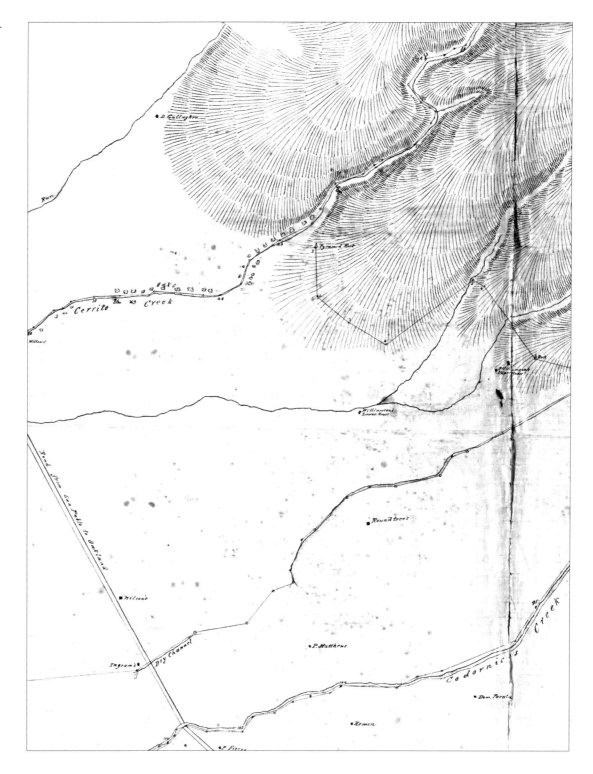

Alameda County to execute a writ of assistance to evict Williamson and his ranch hands, including Reed. It did not go well. Clarke brought his twenty-seven-year-old son, Fred, to the property when Sheriff Morse evicted Williamson, Reed, and others on Thursday, February 16, 1871. Fred Clarke had not been in good health, and H. K. W. Clarke thought the ranch environment would be good for his son. The elder Clarke gave his son some blankets, a coat, and several warnings about protecting the property, then sent him into the large gated inner house to spend the night. Prior to his eviction, Williamson and his family had lived in this part of the compound for many years.

Sheriff Morse told Williamson that he had the day to remove his possessions, which consisted of various ranch implements, harnesses, pans, kettles, and other household equipment. When it became obvious that the job could not be finished in one day, the sheriff told Williamson that he could return the next day to complete the removal of his property. Williamson moved his furniture using two wagon teams, but all of the other items remained on the site. The elder Clarke also procured another wagon team at his own expense to expedite Williamson's evacuation.

Williamson had told Clarke that much of the livestock on the ranch was not his, but that he had no interest in helping Clarke sort it out. To move the livestock it was necessary to bring all the animals up to the gated compound where Fred Clarke was staying. H. K. W. Clarke believed that Reed had left the gate open intentionally when he went to the pasture so that the livestock would get out and ruin the orchard. While Clarke, his son, and others stood inside the compound, Reed rode toward them on one of Williamson's horses, waved his hand and shouted that he would defend his rights there: "My name is Reed—old Reed. I am prepared for you, and my best heart's blood shall flow freely as water."[2] Then Reed pulled the reins hard and galloped off.

The sheriff heard Clarke tell Reed not to drive stock through the enclosure and witnessed Reed bark out his warning to the Clarkes. After half an hour, Reed felt bad about his blow-up and went to apologize to H. K. W. Clarke. But Clarke would have no part of it; he said that Reed's threats and apologies were alike to him.

The sheriff had to physically remove Reed, who flailed and yelled as he was led off the property and was therefore not permitted to gather his belongings. He was told to return the next day to retrieve his possessions, which were substantial. Friends of the Clarkes warned them that Reed was a dangerous man.

Reed still had a valise in the small house and wanted to leave it there that night, but now Clarke objected and had the sheriff deliver it to Reed. Clarke asked Sheriff Morse to prevent Reed from coming back on the ranch, since he believed Reed was the most important man to remove from the premises in order to maintain control.

Sheriff Morse assured Clarke that Reed was not staying in the small house, and Clarke inspected it and found it empty. Morse then gave Clarke official possession of the property. Williamson, exhausted and still facing much property to move, asked Clarke if he could leave a small wagon on the property overnight. Clarke agreed to that and instructed his son to let Williamson have anything he thought belonged to him. The Clarkes feared Reed, not Williamson.

When Fred Clarke, now left alone in charge of his father's property, went down to the lower compound, he found Williamson's son and an older man there trying to catch the chickens to move them from the ranch. Clarke learned from them that Williamson's crew planned to stay the night and that Williamson's men still had their beds there. Clarke complained to the sheriff, and the beds in the lower compound's small house were moved out.

That night, Reed and a thirty-three-year-old teamster and ranch hand named Charles Huntsman snuck back to the compound and stayed in the small house so that they could get an early start the next morning removing Reed's things from the ranch. Huntsman had lived in that structure while working on the Williamson Ranch for the previous three months. Williamson's old house stood about 900 feet away within the gated compound, where Fred Clarke was now camped to guard his father's interests.

Seeing a light, Fred Clarke walked over to the smaller building. The sheriff had assured the Clarkes that Reed was gone, so Fred demanded that the two men leave. According to Fred Clarke, Reed was upset and threatened him again by touting his ability to defend himself, saying that he could take care of himself and shoot as well as the next man. When Clarke left the small house, he told people that Reed had threatened to take possession of it. Fred Clarke's nervousness was getting the best of him: he was shaken by the day's events and uncomfortable in these unfamiliar surroundings. And there was not even a real bed where he might calm himself with rest. Fred Clarke could not sleep the entire night.

Early the next morning, Reed and Huntsman got right to work removing Reed's belongings. Meanwhile, Charles F. Wait, the nephew of Horace Carpentier, H. K. W. Clarke's law partner, arrived to help. He had been there the day before as well. A woman who lived on the ranch overheard Clarke and Wait talking about their fear that Reed would take possession of a small house on the property and that they thought he had a pistol.

Huntsman took two loads of animal traps early that day to Jacob's Wharf, a few miles away. Henry Williamson had gone to San Francisco to arrange for a boat to take everything from Jacob's Wharf to Alameda, where his family had relocated. Huntsman returned for a third load, consisting of a broken sulky whose shafts were upstairs and other parts scattered around the stable, an old buggy, and some more traps. He was assisted by another ranch hand named James Dyer.

When Huntsman pulled into the back of the stable, he heard a man bringing Fred Clarke to settle a dispute. There was a quarrel over whether a horse belonging to one of Clarke's men could be fed from a pile of Williamson's barley. The day before, Williamson had given Clarke permission to feed the horses, but Huntsman did not know that and tried to protect his boss's assets, calling Clarke a "damn thief" and a "hireling."[3] Clarke became agitated and demanded that Huntsman take his rig, leave immediately, and not return inside the gated compound. Wait and a couple who lived on the ranch witnessed this interaction. Huntsman stomped back to the small house to fetch Reed to help him deal with moving the possessions and the rising tensions at the compound. Huntsman thought that Clarke would calm down by the time the two returned to finish their job. When Huntsman arrived at the little house in the lower area, Reed was in his stocking feet packing up some things. Huntsman looked over the objects in the room—a couple of chairs, beds, blankets, trunks, a valise, and a carpetbag. There were a few items from the big house that had been brought there the night before, some of which belonged to Reed and Huntsman as well as Williamson.

When Reed and Huntsman returned with a wagon and team of horses for another load, Fred Clarke told them that everything must be taken out on this last load. Reed, annoyed by his meddling, responded that maybe they would and maybe they would not finish in one load. Reed and Huntsman left the team inside the gated compound and returned to the lower house. While the men were gone, Clarke and Wait drove the two horses out of the compound.

At 2:30 in the afternoon, Reed drove his wagon up to the gate of the inner enclosure where the last cache of things to be removed was stored. In the back of Reed's wagon was a valise, a pair of pants, and some assorted clothing. Fred Clarke ordered the two men to remain outside the gate. Reed said he had authority to come in and would do his duty. Reed got off the wagon and opened the gate, in spite of a warning from Clarke not to enter. Reed repeated that he would do his duty. Reed waited as Huntsman drove through, holding the horses in a tight rein at a little faster than a walk. Fred Clarke and Wait stood guard inside the gate and tried to stop the horses from coming through the gate but moved out of the way when they realized they would be run down. Reed then closed the gate and got back on the wagon's buckboard, his feet dangling off the side of the wagon, and turned back toward Clarke. Huntsman stood in the back of the wagon still holding the reins.

Suddenly, Fred Clarke zipped out his Sharpe's four-barrel pistol and told the two men that they must leave immediately. Clarke threatened to shoot and leveled the gun at the men from behind their wagon. Already consumed with anger and loss, Reed was in no mood for a confrontation but he felt too wronged to be pushed any farther. "Shoot away," Reed spit back at Clarke.[4]

Clarke began to fire. His first shot, at Huntsman, fell wide of the mark. He emptied the other three barrels at Reed, knocking him backwards. Huntsman did not know that Reed was hit and kept driving the rig another 180 feet. Then he heard Reed gasp, "I am killed!"[5] Zelotus Reed had been shot through the heart. Huntsman saw that Wait was about to hand Clarke a pistol that he'd hidden in his pants. Huntsman yelled: "You have already killed one man and that is enough."[6] Huntsman's anguished rebuke that they were not armed ended the exchange. Huntsman grabbed the valise from the back of the wagon and put it under his friend's head. Fred Clarke grabbed a wet towel and bathed Reed's head in water, yelling at Wait to fetch Huntsman a horse so that he could get to Oakland and bring back a doctor. Everyone was in shock. Huntsman, propelled by adrenaline and horror, raced to Oakland and along the way frantically informed police of the ghastly event.

By the time two doctors returned with Huntsman, Reed lay dead in the back of the wagon. Williamson arrived from San Francisco where he had been trying to arrange for another boat to transfer his final load of possessions from Jacob's Wharf to Alameda. Huntsman and Williamson stayed at the ranch that night and continued the now solemn job of loading the wagons.

Clarke and Wait turned themselves in to the authorities, and were immediately arrested and jailed for trial. Wait's gun was unfired and still loaded with seven shots, but he was arrested for offering the weapon to Clarke while he was attacking Reed and Huntsman. Trials were speedy in those days—a jury was summoned the Saturday morning after the murder—and jurors were permitted to question the witnesses themselves. Notable lawyers represented both sides. Clarke and Wait were questioned for five days in a densely packed Oakland Police Court. The trial was officially a preliminary examination because the incident took place outside the city limits.

The trial revealed a mass of conflicting reports, some justifying the shooting, others describing it as the heinous murder of an unarmed man. The defendants pleaded not guilty.

Detectives searched a large trunk owned by Reed and found no guns; neither Reed nor Huntsman was carrying a gun at the time of the shooting. But Fred Clarke, nervous and fearful, had convinced himself that the unarmed men were prepared to kill him for defending his father's land. During the preliminary examination, Clarke and his witnesses tried to present the stories they had heard indicating that Reed was a dangerous man, and how he had once threatened a man with a knife over some property in Moraga. Though there were many stories, no one presented any proof that Reed had ever physically harmed anyone. At one point the prosecutor asked one witness, as he did each who took the stand, if they knew of an incident where Reed had injured someone. This man answered, "Not bodily," to which the prosecutor shot back, "Did he injure their souls?" For a moment in this sad affair, laughter broke out in the courtroom.

Many witnesses testified to the good character of the defendants, including Edson Adams, one of the founders of Oakland and an old law partner of Horace Carpentier; and F. K. Shattuck, who previously had been mayor and a city councilman in Oakland and an Alameda County supervisor. In 1868 Shattuck had built a magnificent estate on Shattuck Avenue, in an area where he owned a lot of property. Shattuck was so politically powerful that in 1876 he persuaded the Central Pacific Railroad to extend its line from Oakland into the remote area, now downtown Berkeley. Shattuck's first job with the city of Oakland was as a clerk appointed by Horace Carpentier, H. K. W. Clarke's law partner.

The defense pushed the concept of justifiable homicide and tried to show that Wait did not have any motive to assist in a murder. The prosecution in turn tried to show that this was a murder by two men who were trying to take the law into their own hands, and that the only thing that would discourage this kind of behavior was strict administration of justice.

Judge Anselm H. Jayne found that there was sufficient cause to believe Fredrick F. Clarke guilty of murder and handed him over to the sheriff to be tried in the Alameda County court. Jayne considered Wait to be a truthful witness who did not attempt to shield his friend. The judge found that there was no evidence to charge Wait, and he was released. Fred Clarke was soon released on $30,000 bail, but, through the seemingly intentional inaction of a grand jury, never paid any of it.

Clarke was brought before another grand jury two months later, in April 1871. This jury, like the first, consisted of some of the area's most prominent men, including Anthony Chabot, the man who developed Chabot Reservoir;

J. A. Folger, the coffee and spice magnate, who owned a large tract of land spanning Oakland and Berkeley's western end and for whom Folger Street is named; and William Brey, a prominent Oakland businessman. Amazingly, this jury also ignored the bail, exonerated Clarke's bail, and simply discharged the defendant. Many people were shocked at this turn of events. The district attorney tried to get the case resubmitted due to errors in the proceedings, but was unsuccessful. Other points were argued, but the case ultimately was shelved for two years and only reconsidered after great public outcry. The case was referred to yet another grand jury, which also ignored the bail, and the case was dismissed on March 23, 1880, never to be tried. It was commonly believed that Clarke's well-connected father had pulled many strings to ensure the release of his son.

An Oakland editorial described community reaction to dismissal of the case:

> There was a great deal of feeling in this case, not only in Alameda County, but outside it. It was presumed that the wealth of the accused and his social position had much to do with his escape; it was charged that he received the favor of the legal fraternity; that his father was a lawyer; that members of the judiciary became his bondsmen; that the Supreme Court Judges favored him; that all the land-grabbers in the country gathered around him; that Horace W. Carpentier had used his wealth and influence unsparingly for his protection; and all because the man who was slain had in his capacity, as a settler on some disputed lands in Contra Costa County, rendered himself obnoxious to these parties in defending his own and his neighbors' rights against their encroachments.
>
> Much space is given here to this celebrated case, because it is looked upon as one to be ever held up as an example, showing the danger to life and liberty, even under our free and popular system of government, when certain influences are allowed to be exercised. Indeed, the whole affair is looked upon as marvelous, and such as not to be credited only that the evidence of it is so recent, and all the facts are so patent, with what assiduity and ability the mind must have worked and the hand directed, that produced such extraordinary results and defeated justice, shielding a culprit and threw the darkest shades of suspicion on the machinery of the law![7]

Years later, Fred Clarke was charged with embezzling money due the estate of his father.

More than twenty years after California became a state, squatters' rights

and many land title disputes remained unresolved. The confusion surrounding many sales and unusual transactions caused chaos, division, and even death in the East Bay.

The tragic murder of Zelotus Reed was archetypal for many early California citizens, a classic saga of rich against poor, murder, government corruption, and the illegal influence of money, all over a piece of land made lush by a life-giving creek. In the 1870s and 1880s, the ranch house of the gated compound was dubbed a haunted house by many Berkeley children who wandered the hillsides beyond the town limits but fearfully avoided it, having only the vaguest of notions of what had occurred there many years before.

Blackberry Creek ran open through the Thousand Oaks School yard (developed in 1921) until the 1940s, when it was covered with a culvert. The creek was uncovered again in 1995. Today, it murmurs quietly toward Ensenada Avenue and offers a glimpse of the natural grandeur that once prevailed in the open and remote country we know as North Berkeley.

THE STRUCTURES IN THE MID-LEFT OF THE PHOTOGRAPH ARE PROBABLY THE REMAINS OF THE WILLIAMSON RANCH UPPER COMPOUND. THIS PHOTO, CIRCA 1908, CAPTURES THE STATE OF THE AREA AROUND TODAY'S SOLANO AVENUE.

A PHOTO OF MARY TOWNSEND THAT WAS KEPT AMONG
THE FAMILY PHOTOS OF THE TEAGUE FAMILY. SHE
PROBABLY WORKED FOR THE FAMILY SINCE SHE WAS
NOT RELATED. THIS REFLECTS THE HIGH REGARD MANY
OF HER CLIENTS HAD FOR HER.

6

THE RAILROAD MEETS THE BERKELEY SPIRIT: THE MARY TOWNSEND SAGA

IN THE MID-1870S, SHATTUCK AVENUE WAS JUST BEING SETTLED. THE university had just opened in 1873, and only a handful of permanent residents lived in the area. The town's first commercial center was at Shattuck Avenue and Dwight Way, where a general store called Stewart & Trowbridge occupied a wooden building on the southeast corner. If you were looking for a shirt, instead of looking for a brand or style, you would pick the one with the fewest specks of dirt.[1] Blacksmith Charles Cain worked right next door on the south side of the general store. Dwight Way, Alcatraz Avenue, and University Avenue were the only roads connecting San Pablo and Shattuck avenues. The lines between town and farmland were blurry, so it wasn't uncommon to find commerce mingling with cornfields like the one planted on the 2000 block of Center Street. A huge muddy lake bordered the east side of Shattuck Avenue between Addison Street and University, delaying any development there for years. It functioned as a natural swimming hole and frog pond, and its fecund banks of shrubs and dense willow, alder, oak, and buckeye trees offered birds and boys a place of refuge.

While the town still boasted more fields than houses, those with keen eyes for future development were already securing prized parcels. Near Stewart & Trowbridge, the estates of Francis K. Shattuck and James L. Barker, two well-connected capitalists, blossomed with the splendor of their hard-earned success. West of Shattuck Avenue was open land; the farm of James McGee, who had worked this parcel since 1852, occupied the area that today is bounded by Dwight Way, University Avenue, Martin Luther King Jr. Way, and San Pablo Avenue. His farm had been the impetus for the construction of a road, originally called Higgins Lane, running east from San Pablo Avenue to the entrance of his farmhouse, which was close to the street later named after him. Higgins Lane was later

STILL HOLDS THE FORT

Gray Haired Old Dame Townsend Defies the Authorities

She Moves Her House Out Upon Shattuck Avenue Claiming the Ground Is Her Own.

BERKELEY GAZETTE, NOVEMBER 6, 1896.

ABOVE: CORNER OF SHATTUCK AVENUE AND DWIGHT WAY, THE GENERAL STORE IN EAST BERKELEY. ITS NAME CHANGED MANY TIMES AS THE BUSINESS CHANGED HANDS OVER THE YEARS.

RIGHT: F. K. SHATTUCK'S HOUSE CIRCA 1885. SHATTUCK WAS AN OWNER OF A VERY SUCCESSFUL LIVERY BUSINESS IN OAKLAND, AN EARLY MAYOR, AND AN ALAMEDA COUNTY SUPERVISOR. HE OWNED MUCH OF WHAT WE CONSIDER DOWNTOWN BERKELEY WHEN THE AREA BEGAN TO DEVELOP, THE RESULT OF HIS UNTIRING EFFORTS AND HIS CIVIC AND ENTREPRENEURIAL ZEAL.

THE JAMES BARKER HOUSE AT 2031 DWIGHT WAY, CIRCA 1877. BARKER IS STANDING ON THE RIGHT, PRESUMABLY WITH HIS WIFE. HIS FAITHFUL CHINESE "HOUSE BOY" IS STANDING AT THE TOP OF THE STEPS, OBVIOUSLY A TRUSTED MEMBER OF THE FAMILY TO BE ASKED TO POSE IN THE PHOTO. (OR WAS THIS A SHOW OF STATUS? OR BOTH?) BARKER HAD PURCHASED FORTY ACRES BOUNDED BY DWIGHT WAY TO BANCROFT WAY AND SHATTUCK AVENUE TO GROVE STREET (NOW MARTIN LUTHER KING JR. WAY) FROM F. K. SHATTUCK. HE HAD MADE HIS MONEY AS A PLUMBING SUPPLY AGENT FOR A SAN FRANCISCO COMPANY, BUT CAME TO BERKELEY TO SPECULATE IN REAL ESTATE.

extended to Shattuck Avenue and renamed Dwight Way.

But even those of modest means managed to stake significant claims. Mary Townsend, a well-respected Civil War widow, was one of the neighborhood's early residents and landowners. She lived on Shattuck in a modest little wooden house that she had moved by oxen from Ellsworth Street.[2] A hardworking soul in her fifties, Mary began cleaning houses, taking in laundry and ironing, and performing whatever tasks she could to make ends meet and provide for herself and her teenage son, Charles. As the town expanded, Mary spent the next several decades working for some of the best families of Berkeley. These families had great affection for her. Their warm feelings grew into esteem as Mary again and again demonstrated an unfailing work ethic and conscientious nature that made her all but indispensable. One Berkeley pioneer family, the Teagues, even kept a photo of Mary with their own family pictures.[3]

There was never a shortage of housework in those days. There were pieces of furniture to move and rugs to drag outdoors and beat. Unpaved roads and limited landscaping meant that dirt, dust, and mud were tracked into homes so that

FRANCIS KITTREDGE SHATTUCK.

floors required almost constant attention. There was also wood to chop for the wood-burning stoves, and there were kerosene lamps that needed filling and whose wicks required snipping. In addition, all laundry was done by hand, and someone would have to walk to the store each day to buy fresh vegetables and meats for the daily meals, which were all prepared from scratch. These were just a few of the many tasks Mary might be asked to help with.

Frugal Mary was both industrious and savvy enough to have purchased property around town in its early stage of development. She also took in boarders. As a single working mother, she could only depend on herself. Her son, Charles, could be more of a hindrance than a help, such as when he was arrested in San Francisco in possession of a watch and $85 belonging to one of his mother's boarders.[4]

Townsend's employers admired her fortitude. Years later, Dr. Mary Bennett, a Berkeley physician, fondly remembered Mary Townsend:

> *Mrs. Townsend, a character of early Berkeley days, took care of our house. When the railroad was laid on Shattuck Avenue a lot owned by her was condemned against her will. She vowed no train should run over that lot except across her body. When that great event, the approach of the first train occurred, she sat down in the middle of the track, on her lot. The train was forced to stop, but Berkeley's burly policemen, with adequate assistance, succeeded in carrying off the kicking, scratching woman whose property rights she considered had been unjustly usurped. This incident was a classic of early Berkeley history. Later the same fiery little woman served me faithfully and cheerfully in various capacities for many years. Whenever I needed extra help I could rely upon Mrs. Townsend.[5]*

Dr. Bennett's story about Mary Townsend is echoed in similar accounts by other early town residents. According to the May 9, 1900, edition of the *Berkeley Daily Gazette,* "Several pioneers say that they can remember with vividness the scene that Mrs. Townsend enacted when the first train was run through. They allege that she lay upon the rails and had to be removed by force." Another article published in 1913 reported similar accounts: "Older residents of the city recall the day that Mrs. Townsend, with a revolver in her hands, threw herself across the railroad track at Shattuck Avenue and Haste Street and literally defied the engineer to bring his engine nearer. The engine was stopped and after a hasty but temporary compromise, the first Southern Pacific passenger train entered the city."[6]

How did this modest housekeeper come to fight such a formidable foe?

Mary's accomplishments were borne of her strong will and principles. Some of the town's most powerful residents ran up against those traits when they tried to force the small workingwoman to do something she did not think was fair.

In the mid-1870s, Francis Shattuck and James Barker convinced the Central Pacific Railroad to continue its Oakland steam railroad up Shattuck Avenue, where both men owned large tracts of land. The two had wanted to develop their properties and would benefit by the extension of the new rail line to the isolated area, where the few roads were in terrible condition. By 1876, the preparations were almost complete; the railroad held easements to the frontage portions of all lots on Shattuck Avenue, save two.

Track was laid right up to the homes of Mary A. Townsend and Peter Maloney, who both lived on the east side of Shattuck Avenue south of Channing Way. (Haste Street had not yet been cut through to Shattuck Avenue.) Townsend and Maloney refused to sell their land or grant easements across their front yards. Their lots were shallow, and if they ceded the fifty-foot portion requested by the railroad, their houses would be pressed right up to the tracks. The railroad there-fore made a loop around their properties, known as the "Maloney curve," while the county started legal action to condemn the disputed land for fifty years, the life of the railroad franchise.[7]

Barker offered to give Mary Townsend a lot behind her current property if she would give the railroad her fifty-foot frontage on Shattuck Avenue. He emphasized that the lot he offered measured 178 feet in length, while hers was only 138 feet long. Mary respectfully explained that this larger lot was surrounded by other lots and had no street access. She countered that she would accept a lot "foot for foot" across the street, which would still have road access after the tracks were laid, if the lot was within 250 feet of Channing Way. She also requested that he move her house and pay her $1,000 for her trouble. Her counter offer was not accepted.[8]

House moving in these days was much easier than it is today, especially for small cottages. There were no electric wires and no indoor plumbing. A house was simply placed on a big pulley (called a "hawser"), attached by rope to a team of horses, and pulled to another location.

It raised Mary's working-class hackles that Shattuck and Barker were offering her deals that she felt were unfair. She did not want to move and believed that these men were interested only in their own financial gain. Mary felt their offers and behavior demonstrated a lack of respect, and this roused her fighting sensibilities. She made no effort to hide her indignation when dealing with these men

JAMES L. BARKER.

Report of committee on streets and highways appointed to examine into the matter of Mr. Maloney and Mrs. Townsend and the Berkeley Branch Railroad, which railroad occupies a portion of Shattuck avenue, between Dwight and Channing ways. We, the undersigned committee, have examined said railroad, and we find it is an obstruction and an inconvenience to the traveling public, and a damage to Mr. Maloney and Mrs. Townsend's property, and it is the opinion of your committee that said railroad ought to be removed.　C. SCHNELLE, JAMES McGEE.

BERKELEY ADVOCATE, JUNE 6, 1878.

THE USE OF HAWSERS AND HORSES TO MOVE BERKELEY
CITY HALL IN THE NINETEENTH CENTURY.

or with Alameda County officials (the city of Berkeley was not incorporated until 1878), who continued to give her the runaround. Mary finally hired an attorney, who repeatedly petitioned the Alameda County Board of Supervisors to remove the tracks from Shattuck Avenue entirely, claiming that they constituted the use of a public street for a private enterprise.[9] On October 11, 1877, the *Berkeley Advocate* reported on events at an Alameda County Board of Supervisors meeting related to Mary's struggle:

> *Mrs. Townsend, who was present, stepped up to the railing that separates*
> *spectators from the board, and, raising her veil, gave that exceedingly*
> *grave body a piece of her mind. She said the matter had been referred*
> *again and again to the same delegation without any action whatever*
> *having been taken, and she protested against being put off in this manner.*

Later in the meeting Mary used more than words to convey her outrage:

> *Mary Ann Townsend, of Shattuck avenue railroad notoriety, attacked*
> *Mr. Shattuck, who made some remarks not to her liking. She seized him*
> *by his long beard and gave him several lusty jerks. As he was about to*

resent her attack, several Supervisors loosened Mary Ann's grip and led

her out of the Court-house. The matter of interfering with the railroad was

postponed for six months by a vote of six to one.[10]

Shortly after the city of Berkeley was incorporated, Mary filed suit against both the County of Alameda and the City of Berkeley for illegally granting use of a public street to a private (not municipal) railway. The court ruled that Mary Townsend and Peter Maloney should be paid the costs of moving their houses further back on their lots, but confirmed that the track would be laid on their land. The pair kept title to their lots, and the railroad was granted an easement for fifty years. After paying her legal fees, Mary saw only a small amount of the $1,030 awarded her.[11] Charles Crocker, the railroad magnate of the Central Pacific, wrote a letter to the *Berkeley Advocate* informing the public that he would not pay the Townsend award, and that he had never received the right-of-way nor was he paid for his tracks, and that if the neighbors did not pay Mary's fees, he would rip the tracks up. The owners of the surrounding properties promptly paid Mary's judgment. Furthermore, Central Pacific built a special driveway to her house over its tracks.[12] She was left with the little cottage, a tiny lot (now fifty feet by thirty-six feet), and great resentment. By about 1880, Mary and her son had moved to her property near Rose and California streets, but she kept her Shattuck Avenue property, most likely renting it out.

Some twenty years later, Shattuck Avenue had become a thriving business district. Francis Shattuck had built some commercial buildings south of University Avenue and businesses had sprung up on both sides of the street offering many goods and services not available in the area previously.

Over the years, the muddy swimming hole at the east end of Shattuck Avenue between Addison and University had become an unofficial garbage dump. Though the railroad had rights to the property, complaints by citizens forced the railroad to permit the townspeople to beautify the site.[13]

Berkeleyans also complained about the unpaved areas between the railroad tracks in the downtown area. People often tripped over the ties, and the spaces between them gathered trash. In the winter of 1896, the city started paving between the tracks. Work went smoothly right up to the property of Mary Townsend, now in her seventies, who refused to let the project continue. She said that twenty years ago she had agreed to allow the railroad through, but she had not granted the use of her land as a public street. The city attorney advised the workers to continue paving as a matter of public safety.[14]

A Woman's Anger.

At the last meeting of the Alameda Supervisors, Mary Ann Townsend, of Shattuck avenue railroad notoriety, attacked Mr. Shattuck, who made some remarks not to her liking. She seized him by his long beard and gave him several lusty jerks. As he was about to resent her attack, several Supervisors loosened Mary Ann's grip and led her out of the Court-house. The matter of interfering with the railroad was postponed for six months by a vote of six to one.

BERKELEY ADVOCATE, OCTOBER 11, 1877.

The Price of Progress for Steam Trains in Berkeley

Most folks looked upon the new steam rail line as progress, particularly those who did not live adjacent to the tracks. Those who did live near the line would fly to their windows at the first sound of chugging to shut them tightly. Otherwise, black soot would shoot through the rooms while smoke stole the breathable air. Soot settled everywhere, and a burnt smell would linger for the rest of the day. Although the steam train brought visitors to town and carried commuters to work, the price of progress for people living close to the tracks was considerable.

RIGHT, TOP, AND BOTTOM: PEN AND INK DRAWING OF THE WEST SIDE OF SHATTUCK AVENUE IN 1896 FROM UNIVERSITY AVENUE SOUTH BEYOND CENTER STREET.

SHATTUCK AVENUE.—BERKELEY.

SHATTUCK AVENUE.—BERKELEY.

Maloney had already ceded a fifty-nine-foot-wide strip of land, and this area was quickly macadamized using crushed stone and tar. The city had no claim to the land in front of Mary Townsend's place, so the macadamizing company refused to pave it. Indeed, the city inadvertently contradicted itself by taxing individual property owners for the amount of the macadam—a tacit acknowledgment that the lots were private land.[15]

The town trustees, the old equivalent of the current City Council, repeatedly attempted to condemn Mary's land. In 1896, the town attorney advised the trustees that Mary's land could be claimed, since the city had been in "peaceable

possession of it as a thoroughfare for the past five years."[16] But Mary Townsend claimed the right to her private property and refused "to surrender until the town obtains a legal title by regular process of law."[17] Thus, the imbroglio began anew.

Mary, recalling her previous experience, believed that officials again intended to muscle her into giving up part of her lot. She felt she had a right to her hard-earned property and was outraged at what she saw as the law being bent on behalf of big business. Once again, Mary's strong working-class values fueled her public vow to fight city hall.

On Saturday, October 30, 1896, Mary employed Berkeley contractor W. P. Grant to procure a permit from Berkeley Street Superintendent Guy H. Chick to move her house. The permit was issued, according to the *Berkeley Advocate* of November 6, 1896, for removing the house to a lot Mary owned on the south side of California Street, near Rose Street. It was assumed that she had decided to go along with the city's paving plan.

The assumption was wrong. Grant moved Mary's house back to its original location, about twenty-five feet forward, placing it squarely on top of the railroad tracks. Superintendent Chick confronted Mary over her use of the permit, and Mary rebuked him with "such sarcastic language" that he had her arrested and taken to Town Hall for a hearing.

While Mary was thus engaged, the city moved the house back off the tracks to its previous location.

On the night of November 5, Mary, now back at home, had contractor Grant again move the house, now known by the townsfolk as "Fort Townsend," back

W. P. GRANT, BERKELEY HOUSE MOVER. GRANT, A WELL-KNOWN BERKELEY CONTRACTOR, MOVED MARY TOWNSEND'S HOUSE BACK ONTO SHATTUCK AVENUE. GRANT WAS ALSO A VOLUNTEER FIREMAN. NOTE HOW HIS WORN TIE IS CUT SHORT. HIS HELPER, ON ONE KNEE, TURNS A SCREW JACK WITH A LARGE WRENCH TO RAISE THE POST.

onto the railway. She then cut the rope to the hawser with a hand axe, paid Grant, and sent him out of the battle zone.[18]

Next, the deputy street superintendent appeared, accompanied by a house mover, and ordered that the house be removed from the tracks. To his surprise, well-known attorney Thomas Graber stood by Mary's side. They ordered the city men off the premises, threatening charges of trespassing. At one point Graber laid his hands on the deputy and was almost arrested himself.[19]

Mary took her post guarding the house. Her friends and spies about town got word that Chick, along with the town attorney and a house mover, were planning to move the house yet again at midnight. Mary prepared herself. Her son, Charles, arrived to help. A wagon full of city men appeared, but upon seeing Mary "with determined mien and a gun in hand," beat a hasty retreat.[20]

The morning autumn sun of November 6, 1896, peeking above the Berkeley Hills, was reflected in the shiny nickel revolver in Mary's hand. According to the *Berkeley Advocate* of November 6, 1896:

> *Early this morning passers by were surprised to see her cottage out over the line of the sidewalk, with the determined little gray haired woman on guard on the porch to protect her house against all intruders, whether burglars, or town officials. . . . The plucky woman had stood guard all night, and is still on guard, apparently suffering not at all from lack of sleep.*

As Mary stood on her porch, Chick arrived with his men, intending to quickly move the house back. But "Mrs. Townsend, revolver in hand, cautioned him not to advance a step upon her property, and pointed the gun with such excellent aim that he and his supporters deemed it best to withdraw to a safer distance."[21] Mary waved the building permit for moving her house at Chick. As far as she was concerned, she had paid for the permit and was in compliance with the terms—the permit allowed her a full thirty days to complete her move.

Chick withdrew to City Hall and procured a new weapon—a warrant to arrest Townsend for threatening assault with a deadly weapon. His men stayed by their wagon all afternoon, just beyond range of Mary Townsend's revolver. Trustee President J. W. Richards and Town Attorney Brewton A. Hayne were convinced that Townsend had no right to the property, and therefore no right to defend it. But Mary felt that it was more than legal to draw a revolver on men who trespassed on what she was sure was her property, particularly after her many warnings.

Deputy Marshal Kerns was chosen to serve Townsend the warrant. Nobody wanted to serve it on the old woman—and nobody wanted to be shot dead in the process. Mary Townsend's many friends rallied to her side to help her guard the house.

Plucky Mary and her son stood guard for forty-eight hours. By November 7, exhaustion was taking a toll on the elderly woman. Though forced to take to her

SAN FRANCISCO CALL, NOVEMBER 11, 1896.

bed, she moved it so she could view the street while lying down, revolver at her side.[22] Her perseverance was her strongest weapon against these mighty foes.

On this day, Marshal Richard Lloyd visited Mary at her house to arrest her. Lloyd soon realized that she was in no condition to be taken to prison and decided to wait a few days before serving the warrant.

The *San Francisco Call* published an interview with Mary Townsend on November 8, 1896:

> *Although I am down with nervous prostration, I am not conquered . . . With me there is no such thing as retreat. I fear neither police nor prison in this matter. When Marshal Lloyd comes to arrest me I shall submit peacefully to the mandate of the law and give bail for my appearance in court. I do not believe in murder as a general proposition but in this case I believe I would be justified in killing any man who attempted to remove my home off this disputed land. I have given everybody interested fair warning that I shall shoot the first intruder. In fact I will shoot a dozen men before I will submit to them trampling upon my rights.*
>
> *I have two great corporations to fight in this matter—the town and the railroad company. It is true that I am only an old lady, but I know how to handle a pistol and I guess I can hold my own against all comers. Now I do not want to be driven into the position of shooting anybody, but I am so thoroughly convinced that I am right that I shall not hesitate a moment to shoot if occasion requires.*

On November 23, the Board of Trustees ordered the marshall to remove the "obstruction" from Shattuck Avenue.[23] A large number of townsfolk gathered to observe the affair, but the house mover failed to show up. The following day, the president of the Board of Trustees and Mary's attorneys drew up a compromise, which Mary refused to sign, since it called for the house to be moved away from the tracks while the courts settled the matter.

On November 25, Chick again had a house mover at Mary's cottage, ready for action. Marshal Lloyd knocked on the door.[24] Mary opened it and, upon seeing it was Lloyd, promptly attempted to slam it shut. Lloyd forced the door open and suddenly felt the cold barrel of a revolver against his chest. It was known that Mary had two guns, only one of which was loaded. When she pulled the trigger, the marshal's deputies instantly overwhelmed and disarmed her. Fortunately, the gun aimed at Marshal Lloyd's chest was the empty one, and Lloyd, although

slightly scratched and bruised, remained among the living. Mary became hysterical and was taken to Town Hall in a wagon.

Mary was arrested, pleaded not guilty, and was released on her own recognizance. Within an hour of Mary's being thus engaged in court, city officials had her house moved back to where they wanted it.

By the end of November 1896, Mary had succeeded in getting an injunction against the continued macadamizing of her part of Shattuck Avenue.[25] She also asked for $500 in damages to her property. Still at issue was who owned the property; if Mary prevailed, the city still intended to condemn it.

On December 2, 1896, Mary was in court on Chick's latest charge of assault with a deadly weapon.[26] This felony case was dismissed, partly because Mary had possessed a loaded weapon but had chosen not to use it. Upon dismissal, she was immediately rearrested and charged with a misdemeanor for exhibiting a deadly weapon in a rude, angry, and threatening manner. The legal battles would continue for years.

Mary Townsend's name disappears from the Berkeley directories in 1898. In July 1901, the disputed portion of her land was reported to finally be in the legal possession of the city.[27] According to the *Berkeley Daily Gazette*, March 23, 1901:

*After successfully holding up the Southern Pacific Railroad Company
and standing off the town of Berkeley for twenty-five years, Mrs. Mary
Townsend, the famous defender of her property rights at Haste street and
Shattuck avenue, has withdrawn from her citadel with all the honors of
war and a full indemnity from her enemies she has battled with so long.
The town has given up its long fight and the condemnation proceedings
by which it sought to dispossess Mrs. Townsend of the little strip of land
extending half way across Shattuck avenue and the railroad tracks at
Haste street have been compromised by the payment of $500 to the aged
defender.*

Mary actually received a settlement of $475. The Southern Pacific Railroad
(the Southern Pacific had acquired the Central Pacific) released any claim it had
on the land, only twenty-five years into its fifty-year franchise. Mary and her son,
Charles, had arrived in Berkeley when it was a rural village. After decades of fighting for her property rights, she and Charles made the decision to move back to
a country environment. In 1901, they moved to rural Santa Rosa in the Felton
precinct and farmed there until Mary's death in 1908.

In 1903, the city of Berkeley wanted to open Haste Street down to Shattuck
Avenue. Mary sold the city a portion of her now tiny property (about thirty feet by
thirty-four feet) that occupied land where the street was to be built for $75.[28] In
late 1906, after the town had filled with refugees from the 1906 earthquake and
real estate was in great demand, Mary, no longer a Berkeley resident, decided to
let her Shattuck property go. She sold her property and house to Enoch Morrill,
who soon built apartments on her lot to accommodate the city's huge population
boom.[29] Mary even carried back the loan to Morrill.

Mary's son grew up to sport a new career almost every year. In Berkeley,
Charles was a plumber, a porter, a clerk, a sexton for the First Congregational
Church, a laundryman, a dairyman, and a farmer; he also worked as a stove
mounter in San Francisco. After his mother's death, he returned to Berkeley and
took a job as a general office man for the Mills Company, a real estate firm. In the
spring of 1913 he suffered from heart trouble and died at Alcatraz and Telegraph
avenues while walking to a church event with a friend.

It was noted that the strip of land in front of Mary Townsend's place
remained unimproved—neither graded nor macadamized—to that day in the
summer of 1901 when her lawsuits were settled, a visible reminder of the determination of Berkeley's own Mary Townsend.[30]

A Helpful Suggestion from John E. Boyd

A John Boyd editorial in the *Berkeley Gazette,* November 25, 1896:

If ever a man had a reason to complain of the injustice of our town officials, I am that unfortunate individual. Talk about the atrocities committed in Turkey, talk about Spanish cruelties in Cuba, they are no comparison to the faithless action of our Town Trustees toward your humble servant.

But to explain, Mr. Editor, for years it has been my ambition to hold some town office. I was not particular as to what office it was as long as the salary was good, I looked the offices of Marshal, Clerk and Assessor over, considered the merits and demerits of each and finally decided that the office of Superintendent of Streets would about suit a man of my gigantic intellect.

But to depose Mr. Chick, ah, there's the rub. As Mr. Chick is a young man (almost a spring chicken) there was very little hopes of his dying or resigning, why, I might be somewhat advanced in years myself before that desirable event happened, but luck was in my favor. Mrs. Townsend had moved her home out into the street and the Town Trustees had ordered it back again, and, as the old lady had threatened to shoot the man who laid hands on her property, it was now my lucky star in the ascendant. It would be Mr. Chick's duty as Superintendent of Streets to lead the battle and do the work that others might fear to do.

I made it my business to see President Richards and strongly urged the matter that Mrs. Townsend's house should be moved back at once. But, said Mr. Richards, would it not be a good idea to go slowly and try to have the matter settled peaceably. "No," said I, " just consider the matter, What would Spain say? What will be the opinion in the British House of Parliament if the report goes abroad that the Town Trustees of Berkeley have been bluffed by Mrs. Townsend. No, sir, it is your duty to force this matter and it is Mr. Chick's duty to lead in the assault on the fortress." "But," said Mr. R., "suppose that Mr. Chick should be hurt by Mrs. Townsend's gun?"

Well said I, in that case we would bury him with the honors of war and erect a monument to his memory.

It was finally agreed that Mr. Chick was to move the house next morning. I at once called on Mrs. Townsend and inquired if she had plenty of ammunition and offered to furnish a dynamite cartridge if necessary.

She very curtly told me to mind my own business and she would tend to hers and when I asked her if her pistol was "sure pop" she said that if I didn't get out of the house she would try it on me. I took the hint and left first advising her to take dead aim at the Superintendent of Streets if he came near her mansion.

But man proposes and Dick Lloyd disposes; instead of going down and doing the thing as I anticipated and getting Chick shot and thus creating a vacancy, Marshal Lloyd had to go and spoil all my plans by arresting Mrs. Townsend, and Mr. Chick never had a ghost of a chance of getting shot.

I believe it was a put up job to keep me out of office, and Marshal Lloyd better beware how he crosses my path.

To say the least Mr. Editor I consider it a piece of rank injustice and that a foul wrong has been done me. For if the Marshal had not interfered, if Mr. Chick went boldly about his business, if Mrs. Townsend had used the right end of her gun I might have proudly signed myself.

—John E. Boyd
Superintendent of Streets,
Town of Berkeley

THE CLASSIC POSE OF JOHN BOYD FOR THE COVER OF HIS BOOK, *THE BERKELEY HEROINE*, PUBLISHED IN 1900. AT THIS TIME MARK TWAIN WAS THE SENSATION OF THE WRITING WORLD AND IT IS LIKELY THAT BOYD WAS EMULATING A HUCK FINN–STYLE CHARACTER. NOTE THAT HIS LEFT EYE IS DROOPED, THE RESULT OF AN INJURY SUFFERED FROM A FALL INTO STRAWBERRY CREEK AFTER A DRINKING BOUT. JOHN WAS BERKELEY'S WORKING-CLASS HERO.

7

JOHN E. BOYD: THE BOSS BAGGAGE BUSTER
OF BEAUTIFUL BERKELEY

JOHN E. BOYD, THOUGH A COMMON WORKMAN, INFLUENCED OLD
Berkeley in ways that belied his social status. An expressman, he dressed in tattered work clothes and often endured the trivial demands of unrealistic clients,
but as a self-proclaimed seer in an absurd world, he used his writing and his biting
wit to claim respect from his fellow citizens and create order in his own troubled
life. Through letters to the editor and editorials in Berkeley papers, he assumed
moral, humanistic, and humoristic oversight over his realm. It was as if he could
imagine that he was in control of the town and its moral trajectory, and then, with
his riveting turns of thought, compel and entertain readers into following his
sometimes laughable logic. Through writing, John E. Boyd made the unbearable
bearable and the uncontrollable his very own circus.

Boyd was in his day compared to Mark Twain because of his conversational
writing style, and later to Will Rogers because of his wit and manner. He might
also be compared to Charlie Chaplin's immortal character of the tramp, the common man who used his limitations and humor as weapons against an imposing
world. Around 1910, a *Berkeley Daily Gazette* writer named Francis W. Reid stated,
"We have today in America only two living humorists of the first rank. One is Mr.
Dooley's with a national reputation and the other is John E. Boyd. A good press
agent and business manager could easily secure for him an income of at least
$1000 a week by getting him to discuss national politics." John E. Boyd was a
fixture in old Berkeley from the 1870s well into the second decade of the twentieth century. Berkeley residents first got to know John when they would see him
in his express wagon transporting goods and people at all hours of the day and
night. Whether hauling freight, joking and arguing with customers, or taking
naps on his rig, Boyd was perpetually on the streets of Berkeley. He acted as if he

—Boyd now appears on a brand new
wagon, and his faithful horse has donned
a new harness, giving him an unfamiliar
but an improved appearance.

BERKELEY ADVOCATE, MARCH 10, 1883.

The snow has gone from Grizzly Peak,
The hills wear a greenish dress;
The Town of Berkeley is booming,
And so is Boyd's Express.
No matter what kind of hauling you want
done, send for Boyd. For instance, a
resident had a heifer calf die one day last
week, and wishing to get rid of the body
sent for Boyd, who soon had the animal in
his wagon, and it was quickly disposed of,
and left the gentleman's mind free from all
anxiety. Stand corner Shattuck avenue
and Center street.

BERKELEY ADVOCATE, JANUARY 18, 1888.

J. EVERGREEN ON FIRE INSURANCE

Describes Methods of New Company He Contemplates Organizing on This Side of the Bay.

Editor Gazette: Among other public spirited enterprises which will add to the glory of our town, I am glad to inform your readers that a new insurance company to be known as the Honswagle Fire Insurance Company, has been formed and will have its headquarters in Berkeley. We will insure anything and everything, providing our clients have the cash. In case of loss by fire we will have an adjuster sent to interview the party.

We faithfully promise our customers that they will have no trouble in securing a policy from us (providing they have the cash to pay) and in case of loss by fire our adjuster will furnish the customer with a paper with the following list of questions which must be truthfully answered and sworn to before a notary public:

1. How many children have you got?

2. Did you have mush for breakfast the morning of the fire.

3. Do your children ever play "Peter, Peter pumpkin eater."

5. How old was your grandmother when she had mumps?

5. Is your fire chief blonde or brunette?

6. Did you ever try beans as a steady diet.

7. Do you believe in woman's rights?

8. Do you play poker?

9. Did you buy your wife an Easter hat?

10. What will you do with the insurance money if you are lucky enough to get it?

After answering the questions truthfully and without prevarication, our client will be required to call at our office every day for four months and each time we will assure him that we are working night and day to effect a settlement in his case and when we have him tired out and swearing mad we will agree to settle with him if he will accept a discount of 85 per cent, which amount will certainly allow him what he has spent for car fare and if the silly fellow does not accept our terms. We can repudiate the debt or go into insolvency.

JAY BIRD EVERGREEN,
President Honswagle Fire Insurance Company.

Berkeley Advocate, no date.

owned the roadways, and perhaps he deserved that right. Even in the worst weather, John plodded through the muddy town, hauling everything from furniture to lovers on their way to a dance hall.

While John's daily work may have seemed mundane, it offered him a constant view of the changing city, and time to fuel his inner life and the gossamer visions that inspired his writing. The *Berkeley Daily Gazette* reviewed his book of poems, *Ancient Poetry,* on March 8, 1902:

> *Professor Boyd gives a few verses on trunkology in Berkeley, reciting some of the woes which fall to the trunkologist. Thus he tells how the sensitive expressman is greeted by a hard-faced woman after he has carried a 200 pound trunk up four flights of stairs:*

> *Whenever you go to a home with a trunk*
> *They certainly imagine that you are drunk,*
> *For they never fail to loudly bawl:*
> *"Don't put no scratches on that wall."*

> *But boys, when life's moving days are o'er,*
> *And you're checked right through to Heaven's shore,*
> *The angels, they will gently call,*
> *"Come in, and never mind the wall."*

> *Mr. Boyd ends his treasure something after this fashion:*

> *"In conclusion, let me express the hope that my readers will feel as much pleasure in perusing this little gem as my printers did when I planked down the cash for the printing."*

Though John was a proud and vocal eccentric, he was also an active member of his community and a brave Civil War veteran. His participation in civic affairs predates Berkeley's founding, for he voted in the election that officially established the city in 1878. Over the years, he held a number of positions in city government, though his tenure never lasted very long.

Boyd possessed a lot of energy and strong opinions that he was always eager to share with fellow townsfolk. Though John worked hard as an expressman to support his family, he thrived through writing his "shake your head back and

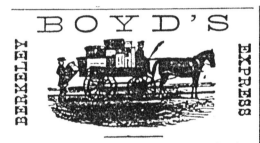

forth" vision of a fumbling world and its leaders. His frequent contributions in local publications would stir readers to respond, and the papers regularly printed his diatribes, despite his notorious and frequent bouts of heavy public drinking.

John was proud of his eccentricities and edited neither his opinions nor his true nature. He loved the attention his writing garnered and was always working on his next piece, whether sitting on his rig between jobs, working as a bailiff in local courtrooms, while in jail for drinking, or any other time he could put pen to paper. An observant and jocular man, John Boyd satirized everyone and everything. His words were often cutting, but rarely mean. John knew how to poke fun at everyone, including himself. He used laughter as a way to connect with people and perhaps as a way of coping with pain, for his humor and tenacity came from a life filled with challenges and personal tragedy.

John Edward Boyd was born April 30, 1843, in Long Island, New York. He quit the life of a schoolboy on July 26, 1859, at the age of sixteen to enlist in the U.S. Navy and served until September 1861. John's military records describe him as five feet, eleven inches and 175 pounds with a fair complexion, black hair, and grey eyes.[1] He served first on the *North Carolina* in 1859 and then on the *USS Sumpter* as a "first and second class boy," the equivalent of a seaman third class. The rank of boy was the lowest among sailors and was usually reserved for young recruits. Pay was eight dollars a month. Boys performed tasks such as laundry and cleaning for the officers, kitchen work, and other jobs like hauling black powder and cartridges from the ship's magazine to its cannons during combat (thus earning them the nickname "powder monkeys").

Early in Boyd's Navy career, a cannon wheel rolled over his left big toe during

JOHN BOYD POSES IN THE DOORWAY OF HIS HOME WITH HIS SON, SHERMAN, DAUGHTER (PROBABLY THORA), AND HIS WIFE, SARAH.

Boyd's Express boxes are called at daily, and orders attended to. They are located at the following places: — East Berkeley, Olive Branch Hotel; Chappie, Tallman & Co. grocers; Post-office box H; Shattuck av. Gottshall & McClain's; West Berkeley, Wright & Co's: San Francisco, 717 Montgomery and 320 Sansome st.

BERKELEY ADVOCATE, APRIL 17, 1879.

a gunnery exercise on deck, sending him to the sick bay for a week. This toe remained a painful nuisance to him for the rest of his life. The crew of the *Sumpter* went on patrol with four other steamers around Cuba and along the coast of Africa, intercepting slave ships to capture the slave traders and free their victims. On one mission, Boyd acted as a spy, infiltrating the crew of a slave ship and leading the Navy to the ship's anchorage upriver.[2] The *Sumpter* sailed from the west coast of Africa on August 10, 1861, and returned to the United States on September 15. Boyd received an honorable discharge eleven days later. In 1863 the *Sumpter* joined the blockade of Charleston Harbor, collided with the Union transport *General Meigs* in a heavy mist, and sank.[3]

Shortly after leaving the military, John married fifteen-year-old Sarah E. Sutliff in Gloversville, New York. In 1874, they moved to San Francisco, where Boyd worked as a grocery man with his brother James. After a couple of years in the crowded and sooty city, John and his family moved across the bay to Berkeley.

In Berkeley, Boyd became an expressman, transporting people and baggage to and from the train station in a distinctive blue and white wagon. His business cards read "John Boyd, Boss Baggage Buster of Beautiful Berkeley," and this slogan became his proud trademark.

Upon their arrival in Berkeley, the Boyds moved into a house on Sixth Street

near Delaware Street. John later moved with his wife and two children to a house on Delaware and Sacramento streets. On November 24, 1890, the family moved to a two-story house on the Hann Block of Center Street above Shattuck Avenue. John's "office" was said to be "in a shelter of planks" behind the Southern Pacific Depot at Third Street and University Avenue.[4]

During the day, Boyd and his son Sherman handled the loads, sometimes transporting furniture and delivering supplies around town. In the evenings, Boyd used his rig as a taxi; he installed board benches for passengers, who joked and jostled on their way to dance halls in west or south Berkeley.

The first known reference to John Boyd in a Berkeley newspaper appeared in March 1877. The article quoted John as saying that he was fortunate he was not "kilt entirely" when a goat butted his horse, causing him to be thrown from his rig.[5] The combination of Boyd's pain, both physical and mental, and playful notoriety in the news would follow him the rest of his life.

There were stories around Berkeley that Boyd had attended Harvard University, but Harvard records reveal no trace of a John E. Boyd. This was one of many rumors that dogged John about town, and it was one that he thoroughly enjoyed. He also relished his many nicknames. He claimed his middle initial stood for Evergreen, and was sometimes known around town as "Jay Bird Evergreen," after readers of the paper finally figured out that John Boyd was the man behind this pen name. By 1905 Boyd and his antics were so well known in Berkeley that his

LOOKING EAST FROM A BUILDING ON SHATTUCK AVENUE TOWARD OXFORD STREET (LEFT TO RIGHT AT BOTTOM OF THE PHOTO); NORTH, SOUTH, AND BACON HALLS ARE IN THE LEFT REAR OF THE PHOTO. JOHN BOYD'S HOUSE WOULD HAVE BEEN IN THE MID-LEFT OF THE PHOTO, WHERE CENTER STREET WOULD BE. IT WAS THE LEFT STRUCTURE, THE ONE ON THE RIGHT BEING THE KELLOGG SCHOOL, ESTABLISHED IN 1879. THE LACK OF DEVELOPMENT ALSO HELPS DATE THIS PHOTO AS CIRCA 1879. ALLSTON WAY WAS STILL A DIRT TRAIL FOLLOWING STRAWBERRY CREEK, WHOSE CHANNEL IS LINED WITH TREES ON THE RIGHT SIDE OF THIS PHOTO.

JOHN E. BOYD.

No description of our fair town and its enterprising citizens would be complete without mention being made of our pioneer Expressman, John E. Boyd. We have long endeavored to procure an authentic picture of Mr. Boyd, but his well known modesty has prevented this. Our artist made the picture opposite with a snap-shot camera as Mr. Boyd was rushing to the 11 o'clock train which had a pile of luggage in the baggage car. Experts pronounce it a good likeness, although they say the ears are not large enough. Mr. Boyd is a native of New York and was born some years after Columbus discovered America, which is sufficent proof that there is no truth in the report that he purloined a bottle of gin out of the trunk of the great discoverer

Stop that train!
I see a trunk!

Office Boyd's Express, 2512 Center St.

while conveying it to the Cats Island Hotel on the landing of Columbus. Mr. Boyd has many testimonials from a host of well known citizens for whom he has hauled luggage, among which are King Kalula, Lord Fitzgerald, Lydia Pinkham, Jesse James, Sontag and Evans, Warner's Safe Cure, and others, and is a strict temperance man, having signed the pledge 15 minutes after he was born. He is the owner of the celebrated horse Slow-and-Easy, whose dam was Mahomet, and who has been dam'd by all its subsequent owners. Mr. Boyd is Berkeley's popular poet and is the author of the well-known lines:

The boy stood on the burning deck,
He was terrible warm I guess.
The youth was lost but his trunk was saved,
For 'twas marked "care Boyd's Express."

THIS AD, IN A CHRISTMAS EDITION OF THE *BERKELEY ADVOCATE* IN 1892, SHOWS HOW WELL KNOWN JOHN E. BOYD HAD BECOME AND REFLECTED HIS HAVING BECOME A FIXTURE IN TOWN.

—Expressman Boyd received some cuts and bruises on Thursday afternoon, by falling from his wagon, the wheel of which passed over him.

BERKELEY ADVOCATE, MAY 27, 1882.

Jack and Gill went up the hill,
   To get some water, I guess;
Jack fell down and broke his crown,
   While "nipping" on Boyd's Express.
Don't put off any job you may have requiring an expressman until the roads get bad, but put your order in Boyd's box at once.

BERKELEY ADVOCATE, FEBRUARY 21, 1887.

BOYD, our useful expressman, congratulated himself the other day on not being "kilt entirely." As he was driving along slowly, his horse took fright at a goat suddenly emerging through the brush, and threw him to the ground. Having the reins in his hand, he stopped the horse's progress and saved himself. He looks as well as ever, and is ready for the next load.

BERKELEY ADVOCATE, MARCH 17, 1877.

During the terrible storm of rain and hail on Sunday last, a solitary wagon was seen on our streets. The driver was wringing wet, and the horse (well blanketed as he was) looked as though he would rather be in the stable. Upon inquiry of the driver, Mr. Boyd, we learned that he had faithfully promised to haul some trunks down to the Berkeley station in time for the 12 M. train, and, rain or shine, daylight or dark, he will never disappoint a person who depends on him. His order box is in front of the Postoffice, and he wishes to impress on people's minds that Boyd's Express is reliable and prompt.

AN AD BY BOYD'S EXPRESS IN THE *BERKELEY ADVOCATE* OF MARCH 7, 1888.

On Saturday last, as the local train leaving Berryman station at three o'clock was coming to a stop at Berkeley station, Eddie Boyd, a seven-year-old boy, son of John E. Boyd, in attempting to cross the track in front of the engine, fell and before the train could be stopped a wheel had passed over the right leg, above the knee, crushing it in a frightful manner. The injury extended from the knee to the groin, the muscles being terribly lacerated. Dr. Payne reached the little fellow a moment after the accident and had him removed to the depot building, where he remained with him until he died, at six o'clock, three hours thereafter. The doctor decided to amputate the leg as the only chance for the boy's recovery. At five o'clock, when he had sufficiently rallied to admit of the injured parts being removed, Dr. Payne amputated the leg just below the hip joint, but the shock to the nervous system had been too severe and the patient did not long survive the operation. The coroner was immediately notified and gave permission for the body to be removed to the residence of Mr. Boyd near by. An inquest was held on Monday, at which Dr. Payne testified that to the best of his judgment and belief, the boy died from the shock to the nervous system, caused by the injury. The jury rendered a verdict accordingly and attached no blame to anyone.

Berkeley Advocate, October 23, 1880.

—John E. Boyd, the expressman, has again fallen from grace. He indulged in too much tangle-toe a few days since and tumbled into Strawberry Creek, near F. R. Shattuck's, where he remained waterlogged for over two hours. He was extricated from his dangerous position by some friends, and is now sick in bed.

Berkeley Advocate, May 12, 1883.

Upon motion J. E. Boyd was appointed special Policeman to make arrests for the violation of any of the Town Ordinances.

Berkeley Advocate, October 13, 1883.

—John E. Boyd has made two arrests during the past week—the victims being San Franciscsco drummers.

Berkeley Advocate, December 15, 1883.

—Mr. John E. Boyd has been elected janitor of the new Town Hall at a salary of $10 per month.

Berkeley Advocate, June 1884.

—Mr. John Boyd is taking the school census this week in West Berkeley. John says that "babies reign supreme at this end of town, in fact he don't see where they get them all."

Berkeley Advocate, June 1884.

We are forced to confess that the Town Hall Janitor is certainly "up to snuff." On Monday evening he saluted one of our town officials very politely with "Good evening, Judge." On Tuesday morning he again hailed the same individual as follows "Hello, Alec, old boy; how do you feel?": So much for the influence of position.

Berkeley Advocate, May 23, 1888.

John E. Boyd sent in the following resignation :

The Hon. Board of Town Trustees—Gentlemen: It is with a sad heart and weeping eyes that I address this communication to you, hoping that you will not be utterly desolate at the sorrowful news I am about to impart. Circumstances over which I have no control compel me to resign the important office of Town Hall Janitor, and I hereby tender my resignation of that office, to take effect December 1st, 1890; and, in conclusion, allow me to add that if at any time your honorable body needs any advice in relation to town matters, I shall be perfectly willing to assist you to the best of my ability. Respectfully,
JOHN E. BOYD.

Berkeley Advocate, December 4, 1890.

John E. Boyd has secured a position as a writer on the new evening Berkeley paper. Occasionally he can be found at the depot.

Berkeley Advocate, May 4, 1895.

Boyd, our expressman, says he is not going to wash his right hand for a year. He avows no enmity to the Standard Soap Company, but boasts that on Tuesday last he shook hands with General Grant in front of the Sub-Treasury building on Commercial street San Francisco. When he told us the story, he seemed as happy as a big sun-flower, and declared that he didn't care a continental thingumbob whether the Trustees put the streets in order or not.

BERKELEY ADVOCATE, OCTOBER 9, 1879.

—On Sunday last special officer, John E. Boyd was presented by his wife with a new year's present in the shape of a daughter. Boyd says that the "chief engineer of the flannel and beef-tea department" did not allow him to see the little stranger, and the first glimpse he obtained was when he arrested and locked the youngster up for jumping on the train while in motion. The youngster pleaded short residence in the town and and ignorance of the law, and the judge passed a sentence of milk and gruel for 24 hours.

BERKELEY ADVOCATE, JANUARY 17, 1885.

nickname evolved from "John Evergreen Boyd" to "John Ever-Dreaming Boyd."

Boyd's visibility was enhanced by his many government jobs. His duties ranged from Town Hall janitor to "semi-official deputy marshal," a title that he earned because it was easier for people to find him than it was to find the real marshal. Over the years he also worked for the city as a special police officer, pound master, census taker, and "letter fetcher." Boyd had an entrepreneurial bent and at one point opened a confections and stationery store. But John had a dark side, too, and his actions sometimes surprised people who were used to his playful antics. Once, while acting as pound master, he shot a dog for barking, to the horror of its owner and other residents. This same man was quick to take up collections for people in need—and to habitually drink to excess.

In the summer of 1883, Boyd was walking through Berkeley and fell off a bridge that crossed Shattuck Avenue. He was unconscious for about an hour and permanently lost sight in his left eye, save for vague light. From reports of the incident, it appears that John was drunk when he fell. A later photograph of him depicts the left eye injury.

Boyd occasionally wore a gray Civil War uniform about town, probably to spark outrage, one of his hallmark activities. Berkeley was a Union town and Boyd a U.S. Navy veteran. On at least one occasion, this practice caused great confusion, which was clearly his intention. A southern matron newly arrived in town, upon seeing Boyd in a Confederate uniform and thinking he was one of her own old compatriots, invited him to dinner at her home. The family presented an elegant meal served with all the ceremony of southern hospitality. At some point, the hostess asked Boyd in a syrupy southern drawl, "So Mr. Boyd, you were a Civil War veteran?" Boyd, probably fueled by wine, recounted his Union experiences of "blasting all in hell" a Confederate vessel. He barked on at length, relishing the shock and discomfort of his red-faced hosts. Boyd had calculated well; their manners prevented them from throwing him out, and he made the most of this one-time opportunity.[6]

John Boyd was a complicated man—annoying, cheerful, sarcastic, caring, humorous, hardworking, and contentious, all at the same time. Sadly, his life as a husband and father was marked by a series of tragedies. According to the *Berkeley Advocate,* in the fall of 1880, as Boyd's express business was thriving and his roots in town were growing deep, his family lost an infant son who was only a few days old.[7] Within a few weeks of this tragedy, John's seven-year-old son, Eddie, a fine young boy who was popular throughout the town, was struck and killed by a train on the Shattuck Avenue tracks.[8] Ten years later, Boyd's youngest daughter, Thora, accidentally drank carbolic acid. A doctor saved her life, but her neck and mouth were badly burned.[9]

On January 22, 1891, the *Berkeley Advocate* again reported sad news of the Boyd family: an infant son, two weeks old and weighing only five pounds, had died in convulsions the previous morning.[10]

These tragic events took a great toll on John's wife, Sarah. By 1891 she had lapsed into a perpetual drunken state and began to mistreat her children. Boyd walked into their house one day and found her engaged in an act of adultery. He immediately left her and contacted the town marshal about custody of his children. John Boyd's personal grief about this incident, too, was dutifully reported to all by the local press.[11]

On November 5, the Society for the Prevention of Cruelty to Children, with the help of town marshal Schmidt, came to transport Boyd's four children to the society's Temescal facility. As soon as the officials entered the house and faced Mrs. Boyd, she reached for a bottle of poison and claimed that she would kill her children before she would lose them. The marshal firmly restrained her as the society's officials led the frightened children out the door.[12]

Boyd survived these personal trials and still managed to continue writing. Perhaps he needed to write because of these tragedies. For a man with so little formal education, Boyd possessed an unanticipated degree of skill as a writer. He managed to absorb the spirit of the town, and he conveyed it to others through his numerous editorials in the *Berkeley Advocate*. Because he signed his early editorials "Jay Bird Evergreen," it was some time before readers realized that the easygoing expressman was the author of these biting statements. He gave fresh perspective to controversies, such as the hypocrisy of prohibition or the annoyance of town ordinances, and whatever else captured his attention. In spite of the potshots he took at some of his neighbors, people felt great affection for both sides of this man whom they saw every day driving through town on his express wagon and whose articles they read in the newspaper. One was disheveled, and one was distinguished and disarming; both were John E. Boyd, the Boss Baggage Buster of Beautiful Berkeley.

Boyd had friends up and down the ladder of success, and even in the puddles below it. One of those friends was M. B. Curtis, the most successful actor in the country from the mid-1880s through the early 1890s. After a meteoric rise to fame, Curtis came to Berkeley, contributing much to the town. When Curtis was jailed in San Francisco on murder charges, Boyd visited him and asked his fellow Berkeleyans to remember that Curtis was charged but not yet convicted. Curtis

On the 28th, Mrs. Sarah E. Boyd was brought in on a warrant sworn out by Mrs. Abbott and Mrs. Donovan for disturbing the peace. In a drunken fit she had threatened to set fire to houses and perform other desperate acts which endangered the safety of the community. She was sentenced to thirty days in the county jail, and is now serving out her term.

BERKELEY ADVOCATE, DECEMBER 3, 1891.

Mrs. Sarah E. Boyd who is serving thirty days in the county jail will probably be removed to the Fabiola hospital for treatment as she is very ill. Mrs Boyd has made the statement that the liquor was furnished to her by women—neighbors, and she has given their names. Mr. Boyd threatens to prosecute them as soon as she is able to be out again and make affidavit of the fact. He has been suspicious for months that she had an accomplice, and if it can be proven he intends they shall suffer to the fullest extent of the law.

BERKELEY ADVOCATE, DECEMBER 3, 1891.

A PHOTOGRAPH OF THE CANNON JOHN BOYD PRO-
CURED, BY GREAT EFFORT, WHICH WAS DISPLAYED AT
BERKELEY'S CITY HALL (SEEN IN THE BACKGROUND).
THIS CANNON WAS USED BY ADMIRAL DEWEY AT THE
BATTLE OF MANILA BAY IN THE SPANISH-AMERICAN
WAR. THE WOODEN CARRIAGE FOR THE CANNON,
WHICH ORIGINALLY WAS BUILT TO CRADLE IT IN 1911,
HAD BEEN REPLACED BY A CONCRETE ONE BY THE TIME
THIS PHOTO WAS TAKEN. THIS PHOTO MEMORIALIZES
THE FEBRUARY 22, 1912 CEREMONY OF MOVING THE
DEWEY CANNON TO BELOW THE CITY HALL FLAG POLE
AND ONTO A NEW CONCRETE BASE. THAT DAY THE CAN-
NON WAS REDEDICATED FOR THE PURPOSE OF PEACE
INSTEAD OF WAR.

—Boyd now appears on a brand new
wagon, and his faithful horse has donned
a new harness, giving him an unfamiliar
but an improved appearance.

BERKELEY ADVOCATE, MARCH 10, 1883.

BERKELEY, Cal., June 13, 1888.
Hon. Judge Gresham, Chicago, Ill.—
Sir: Referring to your telegram of the
12th inst., I haste to inform you that
under no circumstances have I consented,
nor will I consent, to my name going
before the convention for either first or
second place on the ticket, so please set
your mind at rest on that score.
My reason for declining so distinguished an honor is that my local express
business here is booming and I cannot
sacrifice it even on the altar of the nation's welfare.   Very respectfully, etc.,
JOHN E. BOYD.

BERKELEY ADVOCATE, JUNE 13, 1888.

was later acquitted of the charge.[13]

John took his military service very seriously and was instrumental in getting
the Grand Army of the Republic (a Civil War veterans group) to establish the
Lookout Mountain Post in Berkeley.[14] Working the crowds at the Berkeley train
station, he would buttonhole every local veteran and say, "Hey, comrade. Why do
we have to go to the city for GAR meetings? Sign up and we'll start a post here."
The new post became influential, with Boyd always in the thick of its activities,
wearing his GAR uniform and sporting his walrus mustache. The *Berkeley Advocate*
of June 5, 1890, reported on the post's members decorating the graves of soldiers
buried at Mountain View Cemetery in Oakland, describing the scene "with John
E. Boyd bearing the new banner draped in mourning, of which he never for a
moment released his hold, fearing some one would deprive him of his precious
burden." Boyd's patriotism inspired his campaign to get a cannon used by
Admiral Dewey at the battle of Manila Bay in the Spanish-American War displayed
at the City Hall plaza.[15] Boyd wrote to the secretary of the navy and various con-
gressmen about this effort. He even raised the money to have a wooden carriage
built for it. The cannon was installed at City Hall on George Washington's birthday in 1911.

John's noble intentions were counterbalanced by a host of bad habits. Boyd
was known not only to drink heavily, but also to argue vehemently. Once, when
arrested in Oakland for drunkenness, he protested that he should be released as

John E. Boyd speaks out on the Lorin District

Here is an example of John Boyd's skill as a writer. This excerpt is from his book *The Berkeley Heroine,* most of which was derived from his previously published editorials. His style recalls the terse comic wit of Samuel Clemens, more commonly known as Mark Twain. Ever poking fun at the establishment, Boyd claimed that his book was copyright by the Confederate States of America. He also wrote in a letter to a UC Berkeley librarian that the book "both astounded and astonished the civilized world." Here Boyd describes a scene in the Lorin district near Adeline Street and Alcatraz Avenue:

I went down to Lorin yesterday and was greatly pleased with its beautiful streets macadamized with mud. I was sent to Trustee ——— house to get some furniture, by a young man who met me and who had an angel on his starboard arm and whom he called dear, and she called him love. Neither one called me love, when I got back, covered with Alcatraz avenue mud, although I was a lovely sight. I inquired of the grocery man at the corner of Shattuck and Alcatraz avenue and he advised me to take a pilot and to keep the deep sea lead going. I asked him if Alcatraz avenue was so bad, and he said that it was in pretty good condition in summer, and for fear that it would be passable through the

winter, the Trustees had ordered a sewer laid so that teamsters would get stuck and swear. However, I went on and as I could see the tips of the horses ears sticking out of the mud, I had no trouble in guiding him. About half a block down I met a teamster with a derrick. He said he had lost a horse, wagon and a quarter ton of coal in a hole just below us, and asked me to help him. After an hour's work we got him out and a gentleman standing near got an old real estate sign and a marking pot and told me to put an inscription on it to warn teamsters. I did so, marked it and stuck it up, and as the sign reads, "This is Hell," I hope teamsters and town officials will keep away. I journeyed on and at length reached the Trustee's house, got my load and returned. Up near the post-office I saw an old bulletin board, lettered, "Public notice, city of Berkeley." I procured a piece of chalk and wrote: Ordinance No. 41,444— It is hereby ordered that the name of this street be changed from Alcatraz avenue to mud lane, and that the teamsters who get stuck shall not cuss the Trustees out loud. This ordinance shall take effect immediately. I met Dr. Rowell down there and inquired: "How is business, Doc?" He replied, "bully," and informed me that he had just been appointed Deputy Coroner for Lorin, and as from four to six men were drowned

Men on horseback ride down a dirt-paved and rutted Alcatraz Avenue.

every night in the mud-holes, he was doing a very fair business holding inquests. He said the inquests were just a formality, as the verdict was always the same. That the deceased came to his death by trying to walk through the streets of Lorin after dark. The Doctor very kindly said that if I would come down some night and take a walk through Lorin that he would give me a first-class inquest and mention my many virtues to the jury, for which I returned him my sincere thanks.

ABOVE: JOHN BOYD HOLDING A NEWSPAPER IN FRONT
OF THE PUBLIC DRINKING FOUNTAIN BY THE DOWN-
TOWN RAILROAD STATION, DONATED BY PHOEBE
HEARST. BOYD'S EDITORIALS AS EARLY AS 1900 CALL-
ING FOR A DRINKING FOUNTAIN HELPED CREATE PUBLIC
DEMAND FOR THE FOUNTAIN. HERE BOYD POSES IN
FRONT OF IT AND THE BERKELEY STATION, THE CENTER
OF HIS TOWN AND HIS WORLD.

RIGHT: *BERKELEY ADVOCATE*, JULY 1, 1901.

PROPOSES FOUNDING A HISTORICAL SOCIETY

Plan to Collect for Preservation Views of Pioneer Berkeley.

Editor Gazette: In view of the fact that the old buildings on Shattuck avenue are to be removed, should not some step be taken to preserve pictures of the ancient buildings for the purpose of letting future generations see how our town looked in ~~early~~ days.

There is a photo of McClain's store as it stood solitary and alone in "80," and several views of different parts of the town as it was years ago, also groups of school children taken at the public schools as far back as "92." Photos of different parts of the town are in many families. Now Mr. Editor could not a historical society of Berkeley be formed for the purpose of preserving old pictures and photos of the town as it now exists could be taken at small expense. Then what better place to hang them than the walls of our public library. The Kellogg school will soon be a thing of the past. Let us preserve a view of the old building where many of our citizens, now men and women, received their education. Will not some of our prominent ladies take this matter in hand and carry the idea to a successful termination. The cost would be small and none would be more ready to contribute than   JOHN E. BOYD.

A Trip to
Berkeley, Cal.
American Mutoscope &
Biograph Company
(c) June 23, 1906

ABOVE: THESE STILLS FROM THE FILM *A TRIP TO BERKELEY* HAVE BEEN SEEN BY MANY VIEWERS AT THE PACIFIC FILM ARCHIVE; IT IS ALSO STORED AT THE LIBRARY OF CONGRESS. THOUGH A POPULAR FILM AND MUCH COMMENTED ON, NO ONE EVER KNEW THAT TWO OF ITS STARS WERE NONE OTHER THAN JOHN E. BOYD AND HIS SON SHERMAN. SHERMAN IS THE LAD WHO RUNS IN FRONT OF THE TRAIN AND JOHN E. BOYD IS THE MAN WHO COMES RIDING UP ON A HORSE AT THE END. OUR TOWN HEROES WERE, UNBEKNOWNST TO US, ALSO MOVIE STARS.

RIGHT: A NEWSPAPER ARTICLE FROM THE *BERKELEY DAILY GAZETTE* OF MAY 25, 1906, DESCRIBING BOYD'S ROLE IN *A TRIP TO BERKELEY*. THE FILM WAS RELEASED WITHIN A MONTH OF THE 1906 EARTHQUAKE WHEN BERKELEY WAS SWARMING WITH REFUGEES FROM SAN FRANCISCO.

THE BOYDS TAKE PART

J Evergreen and Son Sherman Enact Exciting Farce on Euclid Ave. for Moving Picture.

A moving picture artist invaded Berkeley the other day looking for something startling. He got it. He happened to run across a wise man who knows everything and everybody. The gntleman was directed to interview John Boyd, the bold baggage buster, who soon arranged an exciting farce with Hearst avenue as the stage. The photographer rode up on a Euclid avenue car with his apparatus on the front platform. At the top of the hill abreast of Frank Wilson's residence, Sherman Boyd was discovered in the middle of the track. The motorman rang the bell, but the young namesake of Old Tecumseh stood fast and paid no attention to the repeated warnings. At last, when patience ceased to be a virtue, the conductor attempted to force him from the track. He resisted and the motorman jumped off to assist. Boyd Jr. put up a fierce resistance, and the carmen had their hands full in forcing him from the rails. In the midst of the struggle Boyd Sr. drove hurriedly around the corner racing his horse at full speed up the hill to his son's rescue, at the same time pulling off his coat and shaking his fists at the carmen. The street car passengers, who did not understand that it was all "make believe," added greatly to the scene. One young lady who sympathized with the poor dust-covered youth, leaped off the car, and taking her lace handkerchief dusted him off, at the same time expressing her sorrow at the cruel treatment he had received.

"Why, madam," explained the victim, "we get $2 for this cruel treatment."

Several automobiles seeing the tussle hastened to the scene, adding greatly to the picture. The artist handed Boyd Sr. two silver dollars, and returned home to develop the picture, which will no doubt in time make its debut at some variety shows in Oakland or neighboring cities a professional courtesy since he was a deputy marshal in Berkeley. Later he said that it had been a worthwhile and interesting experience to be jailed because he met so many of Oakland's leading citizens, and his cell mates were the only local residents who weren't constantly sneaking out to get a drink.[16]

In 1893, Boyd was examined by a government surgeon, who wrote the following in his report: "Claimant admits taking an occasional glass but does not drink habitually nor was he ever intoxicated and his appearance seems to bear out his claim."[17] John Boyd had a strength about him even while his demons danced.

Boyd's military pension records reveal that he had suffered from rheumatism in the neck and shoulders since 1874.[18] By 1903, John claimed that he couldn't work due to his disabilities: his left eye, his rheumatism, and his crushed toe. In 1904, an Army surgeon described Boyd's condition in a report: "This is an old man with shifting gait and very untidy appearance. He is of large frame and well nourished, formed and developed."[19] The surgeon went on to note that his teeth were poor and his tongue was coated.

But Boyd's infirmities did not keep him off the streets. In 1905, he is listed as living at 1915 Addison Street, a house that still stands in downtown Berkeley. When the Civil War veterans were mobilized in Berkeley to keep order as thousands of 1906 San Francisco earthquake victims flooded the town, Boyd was a ready soldier. Captain Garlock, who commanded Company A of the Veteran Reserve Corps, was very particular about the neatness of his camp, especially the tents and cots. One veteran was admonished because his blankets were not evenly tucked. He replied that "if his wife visited camp and found him an experienced bedmaker she might detail him for that duty on his return home."[20] This impertinent man was, of course, John E. Boyd.

On November 13, 1907, Mrs. Sarah Boyd died, ending the couple's forty-six-year marriage. Four children survived her: Sherman Boyd, living in Berkeley; Belle Nelson, in Colorado; Francis Boyd, in Oakland; and Thora Boyd, in Berkeley. John and all the children who lived nearby were with Sarah when she passed away. The obituary mercifully restricted its comments to Sarah's contributions to the town and her work with the Salvation Army.[21]

In 1911, Boyd, at the age of sixty-eight, was appointed a special police officer and bailiff. As he sat and monitored his charges in the courtroom of Judge Robert Edgar, he would often compose poems about Berkeley. Sometimes he would ride around Berkeley on a police bicycle to do routine investigations; the small town he had criss-crossed in his express wagon days was now a crowded city.

One year later, John's gun slipped from its holster, hit the floor, and discharged

a bullet into his leg. Although the wound healed, he died of a "stroke of apoplexy" on January 27, 1912, at the age of sixty-nine. His funeral was a remarkable testament to his life's impact on Berkeley.[22] The Odd Fellows Hall was packed for his memorial. All of the city officials he had parodied in his editorials were in sorrowful attendance. In honor of Boyd's memory, the flag at City Hall flew at half-mast and courts closed for the day. The whole police department, except for the few officers remaining on duty, attended his funeral. So many members of the Grand Army of the Republic, other local veterans groups, and the Berkeley police force came to pay their respects that a Key Route train was reserved to transport them from the funeral service to the Mountain View Cemetery at the northeastern end of Piedmont Avenue in Oakland. Though John E. Boyd was a man of many moods, the people of Berkeley mourned his passing with a deep sense of loss to the fabric of their lives. No one could or ever would replace him.

John Edward Boyd's grave, located in Plot 45 by a tall flagpole in a veteran's section in Mountain View Cemetery, is identified only by a narrow metal marker

In the aftermath of the 1906 earthquake, Berkeley marshal August Vollmer deputized Berkeley's Civil War veterans to help maintain order in the town, then overrun with refugees. John E. Boyd, with the white walrus mustache, volunteered and is the man eleventh from the left in this photo.

THE ENTRANCE TO MOUNTAIN VIEW CEMETERY, AT
THE NORTHEAST END OF PIEDMONT AVENUE. JOHN
E. BOYD PASSED AWAY AT THE AGE OF SIXTY-NINE ON
JANUARY 27, 1912. BOYD WAS LAID TO REST HERE
BY HUNDREDS OF HIS FRIENDS, FELLOW POLICEMEN,
VETERANS, AND A HUGE NUMBER OF PEOPLE FROM
ALL WALKS OF LIFE WHOM HE HAD TOUCHED. HIS
GRAVE, THOUGH NUMBERED, HAS NO GRAVESTONE
TO THIS DAY.

set in the ground and reading "No. 123." There is no headstone at his gravesite,
nor is there a record that one was ever ordered. Here was a man who was well
known and beloved yet whose grave is largely unadorned. But perhaps that was
his request, and the sparse ground leaves room to admire the humor of his permanent address: 123 . . . 45.

The Capture of the *Sultana* by John E. Boyd

John Boyd wrote about his service in the U.S. Navy off the coast of Africa just before the Civil War. The following is an excerpt from his book *The Berkeley Heroine.* Some of the words will be offensive to modern sensibilities, but since this is a historic document they are presented here unedited:

The Capture of the *Sultana*
by John E. Boyd

A San Francisco newspaper has an article stating that the *"Marion,"* an old sloop of war, is to be stationed in the bay as a practice ship for the naval reserve.

It is now thirty-eight years since I last saw the *"Marion"* on the west coast of Africa. We were blockading the mouth of the Congo on the lookout for slavers. It was well known that one of these was up the river with her slave deck laid ready to take in her dusky cargo.

There was a spirit of rivalry between the officers of the *U.S.S. Sumpter,* on which I was, and those of the *Marion,* each being anxious to make the capture, as in all probability there would be not only the value of the ship, but eighteen or twenty thousand dollars prize money for the "blackbirds."

Our officers held frequent consultations as to the best way to effect the capture. One evening I overheard Lieut. Greer say to the captain: "The best plan that I can form is to find a trustworthy man to act the ship-wrecked sailor or deserter."

After some further discussion the captain went below and I seized the first opportunity to interview Lieut. Greer, urging him to recommend me for the deserter in case the captain decided to act upon his plan. He looked at me in surprise. "Why, you young powder monkey," said he, "what the devil do you think you could do? The captain of the *Sultana,* when he caught you hanging around his vessel, would probably hang you up and give you three dozen."

Undismayed, I continued to urge the matter saying that I would pose as a runaway from the *Harriet Foster,* a palm-oil trader that had sailed the day before for Boston. I received however, no encouragement from my officer and was agreeably surprised the next morning to receive a summons from the captain to his cabin. As I stood cap in hand, all expectancy, he began: "Well, Boyd, so you want to go up and fool the captain of the *Sultana,* do you? I fear, however, that he may fool you with a rope's end, or feed you to the crocodiles."

I was burning to go, for I saw in imagination my share of the prize money and a probable purse from my officers and shipmates, who would feel that they were indebted to me for gaining the prey for them instead of allowing it to fall to the *Marion.* The chance of promotion too was no small incentive.

The captain made every possible objection, and just as I was about to give up hope he said: "I have a notion to let you try your luck, but you must volunteer, I will not detail you."

"All right," I said joyfully, "I volunteer."

It was arranged that two of our Krou men, called Tom Lee and Happy Jack (natives of the African coast) were to take me in a canoe up the river twenty-five miles and leave me within half a mile of the slave ship, and that the same men were to come up daily on the flood tide and I was to meet them and communicate with them when possible and keep them informed as to the progress of events; or if to meet them proved impracticable I was to tie a white rag around some tree to be decided upon as soon as they should begin to load the blacks.

It did not take us long to reach the bend in the river, just above which the slaver lay anchored. After deciding upon a signal tree they left me and returned to the ship, while I walked along the bank of the river.

Our surgeon, Dr. Otis, had made a bet of five dollars with Lieut. Greer, that I would "crawfish" and return with the canoe. I am proud to say that the doctor lost his bet. A fifteen minute walk brought me to the Barracoons (walled enclosures where the captives were housed until the ship was ready to receive them). The report that a man-of-war lay at the mouth of the river caused the delay.

As I came abreast I was approached by a yawl carrying two white men dressed in white linen suits and two black men in cast-off officers' uniforms. As they stepped ashore, one of them eyeing me closely said:

"Where in hell did you come from?"

I replied that I had just come up the river hoping to ship with them.

"And what d—— Yankee or lime juice man-of-war do you hail from?" English vessels are called "Lime Juicers" on account of that article being served out as a ration to prevent scurvy.

I told him that I came from no man-of-war, but had left the *Harriet Foster* the day before she sailed as I had had a row with the mate.

"And now you want us to pilot you home," said he. "Well, go aboard and see the mate. Tell him that I sent you and to let you sign articles."

I went on board, saw the mate, who after a short talk in which I related my story about the *Harriet Foster,* took me down to the cabin and produced the articles, after

which I inquired when they were to sail.

"D——d if I know," replied he, "it all depends upon when these cussed men-of-war will clear the coast."

He then enquired if I had any clothes, and when I told him they were all left on the *Harriet Foster* he said I might draw on the "slop chest" for what I wanted.

I went down to dinner with the crew upon the sounding of eight bells. The fare was better than that usually served upon merchant ships and the men said they had soft tack (bread) three days out of the week and plum duff every Sunday. The work was not hard. All the talk was about when they would take in their "cargo." Then hurrah for Cuba! Every man was promised one thousand dollars upon the safe delivery of the cargo. The crew consisted of twelve men and one boy. They had lost a boy overboard on the voyage out and I was to take his place.

After dinner the crew, instead of being set to work as is usual on merchant ships, lounged around the decks smoking, while two or three without asking permission of the mate jumped into a boat and rowed ashore. The other boy, whose name was Antone, asked me to come ashore and get some bananas that grew plentifully near the barracoon. I did so, and made an errand ashore every day, running when I was

alone down to the signal tree in hopes of seeing Tom Lee and Happy Jack when they came up on the flood tide. I never saw them but once and then I was obliged to motion them away, for just as they were paddling toward the bank I heard Antone calling me.

One afternoon the captain sent a note to the mate who ordered me to go to the galley and tell the cook to have dinner ready at six bells (four o'clock). When I delivered the message the cook said, "I'll bet a month's wages that we're off tonight."

I was astounded. It was too late to tie the signal to the tree as the tide was on the ebb and I knew that the canoe must have returned to the ship for that day.

After supper the canoes began to come alongside with poor human freight. The victims came over one by one, while the mate stood at the gangway counting off in groups of five, and the second mate, assisted by two or three seamen, were packing them in the "tween decks." I say packing, for no other word will describe the process of loading a slaver. They were packed as close as sardines in a box, for every slave was worth from six hundred to a thousand dollars.

Rum had been dealt out freely to both crew and negro drivers.

As soon as the last black was stowed below the hatches were put on, wind sails hoisted, the fore and main topsail and jib loosed and hoisted. The hawsers that had tethered us to the trees were cast off and the mate shouted, "Hurrah for Cuba."

Our voyage had begun! I had intended to slip ashore and make for the old *Sumpter* or hide in the jungle until the canoe should come up; but alas, the mate detailed me to hold a lantern over the main hatch in order to prevent the niggers from breaking their necks, as he said, and I could get no relief.

My only hope now was that one of the men-of-war, either the *Sumpter* or the *Marion,* and I was not very particular which one, would capture us. It was slack water and the tide would soon ebb. The captain and an old negro were on the forecastle acting as pilots. No bells were struck, no lights displayed and no noise allowed.

Everything went well until about eleven o'clock when the captain shouted, "Hard a port! Hard a port! Where in hell are you steering for?"

Presently the nose of the *Sultana* was pointed to the south bank of the river and the tide, which was now ebbing fast, drifted her on to a sand shoal and there she stuck. Almost superhuman effort on the part of officers and crew availed nothing. It was plain that we were there to stay. What was to be done?

Should the slaves be unloaded at the risk of losing large numbers into the bush, or should we lie quietly awaiting the

floodtide? The latter course was finally decided upon. A party was dispatched ashore to cut trees and branches. Long before morning every mast and spar was so decorated that we looked to be a part of the forest.

Having worked a good share of the night we were not disturbed until ten o'clock the next morning. Then began the routine of breakfast, "feeding the cargo." The slave-deck was hosed and there the poor creatures were dealt each a tin of rice and a sea biscuit.

During this process a small squad was directed to "rouse up the stiffs." Shortly the word was shouted up the hatchway that there were three "stiffs," and the second mate ordered me to fix a block and tackle on the mainstay to hoist out the "damaged freight," as they flippantly called the murdered human beings. Just as the bodies were laid on deck the captain came along and began to curse "Old King Hurricane," the boss of the barracoon, for putting on board "sick niggers," finishing his harrangue with a grand finale in the swearing art, accompanied by a threat to kill the old black on sight.

I had been studying all the morning on the serious problem of getting word to the *Sumpter.* The only possible course seemed to be to run down the river a mile or two and hail the boys who would soon be coming up in the canoe. But to steal ashore was

a very difficult matter. For some time I had been working on deck and watching my chance when I heard the captain call out in the bush language, "Aja ma we bo" (come here, boys), and add in the same tongue that he had plenty of whiskey. I looked around and there was the canoe with Tom Lee and Happy Jack. I was thunder struck and frightened. The idea came onto my head that the captain had found out that I had been sent there as a spy and I trembled all over. I eyed him closely while he called the second mate and gave him some whispered instructions. As Tom Lee came over the side the cabin-steward brought a pitcher of rum and handed him a drink. The captain called Happy Jack up out of the canoe to get some and when both were drinking, the second mate and four or five of the crew jumped upon and overpowered them at a signal from the captain. Of course, they were quickly dragged to the hatchway, stripped and sent below, while the captain chuckled and said, "Now we are only one short."

I was even more anxious than before to get off the ship for I feared that Tom, who spoke good English, might disclose the plot and betray me. At an opportune moment I dropped my cap down the hatchway and crawled down the ladder ostensibly to get it. The boys, realizing their situation, looked very unhappy as you may suppose, and the cursing I got in broken English and

Hottentot, almost makes my hair rise now in remembrance. The second mate heard the row and looking down asked me what I was doing there. I told him my cap story, and charging me not to "tease the niggers," he walked away. I stayed long enough to learn the whereabouts of the *Sumpter* from Tom who had ceased swearing, and to assure him that I would get the news to them and they would capture the ship and rescue him. He felt better and urged me to go at once. "Suppose no can hail ship, make fire on beach, quarter-master see 'em, send boat quick."

I promised to obey instructions, and going on deck, lounged around, watching my chance to make the land. Finally one of the sailors, declaring that he was going to have a good fill of bananas before leaving the coast, swung into a tree-top and in that way reached the shore. Two or three others followed and I went with the crowd. As soon as we touched land I strayed from the party and started down the river on a run. Of course this rate of speed could not be maintained, for I had before me a trudge of several hours' duration. While the scenery was grand and the chattering of the monkeys and chippering of birds was interesting, it was far from being a pleasure trip. Not fresh at the beginning, I was very tired after a few miles, and as night approached I imagined all sorts of dangers lay before me. The forest was full, I felt sure, of fierce ani-

mals, all licking their chops for me and all knowing exactly where to find me. The river too, would be difficult to follow in darkness. This was my only guide out into civilization. Once lost in an African jungle, farewell to prize moneys, promotions and all other things earthly. I fell to speculating upon the cheerful subject of which would be the worst death,—by fever or famine, wild beast or wild man; but like many, perhaps most of our troubles, none of these things happened. A very unexpected thing did, however, even as I had about decided between the desirability of furnishing the feast for a lion or a cannibal; I stooped to drink, placing one knee on a log, as I thought. It was just dusk. My support began to wiggle and I beat a hasty retreat. With feet firmly on land I stood dazed as a large crocodile let loose his moorings and floated off into deep water. Just before it became dangerously dark, I rejoiced to see the top of a marble monument which stands on the south side of the mouth of the river, having been erected there by the English government in honor of some naval officer who was buried there. I do not recall the name but it was one of the many of England's great dead.

From this point I turned to the south and walked along the beach, hoping every minute to catch sight of the *Sumpter,* but it was getting darker every moment and I saw that it would be useless to proceed further,

so I began to look about for dry wood to make a signal fire. Presently I saw the outline of a boat and my first thought was that it had been sent from the *Sultana* in pursuit of me, so I hid and listened. In a moment I recognized the regular fall and stroke of oars, in which the crew of the man-of-war were carefully drilled, and soon after discerned the binnacle light, characteristic of their boats.

I hailed, "Boat ahoy," at the top of my voice. The boat stopped. I called again.

Soon "Who is there?" rang out in the midshipman's familiar voice, and I ventured to give my name. When the boat had pulled through the surf and he had leaped ashore, he swung the lantern in my face and inquired, "Have you seen the boys who went up the river this morning?" "Yes," I replied, "they are prisoners on board the *Sultana,* unless they are rescued."

"Where is the pirate," said the middy.

"Aground, fifteen or twenty miles up the stream," I replied.

"Jump in, quick," he cried, "let's go back and report."

In a moment we were headed for our ship and reached her after a pull of an hour and a half.

The sailors were excited when I told my story, and of course they saw prize money within easy reach. Upon reaching the ship we all hastened on deck and the midshipman reported. I was questioned and gave a brief account of my adventures, finishing with the statement that I was hungry. The captain sent me to his cabin, somewhat to the disappointment of the crew who wanted to hear more. He had given directions to the cabin steward to serve me with something to eat. It was then about midnight and I had taken nothing since breakfast. This was the first and last time that I ever ate in the cabin of a man-of-war.

While eating I heard the boatswain's mate piping, followed by the call:

"Away, armed gig's crew, away."

Another blast and the call:

"Away, you armed first cutters, away."

The second cutter's crew was armed and I was ordered after supper to arm and join them. We soon took the lead. In about an hour we reached the mouth of the river. The officers held a consultation. The tide was ebbing and we would make slow progress pulling against it. The second cutter's crew, it was finally decided, should walk up the south bank and I was to accompany them.

We had gone about two miles when the creaking of the blocks of the approaching *Sultana* was plainly audible.

Our officers sent out two men back on the run to give the alarm. The rest of us waited until the slaver hove in sight. Down she came with fore and main top sails set and ebb tide to help. We found it impossible to keep abreast in the race down the river, and when we reached our boat she had already cleared the mouth and appeared to be some distance out.

The *Sumpter* lay stream up and a shot from her 32-pound howitzer gave the slaver a hint to heave to. The crews of the other boats were just boarding her as we shoved off, but we were all anxious to be in at the death so we joined them with all haste, and found our men putting the slaver's crew in irons. The first thing I did was to run to the main hatch and reassure Tom Lee and Happy Jack. A moment later one of our men secured the key and released them. They were overjoyed and displayed their feeling after the manner of their race. They danced, they sung, they shouted and shook hands with each other and our crew and officers. They lauded me until I felt as brave as an admiral.

The *Sultana* was sent to Liberia to unload her cargo, thence to Boston where she was condemned and sold. Out of the proceeds I received two hundred and thirty-eight dollars prize money and my officers added fifty dollars to this. Financially, I should have done much better to have stayed with the slaver, but I have always considered that day's work well worth the doing.

Tom Lee and Happy Jack received a purse between them almost equal to mine. The officers used to chaff them by reminding them that we should all have received more prize money if they had turned them in with the slaves.

Nearly thirty-five years have elapsed and I suppose that most of the *Sumpter's* crew have furled their jibs and anchored on the other shore, but if this should meet the eye of any one of them, I should like to hear from him.

THE EMPEROR NORTON.

8

EMPEROR NORTON IN BERKELEY

EMPEROR NORTON IS GENERALLY ASSOCIATED WITH THE CITY OF SAN Francisco. Indeed, the 1870 U.S. Census lists one Joshua A. Norton living in San Francisco, "Occupation: Emperor." However, contemporary local periodicals reveal that Emperor Norton had a significant presence in Berkeley as well. Far-reaching was the influence of the man who, though suffering from a grand delusion, ruled over the Bay Area and beyond with a most magnanimous hand. As described in one local publication: "There was always such a quiet dignity and impressive air of certainty about him that it seemed impossible to doubt his sincerity of belief in himself or the dignity of his reign."[1]

A PEN AND INK DRAWING OF EMPEROR NORTON'S UNIFORM FROM THE MAGAZINE *OVERLAND MONTHLY* OF MAY 1892.

EMPEROR NORTON IN SAN FRANCISCO

Joshua A. Norton was born in 1819 to English parents living in South Africa. He landed in San Francisco on the steamer *Franzika* with a pack of gold-seeking forty-niners. He had left South Africa after his widower father died leaving a bankrupt business. Norton's own business had failed as well, giving him good reason to try a fresh start in a new place.[2] In spite of his business troubles, he did manage to bring $40,000 with him to California and parlayed his fortune into real estate and general brokerage sales from a rented Montgomery Street cottage owned by millionaire James Lick.[3] At that time, food commodities were all imported into San Francisco, and with the city's population boom even food storage facilities were in short supply. These circumstances led to a vibrant speculative market in foodstuffs. Norton joined the fray and was doing quite well, even avoiding ruin after a May 1851 fire, thought to be started by the Sydney Ducks gang, destroyed all of the waterfront businesses and his competitors, as well as hundreds of houses. Fortuitously, Norton's commodities were stored safely in the belly of a ship offshore.[4] Though his office burned, his fortune was preserved. He regrouped and continued dealing in commodities, mining stocks, and real estate. In 1852, he built the first rice mill on the West Coast.[5] Following his business successes, Norton became a naturalized citizen and a Mason. That would be as good as it got for Joshua Norton.

After the 1851 fire, any merchant not joining the San Francisco Vigilance Committee would have found it difficult if not impossible to do business in the city. As its name implies, the committee had members who favored vigilantism. Though Norton joined the group, he took a firm stand against any act that deprived an accused person of his or her rights. Through strong moral conviction, Norton was able to force this resolution through the Vigilance Committee:

> *On motion of Mr. Norton. Resolved: that no criminal shall be sentenced until he or she shall have an opportunity of pleading guilty or not guilty and assigning his or her reasons why judgment should not be passed.*[6]

In a reactive time, Norton stood fast to the principles of American justice and was convincing enough to persuade others to adopt his standards amid great social turmoil and violence.

Rice was the most sought-after food in the area because it was the basic food for the significant population of Chinese men who had come to the area, either drawn by the gold rush or work building the railroads. Rice prices in San Francisco in 1852 skyrocketed within four months from four cents a pound to thirty-two cents a pound. Supply and price cycles whipped the market. Merchants held back stock from the market in hopes of catching the fluctuations just right for maximum profit. Then, in December 1852, they heard that China had stopped exporting rice due to a famine. Prices rose again. Norton joined the speculation and attempted to corner the market on rice in San Francisco by buying all that was on its way to the port.[7] If the scheme worked, he could retire an overnight millionaire. He and some partners purchased what they believed was all the rice on its way to the Bay based on a sample bag of the product presented to them by a broker. To their surprise, many ships began arriving with more rice than they knew what to do with. Prices plummeted to eight cents a pound by January 1853, and soon dropped to three cents a pound. Norton was ruined and he found himself in debt.

Norton claimed that the rice was not the same quality as the samples he was given and went to court to settle the $24,399.18 debt.[8] He first lost, appealed the ruling and won, only to lose on an appeal to the Supreme Court. His whole life was in limbo for two and a half years. He was not alone in his failure: only one in ten San Francisco merchants who started businesses in 1849 made it to 1855.[9]

Norton lost his real estate in North Beach when he could not meet the payments. The lots were repossessed by none other than William Tecumseh Sherman, who was working as agent for a bank. Sherman, who was released from the army along with many other officers to reduce military expenses following the Mexican-American War, would go on to become one of the most famous Union generals in the Civil War less than a decade later.[10]

Norton had lost his fortune for reasons largely beyond his control, save for having taken the risk in the first place, but he blamed himself. His financial troubles and the ensuing litigation tipped his mental balance, and he was thrown hopelessly into a world of delusion. He must have lived on his personal cash until it, too, ran out. Then on September 17, 1859, Norton's first proclamation was printed in the *San Francisco Bulletin*.

Norton was now Norton I, Emperor of the United States. Joshua Norton had taken refuge in a safer world of his own illusions. Somewhere in his mind he had seized control over a world that had previously taken everything he had. Now he believed that he was in charge, not knowing that the world he chose to dominate was a fantasy of a most intriguing and alluring character.

Joshua Norton rose above the mayhem. His madness took a form that was commanding, yet completely charming. He proclaimed himself "Emperor of North America," later adding "Protector of Mexico" to his title when Napoleon III sent his troops into that country. This first proclamation in 1859 was the harbinger of his burgeoning delusion. He began to lead a simple, predictably scheduled life that included a lot of walking. On rare occasions when someone addressed him as "Mr. Norton" rather than "Emperor," he was said to have appeared sad rather than angry.[11] The Emperor dressed the part, wearing an out-of-date blue military-cut coat, complete with epaulettes and brass buttons, a sash of silk, a saber, and a high hat crowned with feathers or a military pom-pom. Other trademarks were a fresh flower in his coat buttonhole, a large Chinese-style umbrella for shade during hot weather, and a remarkable wooden cane. The cane had a snake head at one end, with its body wrapped around the length of the shaft to the ferrule, where the rattlers were at the ready to shake for shock effect.

Emperor Norton reigned for twenty-three years. In spite of his severe mental illness, his kindness and brilliance shone so brightly that people honored and protected him. He was fed in the finest of restaurants. When he needed a new uniform, the newspaper or the fire department or Board of Supervisors would arrange to procure one, although he often had to wait quite a while.[12] He printed

A PEN AND INK PORTRAIT OF EMPEROR NORTON FROM THE MAGAZINE *OVERLAND MONTHLY* OF MAY 1892.

his own money and levied his own taxes on an optional payment basis—one paid taxes only if one could afford them. He often used the money he received as "tax payments" for charitable purposes, including an annual Christmas party for his youngest subjects.[13] He could walk into any museum or theater and receive the free and special treatment due a man of his "position." The state legislature even reserved a seat for him at its sessions.

Once an old acquaintance from South Africa found him and asked him why he dressed in a uniform and how he came to be called Emperor. Norton responded with a wild story of being a crown prince from France who fled to Cape Town to escape assassination and allowed himself to be adopted, and then stayed there out of love for his new father. He said that the uniform had been given to him by Queen Victoria herself and that everyone in the United States and Mexico was his subject. The horrified friend felt compelled to tell Norton that he thought he was crazy. Norton replied, "And so do a good many others."[14]

During a period of violent riots against the Chinese, a speaker tried to stir up an angry crowd at the corner of Kearny and California streets. When Emperor Norton came upon the scene, he marched up to the platform uninvited and faced the riled-up throng, while the stunned speaker stepped aside. After moments of laughter and then uneasy tension, with bowed head and closed eyes, Norton began to recite the Lord's Prayer, leaning on his famous cane. Everyone fell silent. He asked the audience to pray with him, and many did. Norton then offered his belief that all people were God's children—everyone. He spoke of how imperative it was for all to live together in peace. He asked the men to disperse, then stepped from the stage and disappeared.[15] The crowd could not but follow his request.

Many journalists poked fun at the local royal, but the town's most famous reporter, Mark Twain, would not use Norton as sport or entertainment to the degree his peers did: "I have seen him in all of his various moods and times, and there was always more room for pity than laughter."[16] Twain saw Norton's pathetic side and was surprised that the man was not studied for those human traits rather than the comic entertainment he provided most readers, albeit laced with affection. "O, dear, it was always a painful thing for me to see the Emperor begging; for although nobody else believed he was an Emperor, he believed it."[17]

It is theorized about in literary circles that Twain was so taken by the character of Norton that he used the Emperor as the basis for his character "the Dauphin," the grifter in *Huckleberry Finn*. Scholar William Drury regards this character as a "disguised Norton," noting that Twain's "King" claimed to be a crown prince from France, just as Norton had.[18] Twain perhaps answers this speculation

Emperor Norton reviewed the University cadets on Monday. He appeared
"large as life," with sword in one hand,
and a cane in the other, and was quite as
polite and gallant to the ladies as ever.

BERKELEY ADVOCATE, JUNE 5, 1879.

himself: "I don't believe an author ever lived who created a character. It was
always drawn from his recollection of some one he had known."[19]

EMPEROR NORTON IN BERKELEY

In the 1870s, the Emperor's abiding interest in education brought him to
Berkeley each month to visit the college students.[20] He reviewed the university
cadets in his full regalia, with sword and cane by his side. The UC cadets gave him
the respect due a man of his "title." During these visits, he stayed at the Franklin
House at Third Street and University Avenue.[21] He "engaged rooms" (under the
presumption that royalty requires a suite of rooms), although the claim as presented in a newspaper article reads suspiciously like an advertisement for the
hotel.[22] Norton was, after all, San Francisco's prime tourist attraction. The city of
San Francisco and many of its newspapers, theaters, eateries, clothing stores, and
even the railroad used Norton to advertise their bounty and the specialness of
San Francisco culture. Business always increased after an establishment touted

PORTRAIT OF DOM PEDRO, THE EMPEROR OF BRAZIL DURING THE PERIOD EMPEROR NORTON VISITED THE UC BERKELEY CAMPUS.

patronage by Emperor Norton. Berkeley handled him no differently, though the students were truly in affectionate awe of him. Whether this was based on entertainment value, respect for his fame, or a real sense of his magnetism and character is beyond our knowing.

He almost surely traveled to Berkeley by ferry, at least after 1874, when paddle-wheel ferry service began between San Francisco and Berkeley. A forty-five-minute ride from San Francisco's Green Street slip to the wharf at University Avenue and Second Street brought passengers within a block of the Franklin House. Visitors to UC transferred there to horse-drawn wagons; Brennan & Brothers Livery Stable was located right at the southwest corner of Second Street and University. On arrival at the campus, Norton was always swarmed by excited students begging for appointments to his royal government.[23] One student wanted an appointment as ambassador, another requested one as treasurer. Norton would often bestow these titles on anyone who struck his fancy.

Norton would give speeches to the university students, whom he considered his noblest subjects. He had a powerful manner, exuding kindness and dignity, which endeared him to young people. The speeches always included a warning about being loyal to the Empire (his royal monarchy, not the United States government, a democracy), and he would urge them to strive for the rewards only he could bestow upon them as Emperor.[24]

In 1876, University of California President Daniel Coit Gilman was hosting Dom Pedro, Emperor of Brazil, at a ceremony on the campus. Norton made a dramatic entrance attired in his royal uniform, his hat bursting with colorful feathers. There was one empty seat on the stage, which Norton graciously accepted just as though he'd been invited to the affair. Dom Pedro looked puzzled as Norton climbed to the stage and sat down until President Gilman whispered something in Dom Pedro's ear. Dom Pedro smiled. For a minute, the audience didn't know whether to laugh or remain silent, and respectfully chose the latter. After the ceremony, the two emperors exchanged all the formalities of their respective positions.[25]

At the end of February 1879, Emperor Norton gave a lecture to a large body of university students in the new Harmon Gymnasium. Norton's audience responded like sculpting clay in his hands, laughing and applauding as he stirred their emotions. The Emperor spoke that night about an issue that resounded through the state—Asian immigration.[26] He believed that a fairly large number of Asian immigrants in every state (10,000–15,000) would benefit all parties. He cautioned, however, that larger numbers would be problematic, presumably over-

The Emperor Norton's rooms are now ready at the Franklin House. From the Governor down to the highest private can be accommodated.

BERKELEY ADVOCATE, AUGUST 7, 1879.

FRANKLIN ✱ ✱ HOUSE.

C. MALONEY, Prop'r,

Late of the Franklin House, S. F.

Cor. University and Railroad Avenues,

WEST BERKELEY.

Good Board and Lodging from $5 to $7 per week.

Meals Furnished To Order.

Wines, Liquors, and Cigars of Choicest Brands.

A FRANKLIN HOUSE AD CIRCA 1885.

taxing the labor market. This was among the most pressing questions of the day, and Norton was on the liberal end of opinion in his era.

The UC Berkeley audience was so enamored of Emperor Norton that the students rose up and sang a song for him when he finished his lecture, then shouted three cheers for their Emperor. When the festivities were officially over, Norton discussed the chances of the United States becoming an Empire to those who crowded around him.

Despite his eccentricity, Norton exhibited an insightful mind in some of the decrees he issued. They were posted in public places and printed in the newspapers, occasionally including the *Berkeley Advocate,* increasing sales of the papers every time. Presciently, Norton declared that a suspension bridge should be built to connect Oakland and San Francisco. Sixty-seven years after his edict, construction of the Bay Bridge was completed less than three blocks from the spot he had chosen as the San Francisco anchorage. A plaque on the Bay Bridge now reads, "Pause traveler, and be grateful to Norton I, Emperor of the United States and Protector of Mexico, 1859–80, whose prophetic wisdom conceived and decreed the bridging of San Francisco Bay, August 18, 1869." Emperor Norton also issued political decrees such as the abolition of the Democratic and Republican parties, both of which he deplored. He also abolished the federal government and fired Abraham Lincoln.

On January 15, 1880, the *Berkeley Advocate* described him just after his death:

> *Perhaps he was the most eccentric genius in the country, and there was certainly a method in his madness . . . but there are strong reasons for believing that his father was the wild Prince of Wales, afterwards George the IV, to whom he certainly bore a strong resemblance.*

Emperor Norton died on January 8, 1880, at 8:15 p.m., while he was walking down California Street near the corner of Dupont Street in San Francisco. He was sixty-five years old. Thirty thousand people attended his funeral. Flags flew at half mast. He was dressed in a black satin robe, and a tuberose and sprig of maiden's hair rested on his lapel, gently placed there by a young woman who was often the beneficiary of Norton's habit of distributing flowers to people on the street.[27]

Found in his pockets were telegrams from the Czar of Russia and the Emperor of Austria, and Chinese script from Hong Kong. These forged documents were the thoughtful contributions of telegraph operators in support of Joshua Norton's benevolent delusion.[28] The Bay Area mourned the loss of a beloved and true eccentric and leader. Emperor Norton's earthly reign had ended.

> *No more through the crowded street he goes,*
> *With his shambling gait and shabby clothes,*
> *And his furtive glance and whiskered nose,*
> > *Immersed in cares of state.*
> *The serpent carven upon his staff*
> *Is not less careless of idle chaff,*
> *The mocking speech, or scornful laugh,*
> > *Than he who bore it late.*
>
> *His nerveless grasp has released the helm,*
> *But ere the Lethean flood shall whelm*
> *The last faint trace of his fancied realm,*
> > *Let us compare his fate*
> *With other rulers and other reigns,*
> *Of royal birth or scheming brains,*
> *And see if his crazy life contains*
> > *So much to deprecate.*

No traitorous friends or conquering foes
Betrayed his trust or destroyed his repose,
No fear of exile before him rose,—
  An Empire in his pate.
No soldiers died to uphold his fame,
He found no pleasure in women's shame.
For wasted wealth, no well-earned blame
  Turned subjects' love to hate.

No long and weary struggle with pain;
One sudden throe in his clouded brain
Closed forever his bloodless reign,
  With every man his friend.
For death alone did he abdicate.
What emperor, prince, or potentate,
Can long avoid a similar fate,
  Or meet a fitter end?

That under his tattered uniform,
Faded and soiled by many a storm,
There beat a heart that was kind and warm,
  The children all agree.
And over his grave we moralize,
That kings that are held both good and wise
May chance to seem to the angel's eyes
  Less free from blame than he.[28]

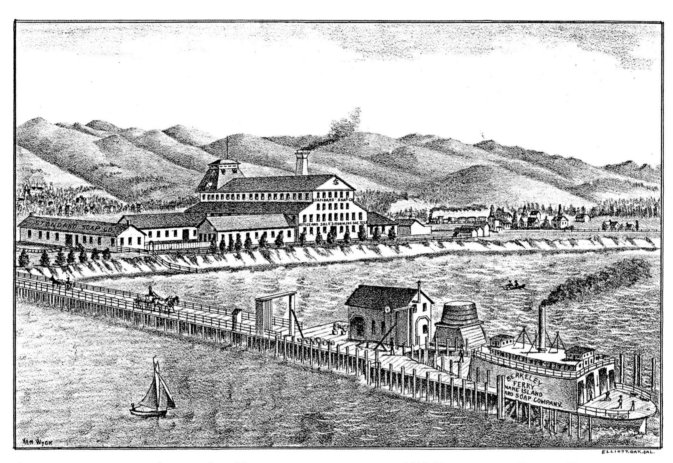

A PEN AND INK IMAGE OF THE STANDARD SOAP WORKS, LOOKING SOUTHEAST CIRCA 1885. NOTE THE EMPTY BERKELEY HILLS AND THE CLUS-
TER OF RESIDENCES TO THE SOUTH OF THE WORKS. THE WHARF TO THE NORTH WAS BUILT BY THE BERKELEY LAND AND TOWN ASSOCIATION
IN 1874. NOTE THE PADDLEBOX ON THE FERRY *MARE ISLAND*, WHICH DISPLAYS THE NAME OF THE STANDARD SOAP COMPANY. RICHARD PARKS
THOMAS OWNED THE SHIP, WHICH USED THIS WHARF. THE ORIGINAL SHORELINE OF BERKELEY SOUTH OF UNIVERSITY AVENUE IS VISIBLE IN
THIS IMAGE. IT OCCASIONALLY ERRODED IN BIG STORMS, SOMETIMES UNDERMINING WORKERS' SHACKS BY THE SHORELINE CLIFF. THE CLIFF
SURVIVES TODAY AS THE EAST SIDE OF AQUATIC PARK. DOWNTOWN BERKELEY IS VISIBLE IN THE MID-LEFT OF THE DRAWING.

9

RICHARD PARKS THOMAS AND
THE STANDARD SOAP WORKS OF BERKELEY

THOMAS'S EARLY YEARS

For decades after its construction in 1875, the massive four-story wooden building of the Standard Soap Company was by far the biggest structure in old Berkeley and could be seen from all quarters of town. This factory, known as the Standard Soap Works, was the largest producer of soap west of the Mississippi. Richard Parks Thomas owned the company and the land and he had designed and built the building. Twelve years prior to building the Soap Works, Thomas was already a proud Berkeley landowner, having purchased ranch land in the Berkeley Hills northeast of the newly established UC Berkeley campus, which opened in 1873. Thomas was a Civil War veteran and one of the town's most active and respected businessmen. His life was filled with his love of animals and gardening, his family, duty, and invention.

Richard Parks Thomas was born August 14, 1826, in Albany County, New York, to Quaker parents. Although a bright and industrious lad, Richard was not a successful student. When his parents discovered that he spent most of each school day chasing woodchucks in a nearby field, they realized he was unlikely to thrive at any school.[1] Richard showed a much greater interest in his father's small country store. His parents, astute enough to see this, arranged a two-year apprenticeship with a Presbyterian merchant. Richard did not last long, since he was found giving more attention to a pet raccoon than to the business.

Returning home, Richard worked in his family's store. The family also operated a potash shed where glycerin was made from the ashes farmers produced by burning their fields after the harvest. Richard's father occasionally made soap, and the process fascinated his young son. The bubbles and steaming mixture mesmerized Richard, and, by his own admission, led to his later career as one of the

A PORTRAIT OF RICHARD PARKS THOMAS PUBLISHED IN THE *BERKELEY DAILY GAZETTE* UPON HIS DEATH IN 1900.

BERKELEY ADVOCATE, OCTOBER 23, 1879.

BERKELEY ADVOCATE, OCTOBER 30, 1879.

nation's leading manufacturers of soap.[2]

Unfortunately, the family store closed, leaving Richard at loose ends. He soon ran away to Boston and, although underage, managed to join the U.S. Navy. For two and a half years he served on a man-of-war in the Mediterranean. When the Mexican-American War began in 1846, he prepared for deployment. Though he was an adult by then, Thomas's parents finally tracked him down just in time to convince the secretary of war to discharge their son before he saw too much of the world.

After the Navy discharged him, Richard bought a store that sold soap and candles, and did quite well until the enterprise burned down.[3] Richard voraciously studied soap making and bought another business in New York, which in 1859 also burned to the ground.[4] During this period, Richard met Jane Watson, a woman who was his match—competent, devoted, smart, and compassionate. Jane had taught art in New York, and her oils and watercolors were known to be fancy and delicate.[5] Richard and Jane married in Skaneateles, New York.

AFTER THE WAR

During the war, Jane Thomas moved to California to be with relatives. Richard followed her out upon his release from the Navy in 1863. In San Francisco, he saw a "help wanted" sign for a soap maker and accepted the position, relocating to San Luis Obispo to set up operations. All was well until a boiler explosion destroyed the entire operation.[6]

Thomas then took a job in San Francisco at Cogswell's Standard Soap, a small factory at Front Street and Broadway. Within six months, Thomas was a partner and soon after that he bought the business outright from Cogswell.[7]

Thomas devoted himself to this enterprise wholeheartedly, and sometimes slept on a cot in the office instead of retiring to his own bed so that he could keep close watch over his business.[8] Within five years he had eliminated his major local competition by buying out the three largest San Francisco soap companies. In 1873, Thomas's nemesis—fire—visited again and devoured his San Francisco Standard Soap Company candle plant. Fires were common in the wooden structures of nineteenth-century commerce, and the constant heating of materials in the soap and candle business only compounded the risk.

But, Thomas persevered. By 1887, he had acquired ten more soap companies.

Thomas and the Civil War

When the Confederates attacked Fort Sumpter on April 12, 1861, Thomas's patriotism propelled him to Syracuse, New York, where he hung a sign: "Men Wanted to Form Cavalry Company."[9] Sixty men responded, forming a battalion that Thomas supported at his own expense. Described in military records as six feet tall, lean, brown-haired, and gray-eyed, Richard Thomas and his battalion enlisted in the U.S. Army on July 24, 1861.

Thomas's battalion was called the Lincoln Cavalry, Company F, and consisted of German immigrants and Americans. A number of fights broke out between the Germans and the Irish Americans, because the two groups were quite different in manners, habits, and language.[10] These men had no uniforms nor any military discipline. An old dragoon positioned a circle of guards to keep the men in camp. Lacking guns, the sentinels carried ax handles as if they were rifles and even practiced the right shoulder shift.

This encampment was established following the battle of First Bull Run. Thomas's company then joined General McClellan's campaign and was renamed the First New York Cavalry. It fought in every engagement led by McClellan, including the bloody battle at Antietam, as well as the battle of Gettysburg, the turning point of the Civil War. Thomas was in the campaign called the Seven Days Fighting, and took a rifle ball in the leg at the battle of White Oak Swamp.

His commander said that Lieutenant Thomas behaved with the most admirable coolness, standing where the enemy's bullets whistled all around him.[11] Thomas was mustered out of the service in 1863 at age thirty-seven by an act of Congress and received one of the very first military pensions granted by the U.S. government.[12]

Thomas later said he could write volumes of what he saw in the war if he were the writing sort.[13] Those volumes were never written, but fortunately other members of the First New York Cavalry preserved their stories in memoirs. They wrote of blackened fields, of exploding tree trunks, and of shallow graves sprinkled with white powder (chloride of lime to prevent epidemics) where the torrents of rain and heat exposed bodies and left them a putrid pool.[14] Even the cavalrymen, high on their gallant horses, were stunned by the stench.

In the Seven Days battle, the men suffered for days without sleep and had only one meal. Brief periods of rest were interrupted by cannon fire and sudden calls to arms. Thomas was among those assigned to escort the changing of troops during the night.

A constant rush of supplies and ambulances supported the fierce fighting, with the roads often guarded by cavalry. When a retreat was called, wounded men were left screaming in the woods.

What Thomas and the others endured was pressed into their souls. When he moved to California after the war, Richard Parks Thomas became a devoted member the San Francisco Post of the Grand Army of the Republic, a Civil War veterans organization, for the rest of his life and traveled to its encampments.

The old oak tree which was blown down on the Shattuck property about a year ago is being made to serve an historical purpose. All the foliage and large branches have been sawed off and taken to San Francisco to be used in the background of the scenery of the Panorama of the Battle of Vicksburg.

Berkeley Advocate, August 6, 1887.

San Francisco Call, January 16, 1888.

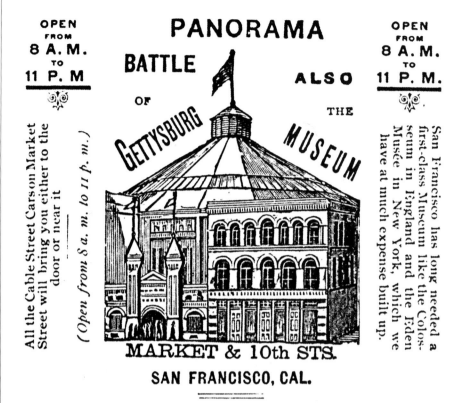

An ad for the Gettysburg Panorama at Tenth and Market streets in San Francisco. The long hours attest to the popularity of the enterprise. The museum burned to the ground in the aftermath of the 1906 earthquake.

RICHARD PARKS THOMAS STANDING IN FRONT OF HIS GETTYSBURG PANORAMA, A MUSEUM OF LIFE-SIZE PAINTINGS INTENDED TO GIVE THE VISITOR A REAL FEEL OF THE BATTLES OF THE CIVIL WAR.

This pen and ink image of the Standard Soap Company graced much of its official correspondence. Note the box and two passenger cars pulled by the one small steam engine and coal car. This view is looking in a generally westerly direction.

The Standard Soap Company has had 400 young gum trees planted along its water front line. It would be well if others who own property would follow its example, the effect of such would be not only beautiful but useful, as a barrier against wind and dust. Go thou and do likewise.

Berkeley Advocate, January, 1880.

A Soap Palace. — Superintendent Thomas has opened a branch store for the exhibition and sale of soaps, from the Standard Company's works in Berkeley, under the Palace Hotel, on Montgomery street, San Francisco. It is termed a "Soap Palace" and attracts a great many visitors daily.

Berkeley Advocate, October 2, 1880.

A cave occurred in the Standard Soap Company's soapstone mine, near San Benito, twenty-five mile south of Hollister, on the 8th instant, instantly killing Mrs. A. B. Kemp, wife of the foreman of the mine. No other person was injured.

Berkeley Advocate, May 13, 1882.

Thomas and Berkeley's Standard Soap Works

After the fire at the San Francisco candle plant, and wanting to consolidate three separate operating locations, Thomas was forced to look for a large factory site. He moved all of his manufacturing operations to Ocean View. Land was cheap in Berkeley, especially compared to San Francisco. A train line was rumored to be in the planning stage that would snake along the bay shore and soon make Ocean View accessible, yet the remote area was almost devoid of industry. Soon thereafter, Thomas purchased an entire block of land and drew the plans for a huge factory himself. He began construction in 1875 of what would soon become the largest soap works west of Chicago. His only neighbor was the Pioneer Starch Works (located on what is now the site of Truitt and White Lumber at Second and Hearst streets). The new building and operation was called the Standard Soap Works. The main office and showroom of the Standard Soap Company remained in San Francisco.

The four-story Standard Soap Works building towered above the area between Addison Street and Allston Way and Second and Third streets, and covered the entire block. Despite his war wound, Berkeley's "Captain" Thomas (the term *captain* was often used as a simple status symbol without real reference to rank) was said to have walked back and forth to work from his home at the foot of La Loma using his gold-tipped cane supported behind his back and held in place by the crooks of his elbows to keep him from bending forward on the steep dirt slopes.[15]

When the Berkeley factory began operating in 1876, a windstorm had already blown off the original roof of 600,000 shingles. The facility measured 300 feet in each direction. Its construction required two million feet of lumber, and 500,000 bricks for the foundation and chimneys.[16] A glycerin refinery, stable, and other buildings made a cluster of the company's facilities. West of this complex stood a grove of almond, willow, oak, and eucalyptus trees, with thimble and blackberry shrubs growing next to the bayshore cliffs. These cliffs still grace the east shore of Aquatic Park.

The Standard Soap Company was internationally known, producing more than 350 kinds of soap, 1.5 million bars per month, including toilet soaps (made principally of coconut oil), shaving soaps, floating bars for the bath, and 130 kinds of laundry soap. It also manufactured candles, both standard and glycerin, from the tallow produced in great quantities by local stockyards.[17]

The cavernous first floor of the factory contained the raw materials—barrels of cottonseed and coconut oils, tallow, lye, and rosin. Also on this floor were the perfumes for the high-grade soaps and four fifty-horsepower boilers providing

THE STANDARD SOAP COMPANY'S SAN FRANCISCO OFFICE AND SHOWROOM, CIRCA 1890. IT WAS LOCATED AT 525 MARKET STREET, ON THE WEST SIDE OF MARKET BETWEEN FIRST AND SECOND STREETS. RICHARD PARKS THOMAS HAD A PAINTING OF THE BERKELEY FACTORY HANGING IN HIS SAN FRANCISCO OFFICE.

THE EARLIEST KNOWN PHOTO OF THE STANDARD SOAP
WORKS, POSSIBLY AS CONSTRUCTION WAS COMPLETED
IN 1876. NOTE THE DIRT ROAD, WHICH WAS THIRD
STREET. ONE CANNOT SEE THE RAIL TRACKS, LAID IN
JANUARY 1877, SO VISIBLE IN LATER PHOTOS, WHICH
RAN DOWN THIRD STREET. THAT FACT DATES THIS
PHOTO TO 1876, BETWEEN THE COMPLETION OF THE
STANDARD SOAP BUILDING AND THE LAYING OF TRACK
ON THIRD STREET.

steam for the machinery. All operations were powered by steam, and human hands never touched the materials until teenage girls packed the bars of soap in boxes.

The second and third floors contained huge vats, twelve feet wide and twenty-five feet deep, in which thousands of pounds of raw materials were boiled.

The toilet soap was manufactured on the fourth floor. Here, blocks of raw soap were shaved by rapidly revolving knives, a process called chipping. The shavings were spread out and dried; colors and perfumes were then added. Next, the chips passed through huge granite rollers, becoming as thin as paper, and were pushed through metal holes in a machine called the plodder, producing long bars of soap. These bars were cut into cakes and a die pressed the Standard brand name and logo onto them. Finally, young girls trimmed and wrapped the bars, placing them in little boxes, three bars to a box.

ABOVE: LOOKING EAST FROM THE BERKELEY LAND AND TOWN ASSOCIATION PIER. THE CONICAL SMOKESTACK TO THE RIGHT OF THE PIER IS THE CAMPBELL GLASS WORKS, OPENED IN 1884. THE STANDARD SOAP WORKS' FOUR-STORY WHITE FACTORY STANDS PROUDLY AT THE RIGHT OF THE PHOTOGRAPH AT BAYSIDE.

LEFT: A PEN AND INK DRAWING OF THE STANDARD SOAP WORKS WAS DISPLAYED AS PART OF AN 1891 POSTER DISTRIBUTED BY REAL ESTATE AGENTS IRWIN AND JOHNSON OF THE LORIN DISTRICT WHEN BERKELEY WAS EXPANDING ITS BORDERS.

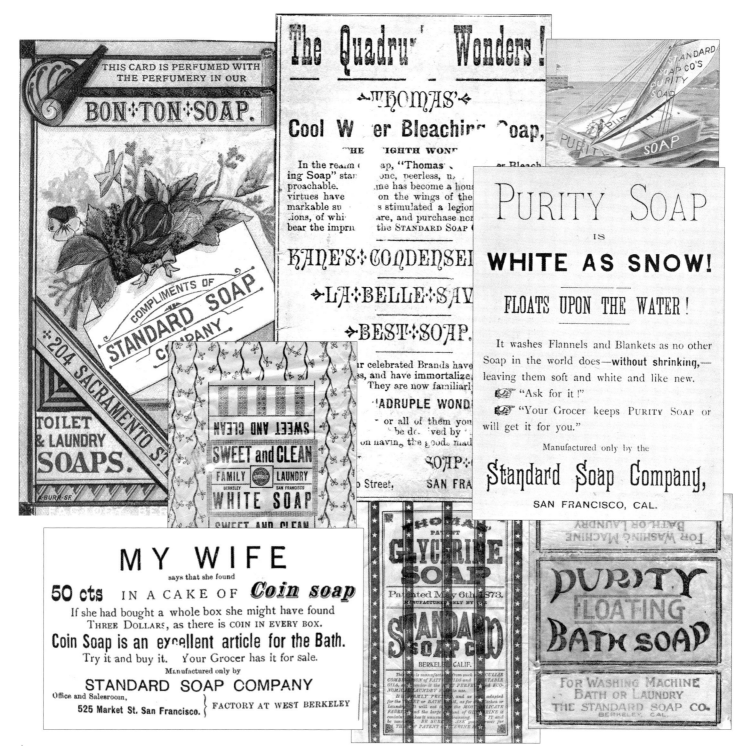

ADS AND WRAPPERS FROM BARS OF SOAP MANUFACTURED BY THE
STANDARD SOAP COMPANY.

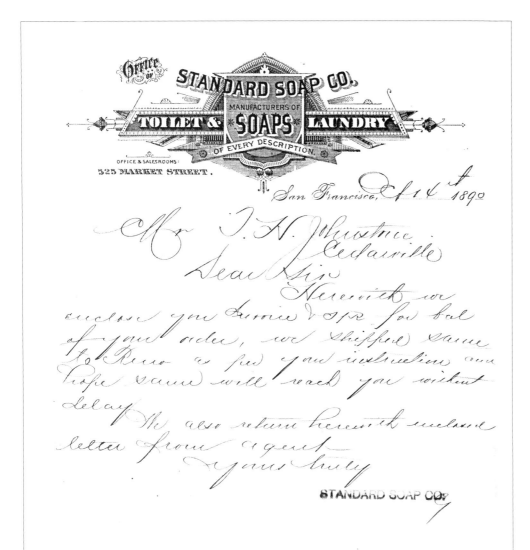

STANDARD SOAP.

WHITE OLIVE,	-	70 $\frac{15}{16}$ lb.	bars.
SEA FOAM,	-	60 1 lb.	"
"	-	100 $\frac{12}{16}$ lb.	"
SEAL IMPERIAL,	-	60 1 lb.	"
LION,	in 3, 4 and 5 lb.		"
CHALLENGE,	-	100 $\frac{10}{16}$ lb.	"
GOLDEN,	-	100 $\frac{12}{16}$ lb.	"
EAGLE,	-	80 $\frac{14}{16}$ lb.	"
GREENBACK,	-	90 $\frac{12}{16}$ lb.	"
MARBLE,	-	80 $\frac{12}{16}$ lb.	"
A. E. LAUNDRY,	-	108 $\frac{10}{16}$ lb.	"
B. DIAMOND,	-	60 1 lb.	"
ROCK OIL,	-	100 $\frac{12}{16}$ lb.	"
PARAFFINE,	-	140 $\frac{8}{16}$ lb.	"
K. CRYSTAL,	-	36 1 lb.	"
"	-	45 $\frac{12}{16}$ lb.	"
CASTILE, cut to order,			

TOILET SOAP.

SEA FOAM, white,	-	36 $\frac{7}{16}$ lb.	"
BOQUET, pink,	-	12 $\frac{7}{16}$ lb.	"
CANDLES,	-	15 oz.	
"	-	13½ oz.	

J. W. SWALLEY.

AN 1890 LETTERHEAD, PRICE CARD, AND 1883 RECEIPT FROM THE STANDARD SOAP COMPANY.

Our town was honored by a distinguished visitor on last Tuesday noon. He was a mammoth sea-lion, and poked his nose above the surface immediately in the rear of the Soap Factory as if to see whether the internal revenue was being defrauded or the article produced was "Standard." After making a satisfactory examination he returned to his favored locality to resume his ablutions—with a a cake of toilet in his paw.

Berkeley Advocate, October 9, 1879.

A barn of rather novel material, unlike any other in the United States, has been erected by the Standard Soap Company. It is made of iron, the waste product, caustic drums. This material has now been pressed into building uses by the utilitarian Superintendent, and will no longer be considered as waste.

Berkeley Advocate, December 11, 1879.

R. P. Thomas, of the Standard Soap Company, showed much liency in not prosecuting W. Hunt for embezzlement. The amount collected was about $100, which, Hunt declares, was either lost, stolen, or strayed from him while under the influence of liquor.

Berkeley Advocate, April 22, 1880.

Berkeley Advocate, November 14, 1881.

LOOKING NORTH ON THE RAIL TRACKS BEHIND THE STANDARD SOAP WORKS. THE GLYCERIN BUILDING IS IN THE FOREGROUND AND THE SOAP MANUFACTURING PLANT IS JUST NORTH OF THAT. THE COMPANY MADE GREAT USE OF THE CONVENIENT RAIL AND MARINE TRANSPORTATION NEAR THE PLANT.

Custom soaps were very popular in the 1870s, and Standard had innumerable dies to make them. There were boats, bulldogs, a fist—you could even get your own initials pressed into the soap. The company also produced a series of commemorative soaps in honor of General Grant. Most of the glycerin soap balls were shipped to China. Standard Soap may have had the only machine on the West Coast for the toilet soap design-stamping process.[18]

By about 1878 there were thirty-five male employees and ten "deft" girls hired as packers. The company had its own railroad spur line on the Southern Pacific tracks, and used the Posen Station at Third Street after it opened in late 1887. Thomas also bought his own ferryboat and painted "Standard Soap" on its paddle-wheel box.

The Standard Soap Company helped Berkeley's newspaper industry. It purchased ads and supported a local printing company that produced both their many labels and the newspaper called the *Berkeley Standard,* known for its clear type setting.[19] This newspaper later evolved into the *Berkeley Daily Gazette.*

Richard Parks Thomas was possibly Berkeley's first commercial recycler.

COMPLIMENTS OF
STANDARD SOAP CO.
San Francisco * Cal.

STANDARD SOAP COMPANY'S EXHIBIT
in the Government Building
WORLD'S FAIR EXHIBITION
AT NEW ORLEANS
From a Photograph

A souvenir of the Standard Soap Works exhibit at the New Orleans World's Fair Exhibition in 1894 and 1895. The man in the hat is the American Indian known only as Billy, whom Thomas wanted to host the company's display.

—Mr. R. P. Thomas and wife failed to make a good start on Monday for the exposition at New Orleans, finding when they reached San Pablo Station that the Indian, who is to be an important figure in displaying the soap exhibit of the Standard Soap Co., was not on the train. They returned and on Tuesday started afresh, making sure of the Indians' presence with them.

Berkeley Advocate, December 1, 1894.

The Indian "Billy" who had charge of the Standard Soap Company exhibit, whose picture is seen in the Standard Soap Herald for May, has returned from New Orleans. He does not like that country, and expressed himself as very tired of the Exposition.

Berkeley Advocate, May 9, 1895.

RICHARD PARKS THOMAS AND HIS ELEVATED TRAIN LINE

Thomas's vision was not limited to his soap company. He promoted a design for an elevated trolley that was displayed at the Mechanics Fair in San Francisco in 1895.[20] Thomas hoped to install this trolley in east Berkeley running up to Grizzly Peak, and he might have built it except for the 1888 failure of the bank of which he was president.

The original idea for the elevated line was not Thomas's but rather one of his brother's, who was blind. Richard Parks Thomas said that his brother

> planned it all out in his darkness and you will see, one of these days, that it is such a perfectly feasible and admirable plan that it will one day supercede the surface roads, both in city and in the country.[21]

The cars would be smaller, lighter, and more aerodynamic than steam engine railcars. Thomas hoped to run this elevated line from San Francisco to Los Angeles through the San Joaquin Valley. The cars would run on a suspended cable ten to twenty feet above the ground, and, powered by electricity, would reach speeds of 100 to 150 miles per hour. He imagined that the cars would be lit and heated by electricity and wired with the latest telegraphic equipment to maintain constant communications with the outside world.[22]

A mechanical device already existed that would prevent the cars from rear-ending each other via a switch that would automatically turn off the electricity. Head-on collisions would be avoided by having cars on each cable moving in only one direction. Thomas claimed that his calculations projected a savings of one-third to two-thirds on construction and maintenance of his elevated system versus steam trains. The only thing that could slow the car down was atmospheric resistance, which could be overcome, Thomas believed, by designing the front end of each car in a pointed shape.

Thomas was so forward thinking that he saw electric power as only a temporary system:

> My plan would be to build compressed air tanks along the road in the country where trains could stop for a moment or two and recuperate the motive supply. I am satisfied that in the end compressed air would be cheaper and more satisfactory than electricity.[23]

In the meantime, Thomas and other like-minded electricians believed the day was not far off when one could travel from New York to San Francisco in twenty-four hours for twenty-five dollars.[24]

RICHARD PARKS THOMAS HANDS OUT SOAP
SAMPLES AT THE MECHANICS FAIR IN 1895 AND
DISPLAYS HIS MODEL OF AN ELEVATED RAILWAY
HE INTENDED TO BUILD UP TO GRIZZLY PEAK.
THE FAIR WAS SPONSORED ANNUALLY BY THE
MECHANICS INSTITUTE OF SAN FRANCISCO.
BERKELEY GAZETTE, SEPTEMBER 15, 1895.

CHINESE WORKERS AND THE STANDARD SOAP WORKS

Although it was reported in the 1870s to historian H. H. Bancroft that no Chinese were employed at the Standard Soap Works, newspaper articles noted Thomas's concern for his Chinese employees, who were housed right by the plant. The report might have resulted from pressure to discriminate against Chinese workers due to the local anti-Asian sentiment of the late nineteenth century and the fear by whites of losing their jobs to Asians, who were very dependable and were willing to work for less. This pressure must have taken a toll on Thomas and the company, because by March of 1880, Thomas had dismissed many of his Chinese workers and replaced them with whites. A court action was instigated over their firing.[25]

Wilhelmine Cianciarulo wrote about the workers at Thomas's factory in memoirs of her childhood in west Berkeley in the 1870s:

Where Allston Way should have cut through to the beach, between Second and Third Streets, there was a village of shacks occupied by the Chinese coolies who worked in the soap factory. Many of these Chinese men were married and had large families that lived in the shacks also. I often watched the coolies when they came out of the factory in a single file, at noon and at closing time. It seemed as if the line would never come to an end. They always walked in single file . . . Chinese women and children dressed very elegantly in native costume, when they went to San Francisco to visit friends and relatives or do their necessary shopping. . . .

The Chinese coolies and their village gradually disappeared as more white people moved to Berkeley and secured jobs in the soap factory. . . .

Adjacent to the Chinese Camp facing Third Street there was a row of three-roomed cabins, painted red. These were built for the white families employed by the soap factory.[26]

Richard Parks Thomas did bow to the pressure of the community at his factory, but he did not in his home. A man named Ah Lung—who was born in China in 1845 and emigrated to the United States in 1855—did all the cooking for the Thomas family. This was one of the few jobs Asian men could hold in Berkeley at this time. Lung wore a black hat with a red knob and was known to love lottery games, which drew him to San Francisco's Chinatown.

The Standard Soap Company have determined to send off the few Chinamen they employ and fill their places with white labor. This they would have done before but for the difficulty they experience in obtaining reliable workmen. The white boys will chuck soap around, go to frolics, and be absent sometimes when large orders are on hand to be make up. The best remedy is to discharge such unfaithful workmen or boys, and hire others to take the places.

BERKELEY ADVOCATE, MAY 29, 1879.

—O those docile and faithful Chinamen! Why, they are natural rogues. Petty larceny is their proclivity. Soap, be it never so standard, cannot wash out this trait in their character. Only the other day a Mongolian servitor of R. P. Thomas robbed his master of sundry household articles, including a watch and a clock and although he was watched he made good time in escaping arrest. The clock and watch stolen belonged to Mr. L. Gerge. The other articles were the property of Mr. Thomas. That John wanted the wherewithal for a new years' frolic was perhaps the cause of the theft.

BERKELEY ADVOCATE, FEBRUARY 18, 1882.

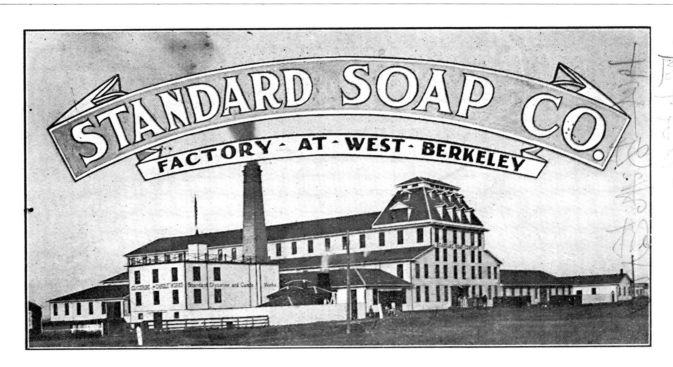

CAPITAL
$500,000

OFFICE
WEST BERKELEY, CAL.
PHONE MASON 643

INCORPORATED
APRIL 9, 1875

A POST CARD OF THE STANDARD SOAP WORKS WITH CHINESE CHARACTERS WRITTEN ON THE RIGHT MARGIN OF THE CARD. THE CHINESE CHARACTERS ATTEMPT TO HELP THE READER PRONOUNCE THE NAME OF THE COMPANY IN ENGLISH. IT WAS PROBABLY USED AS A GUIDE BY THE CHINESE WORKERS AT THE PLANT.

Mr. R. P. Thomas is tunneling for water on his ranch in the foothills, near the University. It is bored a considerable distance, and is being securely timbered. It will be undoubtedly a success, as these hills are rich in the purest kind of water.

BERKELEY ADVOCATE, DECEMBER 4, 1879.

—R. P. Thomas has planted on his ranch north of the University about eight acres of vines. Every attention is being paid to their culture. The vines look healthy and the experiment so far promises to be a success.

BERKELEY ADVOCATE, JULY 1, 1882.

—R. P. Thomas is, we are pleased to say, about to try the experiment of planting grapes upon his foothill ranch north of the University grounds. He will select a location well shaded by trees. Should the experiment prove successful, and we believe it will, much good will result.

BERKELEY ADVOCATE, FEBRUARY 11, 1882.

—R. P. Thomas, of La Loma Park, spends some of his leisure in fort building. He has constructed a fortification on the hilltop of his lofty ranch that commands the entrance of the bay, and in fact everything in sight. He has planted cypress trees around it, into which he will in time cut port holes. We have not yet learned whether he intends to mount Armstrong or Krupp guns. As his position is so elevated, he cannot well use swamp angels. This gentleman was a veteran of the rebellion, and we don't wonder to see the soldier crop out now and their.

BERKELEY ADVOCATE, JUNE 23, 1883.

An old farm boy, he wasted nothing. Bar soap scraps were reworked for laundry soap. Iron from the old barrels of caustic soda was used for fireproof roofs on the barn and stable. All scrap materials were used in maintaining the facilities, and Thomas himself designed all the equipment. He even built a plant in San Francisco using the rubble from a demolished house.[27] In late 1872, he procured U.S. patent no. 138,712, for a process that reused waste glycerin, which saved $100 per day. In all, he had several patents to his credit.[28]

Thomas engaged in other ventures, such as a new meat packing plant in west Berkeley and attempted to procure the franchise for a University Avenue railroad line. He was known as a sophisticated and straightforward businessman.

THOMAS MOVES TO BERKELEY

Thomas purchased a small ranch in the hills of north Berkeley shortly after arriving in the Bay Area in 1863. Soon he owned thirty-two acres—from Cedar Street to Rose Street and from the Berkeley Water Company (just east of what is now Buena Vista Way) to LeRoy Avenue. He built a house and barn, grew grain, and kept horses. He planted an orchard with cherry, peach, and plum trees and even an experimental vineyard. Eucalyptus trees were planted as windbreaks. His ranch offered a commanding view of Berkeley and the bay, as well as a direct view of the Golden Gate. The entire property was bounded with well-maintained whitewashed picket fencing. The entry drive to Thomas's ranch stretched along what is now Greenwood Terrace and began climbing the hill at Rose Street. His carriage horse, Birdie, was said to always seem happy to rush up that hill.

When the city of Berkeley came into being on April 1, 1878, Thomas set off a show of sky rockets to celebrate.[29]

In the summer of 1883, Thomas built a fort of cypress log posts embedded in the earth and mounted two military cannons on the walls, one larger than the other. It was variously known as Fort La Loma (Spanish for hillside) and Fort Soap.[30] It stood at what is now 2900 Buena Vista Way. Thomas built a log cabin next to the fort to display Civil War relics he had picked up during the war, including firearms dropped on the battlefield at Antietam, where Thomas had fought. Thomas's Civil War memories continued to influence his life some twenty years after his wartime service. Nothing ever came close to the intensity and terrible intimacy seared into the minds of Civil War veterans, and for the great majority their wartime experiences framed the rest of their lives.[31]

In 1893, volunteer firemen borrowed one of the cannons from Thomas's adopted son Edgar for a Fourth of July celebration at the railway station at

A VIEW OF THE BERKELEY HILLS, LOOKING EAST ONTO RICHARD PARK THOMAS'S LA LOMA PROPERTY. THIS PHOTO SHOWS THAT THOMAS INSTALLED A PAINTED FENCE AROUND THE ENTIRE PERIMETER OF HIS PROPERTY. FORT LA LOMA IS JUST TO THE RIGHT OF THE WOODED PEAK IN THE MIDDLE OF THE PHOTOGRAPH, DATING THIS PHOTO TO 1883 OR LATER. THE DIRT ROAD AT THE BOTTOM IS COUNTY ROAD, NOW SPRUCE STREET, CUT BY CAPTAIN BOSWELL IN 1888.

Shattuck Avenue and Vine Street. They overloaded the charge and blew the cannon to smithereens.

Although a quiet and modest man, Thomas showed his magnanimous spirit each Fourth of July by opening his grounds to hundreds of people.[32] At dawn he fired the cannons, announcing that the festivities were to begin. Old-timers would say it wasn't the Fourth of July without the sound of Captain Thomas's cannons. These catered affairs featured orchestras, dancing, literary readings, and speeches. The grounds were decorated with flags, flowers, lanterns, hammocks, and banners. Thomas would display his Civil War gear in a special tent, and was conspicuous in his lieutenant's uniform, faded and full of bullet holes.

In the 1890s, Jane Thomas assumed control of the company due to Thomas's failing health, and ran it until 1903. When moving pictures were invented, they were shown to the public in the Standard Soap Works building. An early movie serial, *Officer #44*, about a Berkeley police officer, featured a wild police chase filmed in and around the aging building. Another film involving two men jumping

—R. P. Thomas of the Soap works had a narrow escape from serious injury, if not from death, yesterday morning. While driving down town in his buggy, and when at the junction of University and Shattuck avenues, his horses balked just as they had placed their forefeet upon the track, because of the drain there made to allow the water to pass down the cut. They stopped stubbornly and as the upward quarter-past-eight train was rapidly approaching, the situation was precarious. By a vigorous application of the whip, however, the team crowded ahead and cleared the track just in the nick of time. We are not a pessamist, but we again predict that there will be a serious accident at this crossing some day unless a gate or a flagman be there stationed.

BERKELEY ADVOCATE, NOVEMBER 4, 1882.

A PHOTOGRAPHIC VIEW FROM THE NORTHWESTERN EDGE OF THOMAS'S LA LOMA PROPERTY. IN ADDITION TO A PORTION OF THE FENCE AROUND THOMAS'S RANCH, ONE CAN SEE BERKELEY'S NORTHERN SETTLE- MENTS AND INDUSTRY. FLEMING POINT, BROOKS ISLAND, AND ALBANY HILL ARE AT THE TOP OF THE PHOTOGRAPH. IF YOU LOOK CLOSELY AT FLEMING POINT, YOU CAN SEE THE WHARF OF THE DYNAMITE PLANT AND THE SMOKESTACKS OF THE ACID RECOVERY SYSTEM OF THE CHEMICAL OPERATION. THE PERALTA PARK HOTEL, WITH ITS TOWERS, IS NESTLED IN THE MIDDLE OF THE PHOTO, BETWEEN ALBANY HILL TO THE NORTH AND FLEMING POINT TO THE SOUTH. THE HOTEL ASSERTED ITSELF ON THE HORIZON ABOUT 1889, MAKING THAT THE PHOTO'S EARLIEST DATE. THE ENCLAVE OF NORTH BERKELEY, CENTERED AROUND THE SOUTHERN PACIFIC'S BERRYMAN STATION AT SHATTUCK AVENUE AND VINE STREET IS AT THE MID-RIGHT.

A PEN AND INK DRAWING OF THOMAS'S FORT LA LOMA, LOWER RIGHT, WITHIN A FAMOUS MAP OF BERKELEY CIRCA 1891 AND CIRCULATED BY LORIN DISTRICT REAL ESTATE AGENTS IRWIN AND JOHNSON.

A VIEW FROM THE TOP OF FORT LA LOMA.

FORT LA LOMA AS SEEN FROM THE BASE OF THOMAS'S PROPERTY. NOTE THAT THE DRIVER OF THE EMPTY CARRIAGE IS MOST LIKELY THE PHOTOGRAPHER. THIS ENTRY ROAD IS TODAY GREENWOOD TERRACE.

Our fellow townsman, R. P. Thomas, does not permit mere personal business to distract his attention from passing events of moment. Only a few days since he made a tender of his ranch in this vicinity for the location of the Veterans' home, being himself a veteran of the late war. Now he comes to the front with a proposition to form an "United Brotherly Band of Americans" to give material aid and comfort to Arabi Bey, who is struggling so gallantly against the foreign invasion and domination of his native country, Egypt. The ADVOCATE was among the first of California journals to see through the false mazes of English misrepresentation, and state the plain truths in regard to the situation. It is p'easant to observe that the press now generally entertains like opinions. Neither France nor Italy are in accord with England, while the wanton bombardment of Alexandria meets with the reprobation of many an honest Englishman, notably John Bright, who resigned from the cabinet in preference to giving it even a seeming sanction. Mr. Thomas sets forth his plan of operations in a circular address, which is couched in stirring language. As he is an earnest man and tenacious in purpose, we expect much from his efforts in aid of a cause which must meet with the sympathy of everyone who sympathizes with liberty and right as against tyranny and wrong. Arabi Bey is contending for what our fathers fought in the war of the Revolution and for which Parnell is now struggling to obtain for Ireland—home rule.

BERKELEY ADVOCATE, AUGUST 12, 1882.

The Annual Entertainment given to the EMPLOYEES of the Standard Soap Company.

LA ∴ LOMA ∴ PARK.

INDEPENDENCE ∴ DAY

MONDAY ∴ JULY ∴ 5. ∴ 1886.

LA LOMA PARK.

Mr. & Mrs. R. P. Thomas request the pleasure of your company at their Annual

Independence Celebration and Camp Fire, on Monday, July 5th., at 11 o'clock a. m.

FORT LA LOMA.

Sunrise Gun at 4:23 A. M.
National Salute at 12 M.
Sunset Gun at 7:39 P. M.

FIRE WORKS IN THE EVENING.

R. S. V. P.

PROGRAMME.
---

1. Overture, - - - - Orchestra
2. Prayer,
        REV. G. A. EASTON.
3. Song. - - "The Star Spangled Banner"
4. Reading of the Declaration of Independence.
        MR. CHAS. E. COOPER.
5. Medley of National Airs, - - Orchestra
6. Oration,
        A. H. CUMMINS, ESQ.
7. Song. - - - - "Hail Columbia"
8. Poem,
        MAJ. D. N. HARKINS.
9. Song, - - - - - "America"

COLLATION.

DANCING.

☞ Take 10 A. M. Boat from San Francisco ; Berkeley train to Berryman's Station.

RICHARD PARKS THOMAS GAVE A FOURTH OF JULY CELEBRATION AT HIS BERKELEY RANCH EVERY YEAR. IT WAS ATTENDED BY HUNDREDS OF PEOPLE. THOMAS WOULD FIRE HIS CIVIL WAR CANNONS AT DAWN AND SUNSET. THIS INVITATION ANNOUNCES THE AFFAIR OF 1886, HELD AT FORT LA LOMA, WHICH THOMAS HAD BUILT FOR THE PURPOSE OF MOUNTING AND FIRING HIS CANNONS. PEOPLE FROM SAN FRANCISCO ATTENDED AND WERE GIVEN DIRECTIONS TO TAKE THE FERRY AND THE TRAIN TO BERRYMAN STATION IN NORTH BERKELEY. NOTE THAT THE HOLIDAY WAS BEING CELEBRATED ON MONDAY, JULY 5TH, APPARENTLY BECAUSE THEY DID NOT WISH TO HAVE SUCH AN EVENT ON A SUNDAY. SINCE THE FESTIVITIES STARTED AT 11 O'CLOCK IN THE MORNING, PEOPLE EVIDENTLY HAD THAT MONDAY OFF FROM WORK IN 1886.

One Fourth of July at La Loma

In 1887, during one of the Fourth of July events at Fort La Loma, people were surprised to see the lid of a basket lift up on its own as a feeble wail emanated from within the wicker. Upon investigation, an infant was found inside, neatly dressed and with a half-full nursing bottle. An accompanying note requested that the Thomases adopt him. The baby was accepted with open arms, baptized, and taken in by the Thomases as their own.

Sadly, the child would not remain in their lives for very long. According to an April 18, 1888, article in the *Berkeley Advocate:*

> On the very day upon which they were to have signed the papers giving them the legal control of the little waif left to their tender care Capt. and Mrs. R. P. Thomas were called upon to give it up to a power higher than any earthly court. Nobly did they fulfill the work entrusted to their hands, and their hearts were already gladdened by the love which came with the care of the little stranger. They have the sympathy of many friends in their loss as they had before the admiration of all, for the loving kindness they showed to one of Christ's little ones.

At the Thomas family gravesite at Mountain View Cemetery in Oakland, a small gravestone with the traditional curled lamb motif used for children lies to the left of the family headstone. Carved on it is "Richard age 11 months." The large, elegant family headstone shows the names of Richard Parks Thomas, 1826–1900, his wife Jane Watson Thomas, 1829–1918, and an Edgar Standard Thomas, 1883–1952. Edgar was born in California, and was adopted by Richard and Jane Thomas. He was originally adopted into the family of D. E. Dowling, Thomas's superintendent at the soap works. When Mrs. Dowling died while Edgar was still an infant, the Thomases arranged to become the boy's legal parents and honored the soap works in Edgar's middle name. Edgar Standard Thomas grew up to become a music teacher. Architect Bernard Maybeck, his neighbor, designed his music studio at La Loma Park.

In 1898, Richard Parks Thomas signed a pension document saying that he had "no children living that I know of."[33] Curiously, records show that in 1874, the Thomases had also legally adopted a girl, Jennie.[34] Jennie married and became Mrs. Jennie W. Woltman, and in 1902 succeeded in receiving a share of her father's estate.

THE GRAVESTONES OF THE THOMAS FAMILY. THE LARGE STONE MARKS THE GRAVES OF RICHARD PARKS THOMAS, HIS WIFE, JANE WATSON THOMAS, AND HIS ADOPTED SON, EDGAR STANDARD THOMAS. NEXT TO THE LARGE STONE IS A SMALL LOW GRAVE MARKER WITH A BABY LAMB, THE SYMBOL OF THE GRAVE OF A CHILD. IT MARKS THE GRAVE OF RICHARD THOMAS, AGE ELEVEN MONTHS.

A STILL FROM THE 1925 MOVIE SERIAL *OFFICER #44*. THE EXPLOITS OF A BERKELEY POLICE OFFICER WHOSE BADGE WAS NUMBER FORTY-FOUR WERE SOMETIMES FILMED USING THE OLD STANDARD SOAP WORKS BUILDING, THEN IN DISREPAIR. IN THIS SCENE, A MAN JUMPING FROM THE SOAP WORKS' TALL BUILDING IS ABOUT TO BE CAUGHT BY BERKELEY'S FINEST.

from a burning building used the old Standard Soap Works building for the fiery scene. Two stuntmen jumped while members of the Berkeley Fire Department stood below with nets to be filmed saving the jumpers. The scene did not go as planned. One jumper was hospitalized for six months, and the other was crippled for the rest of his life.

On April 11, 1903, at two o'clock in the afternoon, Mrs. J. W. Thomas transferred ownership of the Standard Soap Works, the land 280 feet by 1200 feet, and seven acres of tidal land adjoining the factory, to the firm of Tillman and Bendel, a wholesale grocery firm from San Francisco. By 1911, the Standard Soap Works of West Berkeley was again operating a thriving soap manufacturing business and was being run by B. J. Williams. In 1916, the Peet Brothers, later of Colgate Palmolive-Peet, bought the structure. The building was eventually abandoned and became a hangout for hobos. In 1924, fire damaged the building, and it was demolished the following year.

LA LOMA PARK

The *Berkeley Advocate* of March 16, 1897, described Thomas's generosity in sharing his property with his fellow citizens:

> *Generous Offer by Which Berkeley May Be Distinguished and Benefited—the proposition of Captain R. P. Thomas to deed over to the town La Loma Park for public use is in that line of munificence which has been happily demonstrated in other directions. . . Its stretches of orange, olive and lemon orchard, and its grassy slopes, that could easily be transformed into a park of wondrous beauty. The acquisition of such a property for park purposes would add vastly to the reputation, which Berkeley has long held as a town of beauty. . . .*
>
> *The gift, however, is contingent upon the acquisition by this town of the Wheeler tract, of about half the acreage, and which, lying lower on the slope, would be necessary as an approach, and for the laying out of picturesque avenues leading toward the summit. . . . Throngs of people come from San Francisco every week, especially on Sunday, for a stroll through the university grounds and over the hills, and I think that Berkeley would be greatly beautified by a good park. . . . Most of the trees on the place have been planted by my own hand during the twenty years of my residence here, and the love I have gained for the place would not permit me to see it subdivided nor put to any other use than for a public benefit.*

The little log cabin among the eucalypti, in which I spend much of my time, is a piece of my handiwork and is a result of seven years' intermittent work. When I came here these thirty-two acres were as barren as any place you ever saw. And everybody in Berkeley is familiar with its unequaled verdure to day and its great variety of arboreal beauty. It is certainly to be hoped that means may be devised by which the great gift can be secured.[35]

LOOKING NORTHEAST FROM THE BERKELEY STATION, THIS PHOTOGRAPH SHOWS THE DOMINANCE OF THE LA LOMA PROPERTY, SEEN ON THE MIDDLE RIGHT OF THE PHOTOGRAPH. THE WOODS WERE PLANTED BY RICHARD PARKS THOMAS, AND ITS FENCE STANDS OUT CLEARLY FOR ALL TO SEE.

Unfortunately, Berkeley was not big on financing parks, evidenced by the absence of a thirty-two acre La Loma Park in north Berkeley. Thomas had made a condition of his offer that the city would have to purchase the land below his property to serve as entrance to the park.[36] Thomas had also offered to donate his property for a veterans' home, but Napa was chosen for the site of that institution.

ABOVE: BASED ON THE LARGE AUTOMOBILE IN THE CENTER MID-RIGHT OF THE PHOTO CIRCA 1908, THIS IS AN IMAGE OF THE GARDENS RICHARD PARKS THOMAS HAD BEEN DEDICATING HIMSELF TO IN THE LAST PART OF HIS LIFE. ALBANY HILL IS ON THE RIGHT AND FLEMING POINT IN THE FAR CENTER. THOMAS HAD OFFERED HIS PROPERTY TO BERKELEY IF THE CITY WOULD PURCHASE THE LAND JUST TO THE WEST OF IT FOR AN ENTRANCE. AS ONE CAN SEE FROM THE PHOTO, HOUSES WERE BEING CONSTRUCTED BELOW THE PROPERTY, THOMAS HAVING PASSED AWAY IN 1900.

RIGHT: THE VIEW AT THE SOUTHWEST CORNER OF THE LA LOMA RANCH.

Looking Out from the Eucalyptus Grove "La Loma" Berkeley

EPILOGUE

Richard Parks Thomas was seventy-three years old when he died on May 28, 1900. On this day, he told his wife that he was going to take a nap in his little cabin on their ranch grounds. When he did not respond to the dinner bell, a search was mounted. His body was found near his beloved rabbit hutch. He'd been felled by a clot in his heart, and died on the ground he loved so much and had worked so hard to beautify. As described in the *Berkeley Daily Gazette:* "Beneath the trees he had planted, he laid him down to sleep, and so, with hands folded peacefully across his breast, his sorrowing family found him."[37]

Thomas's funeral was held on May 29, 1900, at his La Loma property. His military medals were pinned on his chest and his coffin was wrapped in the flag of the country he so proudly fought for. There were but few flowers. A white anchor of hope was placed across the blue of the flag, and over his heart were the offerings of his comrades—a sprig of evergreen, symbol of eternal life; a white rose of purity; and laurel, the crown of victory.[38]

The townspeople knew him as Captain Thomas, a popular term of respect of the day. Captain Thomas's beloved, hand-planted world was subdivided and the tract was named La Loma Park shortly after his death. Edgar Thomas lived in the house after his mother's passing in 1918 as the structure was turned into apartments. Thomas's Civil War museum became student housing. Everything came to an end on Monday, September 17, 1923, when the great Berkeley fire destroyed all the old Thomas property. A neighbor rushed to their home and managed to rescue two William Keith paintings and a few other things.

EULOGY

The *Berkeley Daily Gazette* of June 2, 1900, described Thomas as "one of the most keenest, earnest businessmen of the early days . . . a man identified with every municipal improvement and advancement. . . . Of late he was withdrawn from public life, yet his figure, for a quarter of a century familiar to everyone, will be missed on our streets."

Judge G. Biglow, a speaker of immense understanding and eloquence, gave the eulogy and reviewed Thomas's life:

> *Captain Richard P. Thomas lived to witness the wonderful development of the nineteenth century. As he looked back upon his life from the calm of these Berkeley hills, and thought of the changes that must have been wrought during that time, with steam and electricity, and inventions; with*

G. Standard Thomas

EDGAR STANDARD THOMAS, AN ADOPTED SON OF
RICHARD PARKS THOMAS, WHOSE MIDDLE NAME WAS
TAKEN FROM THE STANDARD SOAP WORKS.

AN AD BY EDGAR STANDARD THOMAS, RICHARD PARK
THOMAS'S ADOPTED SON, FOR MUSIC LESSONS IN HIS
LA LOMA STUDIO.

DESIGNED BY BERNARD MAYBECK, THIS LITTLE STRUCTURE WAS THE MUSIC STUDIO OF E. STANDARD
THOMAS.

A RARE INTERIOR VIEW OF THE MUSIC STUDIO EDGAR STANDARD THOMAS BUILT ON THE LA LOMA
RANCH.

*education and home comforts; it must have seemed more like a rapidly
moving panorama than a reality [the fast changes in living, culture and
science during Thomas's lifetime] that he himself had been no small
factor.*[39]

Biglow spoke of the Civil War and its lasting impact on Thomas:

*Like so many of the others of the survivors of that momentous struggle,
that period of his life counted for more than all the rest, and contained
memories of which he was intensely proud.*

Biglow also described of Richard's beloved La Loma:

*The beautiful spot in which we now stand is a monument of his strong
character; taking it as a wilderness, by persistent effort and untiring
industry he changed it into the veritable Garden of Eden it is today.*

He concluded:

*Farewell, old friend, but not for long; perhaps you cannot return to us,
but we can to you. Death separates, but it also unites. . . . Rest, comrade,
peaceful be thy slumbers. No bugle's blast nor drum's alarm can now disturb your earthly repose. Wherever thy soul, thy mind, the Divine essence
which made thee a living being now roams in the realm of space, we have
faith to believe it is in a better world, a higher and better existence than
that in which we here move.*

A photograph of Benjamin Boswell during the Civil War.

10

Benjamin D. Boswell, the Man behind the Mysterious Boswell Ranch

BERKELEY WAS INCORPORATED IN 1878, BUT FOR TWO AND A HALF decades thereafter development progressed only in spurts beyond the original downtown area, much of it in south Berkeley and Lorin, while the territory north of Berryman Station was divided among a handful of ranches. One of these ranches was operated by the Boswell family and was known for its considerable and unique natural beauty.

Cornelius Beach Bradley, a UC Berkeley professor of rhetoric, included this description of the Boswell Ranch in a book titled *A Berkeley Year*, which was published in 1898:

> **COW STOLEN.**
>
> STOLEN OR STRAYED FROM THE Boswell Ranch a red and white cow, branded "B" on the right hip, with a slit in the right ear; will calve about the middle of October. A REWARD of $5 will be paid for any information concerning her or $20 REWARD for the arrest and conviction of the thief.

BERKELEY ADVOCATE, JULY 17, 1887.

> To one quaint nook only would I offer to conduct my reader, and with the
> more reason, perhaps, because while it is easy enough of access, it seems to
> be very little known. The place is Boswell's, though why so called I have
> never been able to guess. The name suggests human habitation at least,
> if not also vulgar resort and entertainment; but both suggestions are wide
> of the mark. Our visit shall be on some bright morning in April. We take
> the train to Berryman station [Shattuck and Vine], and zig-zagging
> thence northwestward, we soon are clear of the thin fringe of dwelling-
> houses, and out among the fields. Our course so far has been as if for
> Peralta Park [the area north of Sacramento and Hopkins streets]; but
> instead of turning sharply down to the west at the margin of a little creek
> [Codornices], we cross the bridge, and follow the country lane northward.
> When the lane also turns abruptly westward, some half-mile further on,
> we abandon it altogether, continuing our former direction over fields and
> fences, and across two little waterways [two forks of Marin Creek].

THE VIEW FROM SOMEWHERE IN THE VICINITY OF WHAT IS NOW THE ALAMEDA AND HOPKINS STREET, SHOWING THE OPEN RANCHLAND AND THE TREE-LINED COURSE OF CODORNICES CREEK. FLEMING POINT AND ALBANY HILL ARE DISPLAYED BY THE BAYSIDE. THE DYNAMITE AND CHEMICAL WORKS AND THEIR SMOKESTACKS AND BUILDINGS ARE REVEALED THERE. THE CAPTION OF THE "JONES TRACT" INDICATES THAT THIS PHOTO WAS TAKEN CIRCA 1879 (THE FOUNDING OF THE POWDER WORKS AT FLEMING POINT) TO 1892 (WHEN THE FACTORY WAS RELOCATED).

Beyond the second rivulet we reach a broad slope thickly strewn with rocks and boulders, and dotted about with low trees and shrubs. This is Boswell's.

The air all along has been full of the sounds and scents of spring:— the gurgling notes of the meadowlark, the rich smell of newly plowed fields, the warm breath of mustard in bloom. But this untamable rock-strewn area, like the Buddhist monasteries of the far east, has become a veritable sanctuary for plants and living creatures that could not maintain themselves in the open in their unequal struggle with that fell destroyer, man. Here the wood-rat has piled undisturbed his huge shelter of sticks. The warbler and the thrush are singing from every covert. The woodpecker and the squirrel shadow you from behind tree-trunk or rock to discover your intent in trespassing thus upon their private domain; while

the flycatcher flashes his defiance in your very face, if you venture too near his mate on her nest. Nor is it otherwise with the plants. Delicate species that are fast disappearing before cultivation—the blue nemophila, the shy calochortus, the bright pansy-violet—bloom here undisturbed in all their pathetic beauty, "If God so clothe the grass of the field, which to-day is, and to-morrow is cast into the oven, shall he not much more clothe you, O ye of little faith?"

But we linger here too long upon the threshold. The tract is a considerable one, and midway there is thrust up into it from the west a somber wedge of eucalyptus forest, contrasting strangely with the rest of the scene. For here we seem to be in a region three thousand miles away,—in a veritable bit of New England hill-pasture with its labyrinthine paths, its ever-changing short vistas, its endless series of little secluded alcoves walled about with shrubbery and carpeted with grass and flowers. The rocks too are of striking size and form, and culminate near the lower end of the tract in a bold, fantastic crag, in itself well worth the effort to visit it. But the most unlooked-for feature of the place is its air of remoteness and seclusion. Here it lies, spread out on the open hillside, in full view from the bay and from town. Yet as we thread its quiet alleys, or lie dreaming

ABOVE: CORNELIUS BEACH BRADLEY, WHO DESCRIBED BOSWELL'S RANCH IN 1898. IT IS NOT SURPRISING THAT HE WOULD BE SO MOVED BY IT; HE WAS ONE OF THE FOUNDERS OF THE SIERRA CLUB AT AGE TWENTY-SEVEN IN 1892 AND EDITED THE *SIERRA CLUB BULLETIN* FROM 1895 TO 1897. BRADLEY PEAK WAS NAMED FOR HIM BY FELLOW SIERRA CLUB MEMBERS IN 1898. CORNELIUS BRADLEY WAS A RHETORIC PROFESSOR AT UC BERKELEY FROM 1882 TO 1911 AND SERVED AS A MISSIONARY IN THAILAND.

LEFT: A TANTALIZING POSTCARD CAPTIONED "LEAVING BERKELEY," WHICH MOST LIKELY REFERS TO THE SAME SYLVAN ROAD THAT CORNELIUS BEACH BRADLEY DESCRIBED IN HIS VISIT TO THE REMOTE BOSWELL'S RANCH IN 1898.

A SCENIC AREA IN THE THOUSAND OAKS NEIGHBOR-
HOOD CIRCA 1912.

*in the sunshine under lee of its rocks, we seem to have journeyed leagues
from the work-a-day world we left behind us but an hour ago.*

*It is good to be here! And good it is also to return to the world. The
joy of the scene and the season, the clearer brain and quickened pulses we
shall bring back with us as we take up again the effort and struggle. And
more than this we may sometimes bring from such a sanctuary,—some
heavenly vision,—some far-seen glimpse of a transfigured life that may be
ours,—in the strength of which we shall go many days, even unto the
mount of God.*[1]

For those who never visited the former Boswell Ranch, Bradley's words might
have sounded overly effusive. But he was not the only one charmed by the

astounding natural beauty of this place. Just ten years later, a great many citizens
rallied to preserve this Eden-like terrain; sadly, their efforts failed.

Bradley's bafflement as to the origins of the "Boswell" name assigned to the land
he so admired illustrates the sometimes ephemeral nature of collective memory.
The name belonged to Benjamin Demfry Boswell, who leased this enchanted land
from Nevada senator John P. Jones and operated it as a ranch beginning in 1878.[2]
His term on this property was rather brief, as he and his wife left Berkeley in
1896. How quickly this man and his ranch were forgotten is a testimony to the
influx of new citizens into Berkeley in the 1890s and the remoteness of this land
with respect to the original town boundaries.

Boswell was born on September 20, 1837, in Wayne County, Indiana. Despite
his Quaker upbringing, Benjamin felt compelled to join the Union army when
the Civil War broke out and enlisted in August 1861. Boswell's Civil War service
was remarkable. He served almost the entire war and was involved in all of the
early engagements in the Cumberland Valley and all of the major battles in West
Virginia, Tennessee, Kentucky, and Georgia. So vigorous was his action during
Hunter's Raid, an expedition to Virginia by Union cavalry under General David
Hunter, that he ran down fourteen horses during the course of the battle.[3] On
May 19, 1863, during the siege of Vicksburg, Benjamin Boswell was severely

THE OPEN AREA OF NORTHBRAE BEFORE DEVELOP-
MENT. NOTE THE HORSE-DRAWN CARRIAGE TRAVELING
THROUGH THE AREA AND THE EUCALYPTUS GROVE.
EUCALYPTUS WERE PLANTED AS WINDBREAKS, AND TO
PROVIDE SHADE, LUMBER, AND BEAUTY IN THE LATE
NINETEENTH AND EARLY TWENTIETH CENTURIES IN
BERKELEY, COMMENCING AROUND 1875.

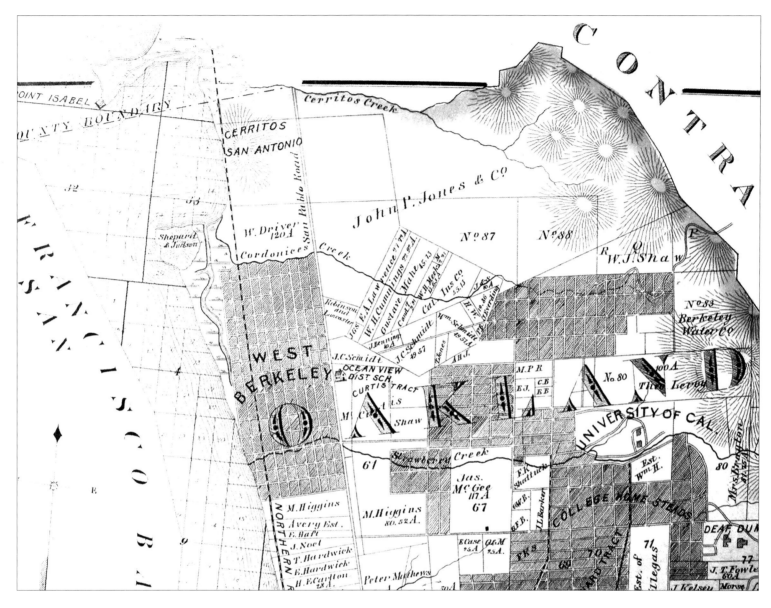

An 1878 map showing the J. P. Jones tract extending from San Pablo Avenue to the crest of the Berkeley Hills and from the proximity of Codornices to Cerrito creeks. This was the land that Benjamin Boswell leased upon his arrival in 1878.

wounded by a minnie ball that passed through his body near his heart. The field surgeon did not expect him to live and gave up on him. Boswell somehow summoned the strength to survive, and was soon sent home to recuperate from his wounds. Within three months, he had recovered and rejoined his unit.[4] This was Boswell's only furlough during his Civil War service. However, as a result of this chest wound and a subsequent case of sunstroke during the battle of Harper's Ferry, Boswell was plagued by a number of serious medical ailments for the rest of his life.

Captain Boswell was mustered out of the service on July 16, 1865, and journeyed to Iowa to complete his law studies. There the twenty-eight-year-old Boswell met nineteen-year-old Emma Elizabeth Pallady, who was living with her parents on their family farm near Allerton. Her mother said that Emma had "never cared for another" and that the couple's relationship was "truly a love match."[5]

Although Boswell had been mustered out of the volunteer army at the end of the war, he applied for a commission and on June 18, 1867, was appointed second lieutenant in the Twenty-ninth Infantry. On June 28, 1868, he took leave on a surgeon's certificate of disability and went to Iowa to marry Emma in a military wedding ceremony. He returned to Washington, D.C., to rejoin his regiment on July 10, 1868.

Following the war, Benjamin suffered a number of recurring ailments, and Emma lovingly cared for him for the rest of his life. Emma said that after the war Benjamin could not tolerate crowds, confinement, or exciting conditions.[6] He would get dizzy and sometimes fall unconscious. When his postwar trauma grew too great, he would lie down and Emma would hold him until it passed. Early on in the marriage, Emma also learned of Benjamin's heart problems. He had poor circulation, could not sleep on his left side, and could not sleep through the night.[7]

In 1868, during the violent period of Reconstruction, Boswell began service as a judge advocate in Jefferson, Texas. He was known to be just and sensitive with both the black and white citizens who came before his court, even though his life was threatened a number of times by whites who did not want to relinquish their power to an integrated society.[8] During this period, Boswell suffered a second sunstroke, remaining unconscious for twenty-four hours before a surgeon was able to revive him. It is unknown whether Boswell was a serious drinker, but his company commander at the time attributed his spasms to delirium tremens resulting from alcoholism.[9] However, a doctor certified after weeks of observation that Boswell suffered "general debility, the most prominent feature of which is nervous asthma . . . he is in my opinion unfit for duty. . . . Miasmic influences, along with the exhaustive heat of this tropical climate may . . . be held responsible [for] the ailment from which Capt. Boswell suffers. I would recommend that an early opportunity be afforded him of changing his residence . . . to a more salubrious district."

He was granted a thirty-day leave on November 2, 1871. When he did not come back after thirty days, he was listed as AWOL and the army cut off his pay. The matter was resolved after extended communications between Boswell and his superiors. Boswell did not want to go back to Texas, and so submitted a surgeon's certificate of disability every month from Allerton, Iowa, from December 1871

BENJAMIN BOSWELL STANDING AT THE FAR LEFT
OF THE LINE OF HIS STUDENTS AT OREGON STATE
UNIVERSITY CIRCA 1873. CAPTAIN BOSWELL WAS
THE UNIVERSITY'S FIRST MILITARY INSTRUCTOR.

through May 1872. One of Boswell's superiors still suspected that he suffered only from too much alcohol consumption. Boswell was ordered before a medical board on July 27, 1872. The board determined that he was "suffering from neuralgic pain of the left arm and leg . . . loss of control of motion. . . . That he was gradually improving and recommended that he be allowed to take up his residence where intermittent fever was not prevalent."[10]

Boswell was ordered to report monthly on his condition using the surgeon's certificate of disability form. Every month he submitted the form reporting that he was "suffering from malarial poisoning causing Hemiplegia and general debility.

(Hemiplegia is a partial paralysis of one side of the body.)" From the trail of certificates, it is possible to trace that he and Emma moved from Iowa to Kansas to Colorado, and then to San Francisco in December of 1872.

Beginning a new year with a fresh start, the Boswells moved to Corvallis, Oregon, on January 1, 1873, where Benjamin's father, a medical doctor, resided. Benjamin found a volunteer job at Oregon State University as the first military instructor at the agricultural college. In fact, he was the first officer on the U.S. Army payroll to serve in this capacity in the western part of the country.[11] (UC Berkeley had two faculty members who were graduates of West Point at this time, but they were not active army officers.) The local newspaper described his class on military tactics as lively and praised his understanding of the art of command.[12] On June 18, 1873, Boswell was appointed to be a regular (not volunteer) professor of military instruction.

Having observed Benjamin's tremors, Dr. John Boswell diagnosed his son's condition as epilepsy rather than alcoholism.[13] Benjamin also suffered from poor circulation (the result of a weak heart) and paralysis of his left side. He pursued retirement from the military due to his health problems—he had been on disability leave for quite some time—and was discharged with a pension in 1878.

BOSWELL RANCH'S COMPOUND OF BARNS AND BUILD-INGS SHOWN JUST TO THE LEFT OF THE LARGE GROVE OF TREES. THE BARNS AND OTHER BUILDINGS WERE BUILT ON WHAT IS NOW PERALTA AVENUE NORTH OF SOLANO AVENUE. THERE ARE ROADS UNDER CON-STRUCTION BUT DEVELOPMENT IS STILL SPARSE. THIS PHOTOGRAPH IS FROM THE ERA FOLLOWING THE 1906 EARTHQUAKE.

On last Sunday afternoon some hunters set fire to the grass in the canyon back of Capt. Boswell's ranch while discharging their guns. The fire ran with the wind up the foothills and was quenched in the gum tree grove near Pat. Curran's ranch, after destroying quite a number of trees.

BERKELEY ADVOCATE, AUGUST 14, 1886.

On Monday evening last about 8 o'clock as Capt. Boswell in company with his wife was driving on Walnut street, near Mr. Hanscom's residence, where a sewer is being laid, his horse and buggy ran into the excavation. As quick as a flash Mrs. Boswell jumped out and escaped uninjured, while the Captain was thrown out and sustained bruise on the side of his head and left arm. The neighbors came quickly to their relief, picked up the Captain, and extricated horse and buggy which were uninjured.

BERKELEY ADVOCATE, FEBRUARY 8, 1888.

BOSWELL'S BERKELEY

Benjamin and Emma Boswell arrived in Berkeley around 1878 and leased land that stretched from San Pablo Avenue into the hills, and from Cerrito Creek south to about Hopkins Street. Solano Avenue was originally a dirt road created to connect Boswell's Ranch to Ocean View, a bayside settlement of immigrants, mostly farmers and factory workers, centered on Fourth and Delaware streets. "Boswell's Road" (now Solano Avenue) extended from San Pablo Avenue to what is now Peralta Avenue, turned north into a gully (now Peralta Park), and led to Boswell's Ranch compound, which included a number of barns and bunkhouses. The combined cow barn and horse stable was huge, about 150 feet long, and held about 250 tons of hay.[14] Jerseys and Holsteins roamed the area. Horses ran in pastures. Boswell even built special pens for his thoroughbred pigs to keep their smell from ever reaching the living quarters. The surrounding land was mostly open, but it was dotted here and there with wooden bridges that linked dirt roads across the area's many creeks. Boswell's Ranch covered all of present-day Albany, much of North Berkeley's Cragmont, Northbrae, and Thousand Oaks neighborhoods, and even the area north to Fairmont Avenue in El Cerrito. It extended east to the Contra Costa County line and west to San Pablo Avenue.

Boswell hired ranch hands from local families to help him harvest hay and oats and raise livestock. One of them was Louis Hagen, son of a pioneer, who in his later years recalled the day Boswell told him to bathe and scrub seven pigs that Boswell had chosen. When Hagen was done, the pigs were put in wooden boxes and transported to San Francisco for a very special voyage. Boswell's stock, according to Hagen, was shipped directly to the royal farm of the Emperor of Japan. Boswell also offered to pasture other people's horses for a fee. The borders of Boswell's land were not well defined—a common problem in those days—and he was forced to deal with several boundary disputes. Once he planted a crop on a parcel that was also claimed by Judge Dameron, who hired two men to occupy the site that he considered his property. But when Boswell rode up on his horse and glared at Dameron's men, they immediately fled.[15] When Boswell's men came to harvest a crop on this land, two men hired by Dameron told them to get off the property. Boswell's men told the guards to get out of the way or they would be mowed under. That was enough of a threat; they moved out of the way rather than be run down by the horse-drawn mower.

Every year, the Boswells held picnics at the ranch for schoolchildren and churches. All were welcome. On June 16, 1888, they hosted a picnic for The Church of Good Shepherd.[16] According to a report of the event, it featured races

Captain Boswell has taken the contract to repair San Pablo avenue north of the school house. He is going to put on that street about 500 loads of gravel taken from the creeks, and will do doubt make a good job it.

BERKELEY ADVOCATE, NOVEMBER 5, 1881.

~Capt. Boswell has been recommended for Roadmaster of Ocean View District. The Board of Supervisors cannot do better than elect him, as he knows just what work is needed and knows how to do it.

BERKELEY ADVOCATE, MAY 12, 1883.

As soon as the announcement of a case of smallpox was made known yesterday, the President of the Board of Trustees, the Marshal and Health Officer took the matter in hand at once. Lumber was ordered, a force of men sent out to the Boswell ranch, and at 12 o'clock last night a fire was burning in the building. It is made as comfortable as possible, has three rooms, good floors, good fires, and the patient is resting easily, under the charge of a competent nurse.

BERKELEY ADVOCATE, JANUARY 25, 1888.

Capt. Boswell, who is a stalwart Republican, has gone into the manufacturing of log cabins on a small scale. They are neat, airy little houses, about 20x20 inches square, surmounted by a small national flag. The gallant captain has kindly presented one to the Advocate. We also notice one in Dr. Hilton's drug store window. These cabins belong to a generation ago, and recall to mind the old political war cry of Tippecanoe and Tyler too.

BERKELEY ADVOCATE, MAY 15, 1888.

The grass on Boswell's ranch caught fire yesterday afternoon and came near doing serious damage. Captain Boswell hurried to Berkeley station and got a crowd of about twenty men who hastened to the ranch, arriving there just in time to prevent the fire from consuming the gum tree forest which extends for several miles along the brow of the hills. After about three hours hard work the fire was completely extinguished, much to the relief of the proprietor of the ranch. The grass was accidentally set afire by a party of picnickers, who were a little overloaded with spirits.

BERKELEY ADVOCATE, JULY 26, 1889.

$10 REWARD.

THE ABOVE REWARD WILL BE PAID upon return to me, or on receipt of information by which I can find A SORREL STALLION COLT, eight months old, white stripe on face. Strayed from my ranch at Berkeley about Monday or Tuesday of last week.
CAPT. BEN BOSWELL.
Berkeley, April 13, 1891.

BERKELEY ADVOCATE, APRIL 16, 1891.

Capt. Boswell Returns to Find Town Changed

Captain B. D. Boswell, an old resident of this city, is visiting Berkeley after an absence of several years. Captain Boswell was puzzled when he alighted from the train. The brakeman had certainly called out Berkeley but it was not the pioneer Berkeley. Where was Joe McClains old corner? What were those electric cars doing here? Where was the old field where C. K. Shattuck used to raise those plentiful crop of squashes? That might be I. O. O. F. hall, but if it was it had certainly a different appearance. And the old Atchinson Hotel had certainly grown another story. In fact whichever direction the visitor turned something new met his eye.

Captain B was for many years lessee of the Jones ranch, but is now located in Oregon at a growing town known as Boswell Springs. The captain is the owner of a number of springs renowned through Oregon for their medicinal qualities. Captain B is an old veteran of the Civil War and was warmly welcomed by his old G. A. R. comrades.
J. E. Boyd

BERKELEY ADVOCATE, JANUARY 27, 1902.

for boys, girls, and even one for married women. Boswell was described by towns-folk as sympathetic, a lover of nature, and always ready to help those in need. According to the local newspaper, everyone was said to be fond of him, especially the children.

By 1881, in addition to being a rancher, Benjamin Boswell received the contract to repair San Pablo Avenue using five hundred loads of gravel shoveled from the nearby creeks. He was then elected Road Master of Ocean View for the County of Alameda. By 1884, he was able to report to the Alameda County Board of Supervisors that the roads and bridges in Ocean View were in "remarkably good condition."[17] He continued in that job into the 1890s.

While the city of Berkeley coordinated paving efforts within the city limits, property owners had to pay for paving the length of road in front of their houses. Some residents chose to have their streets paved privately to ensure better quality rock and workmanship. In the early 1890s, the *Berkeley Advocate* noted that Boswell had rocked or paved several important streets, grading and macadamizing them at thirty-seven dollars per linear foot, including sections of San Pablo Avenue, Sacramento Street, Fulton Avenue, and many others.[18]

As a veteran of the Civil War, Boswell became a charter member of Berkeley's Lookout Mountain Post No. 88 of the Grand Army of the Republic (GAR) in 1885. On Memorial Day 1890, he drove his double team pulling a wagon of flowers collected by Berkeley residents and schoolchildren to the veterans' graves at the Mountain View Cemetery, which was located at the end of Piedmont Avenue in Oakland.[19]

Around 1893, the Boswells left Berkeley for Snowdown Springs, Oregon. The owners of several mineral springs there had developed a spa after noticing that cows grazing near the springs were larger and maintained more vibrant coats.[20] The Boswells ran a health spa during the warmer months, but they continued to spend winters in Berkeley.

The Boswells purchased the Snowdown Springs property, which included a three-story hotel, in 1896 and renamed it Boswell Springs. Following the transaction, the *Roseburg Oregon Review* reported that "the Capt. intends to make a first class watering place of the already popular health resort."[21] The spa offered many recreational—and curative—activities, including boating, hiking, golfing, swimming, fishing, and relaxing on the long veranda. New train service from San Francisco to Portland brought guests who could simply leave the train, cross a wooden platform, and ascend the stairs to the hotel's grand entrance. Emma ran the hotel's kitchen and was responsible for its famous home-cooked meals.[22]

Their advertisements listed the diseases "cured" by the springs—ague, catarrh of the stomach, nasal catarrh, dropsy. Perhaps the Boswells were drawn to purchase the spa in hope that the springs' curative powers would ease Boswell's own ailments.

Ben and Emma saw even more opportunity in the water of Boswell Springs. They began bottling their water and a Portland pharmacy became their exclusive sales agent. Their spring water was entered in a competition at the Louisiana Purchase Exposition in St. Louis in 1904 and won an award.[23] Boswell Springs water also had a booth at the Lewis and Clark Exposition in Portland in 1905.

Business was always slack in winter at the spa, yet the previous owners had kept it open year-round. The Boswells chose a different approach, and locked the doors for what the *Nonpareil* of nearby Drain, Oregon, called "their annual sojourn to California."[24] Emma Boswell said in 1910 that they typically summered

A TRAIN PULLING INTO THE BOSWELL SPRINGS RESORT BRINGING PATRONS FROM UP AND DOWN THE COAST.

THE PORCH AT BOSWELL SPRINGS. IF YOU LOOK CLOSELY AT THE REAR OF THE PHOTO, YOU WILL SEE A MAN IN A HANGING PORCH CHAIR. HIS FACE, WHEN ENLARGED, HAS ALL THE FEATURES OF BENJAMIN BOSWELL. NOTE THE SIGN ON THE RIGHT ADVERTISING LONG DISTANCE TELEPHONE SERVICE.

in Oregon and wintered in Berkeley or San Francisco. Boswell must have been in the Berkeley area in early 1895 because he was one of the signers of a petition to release a farmer from Wildcat Canyon, Robert Lyle, from San Quentin, where he had been held for many years on a murder conviction.[25] Also in 1895, Boswell was elected commander of the local Berkeley GAR post, a position he had held before.

As in Berkeley, he became a beloved figure in their Oregon community and sometimes figured prominently in public events—for example, giving the Memorial Day address in 1895.[26] Boswell was active in the local Masonic Lodge. He volunteered at Corvallis College and was also active at the Central Oregon State Normal School, where he served on the Board of Regents, executive committee, and a faculty selection committee. He gave occasional lectures at the school, and these events were sometimes covered in the local newspaper. One student commented that Boswell's lecture on promptness was "short, neat, right-to-the-point." His involvement was such that he even invited the school's faculty, friends, and students to Boswell Springs as guests. He once invited local school-children to the springs for a New Year's picnic.

By the 1890s, Boswell had developed a reputation for occasionally drinking to excess. An acquaintance said that both Mr. and Mrs. Boswell were "in the habit of getting publicly drunk at Boswell Springs."[28] Others said that Boswell drank to ease his health problems. Aside from those in the temperance movement, people in this age did, on the whole, drink substantially more alcohol than their twenty-first century counterparts: in its early days, the small town of Ocean View had twenty-two saloons.[29]

Benjamin Boswell died May 19, 1907, of heart failure, one season shy of his seventieth birthday. His body was brought in a metal casket from Boswell Springs by his Berkeley friend, attorney Thomas Graber. Graber helped Emma with the estate and the funeral. He described Boswell as "one of God's noblemen,"[30] and also wrote an article in memory of his friend, in which he noted Boswell's "high sense of justice."[31] Graber recalled that every year Boswell resided in Berkeley,

CAPTAIN BENJAMIN D. BOSWELL'S GRAVESTONE AT THE PRESIDIO CEMETERY, SAN FRANCISCO.

> *he provided among the oak trees, picnics for the schoolchildren and*
> *churches. All were welcome, all loved him and the children know him as*
> *a very dear friend. . . . His love of children and his desire to afford every*
> *opportunity to them for education was so well known that for years and*
> *at the time of his death, he held, by the Governor's appointment, the posi-*
> *tion of Regent of the Central Oregon State Normal School at Drain. His*
> *friends were legion; he is mourned by them all.*

Captain Boswell was buried with full military honors on June 9, 1907, at the Presidio Cemetery in San Francisco in an officers' section of the cemetery (OS), plot sixty-three, grave three. His formal eulogy, however, was given by Reverend Harbit on the porch of the Boswell Springs Hotel. Boswell's funeral services were attended by "his Masonic friends and the entire faculty and pupils of the Drain Normal School. The casket was placed on the front piazza, which was banked with choice roses . . . covering his bier." The eulogy was touching. Harbit said that good works live on and strengthen as time passes, and he encouraged parents, teachers, and pupils to keep alive the splendid efforts and encourage the cause of

EMMA BOSWELL LOST THE HOTEL TO FIRE ON JUNE 14, 1908, AND SPENT SEVERAL YEARS TRYING TO CLAIM HER HUSBAND'S PENSION (RANGING FROM $12 TO $30 PER MONTH) FOR HIS STELLAR MILITARY SERVICE.[32] SHE DIED IN LOS ANGELES ON JUNE 4, 1924. BOSWELL SPRINGS SLOWLY RETURNED TO A NATURAL STATE, INSPIRING A LOCAL NEWSPAPER DESCRIPTION THAT "THE DEER, WILD PIGEONS, AND OTHER ANIMALS WERE THE ONLY ONES MAKING USE OF THE MINERAL WATERS." WHILE EMMA HAD HOPED TO DONATE THE SPRINGS TO THE STATE OF OREGON AND ESTABLISH A MEMORIAL THERE TO HER HUSBAND, THE PROPERTY WAS ACQUIRED BY A GROUP OF BUSINESSMEN WHO BUILT A NEW HOTEL AND OPERATED A RESORT UNTIL 1949. THE PROPERTY THEN HOUSED A CHIROPRACTIC CLINIC, CERAMIC WORK-SHOP, AND ANTIQUE STORE UNTIL THE MID-1960S, WHEN IT WAS ABANDONED.[33] THIS 1920S PHOTOGRAPH SHOWS THE NEW HOTEL, BUILT AFTER THE 1908 FIRE; IT LOOKS MUCH LIKE THE ORIGINAL BUILDING.

education as exemplified by Captain Boswell; a fitting and well-deserved tribute to the splendid life's work of the dead soldier.

Nature was in her loveliest garb, and amid the fragrance of blooming roses and bright sunshine, his memory like a sweet benediction, pervading the atmosphere, the old warrior, patriot, philosopher and friend, was laid tenderly at rest in a bed of roses, the birds singing his requiem. A more fitting restful, hopeful expression and tribute of love could not have been sown.

Upon his death some clippings that Boswell had saved were read by Graber and were published with his obituary as representative of the spirit of Benjamin Demfry Boswell:

Then do kind deeds while living hearts may quicken,
Speak loving words while living ears attend,
And send thy flowers to gladden with their presence
The home which doth shelter living friends.

At the funeral, Graber followed his reading of this poem with some thoughts of his own: "A kind, loving husband, devoted to his home and his country; a lover of all that is beautiful in nature, liberal, sympathetic, his hand ever ready to assist, his influence ever extended for good, the State has lost one of its most esteemed citizens."

The 1908 Bond Measure to Create a Huge City Park Within the Old Boswell Ranch

On April 29, 1908, Berkeley residents were asked to vote on a bond measure for a park and playground. The measure proposed creating a city park out of the area a few blocks below Arlington Avenue bounded roughly by Santa Fe Street on the southwest and Ensenada on the southeast, and with the northern boundary following Cerrito Creek. The park had a center point at what is now Stone Face Park at Thousand Oaks Boulevard and San Fernando Avenue. At the time, the whole area was in a natural condition and represented the central portion of Boswell's Ranch. It was described as a "spot dear to everyone who has tramped or picnicked there."[34] The ninety-eight acres of pristine land were valued at $98,000. In 1908, Berkeley's bond indebtedness was less than half that of most other California cities. Financing the entire park would have added $.08 to the $.11 tax levied on each $100 of valuation of Berkeley property.

The local Chamber of Commerce distributed a pamphlet praising the proposal:

> The park is less than two miles from Town hall—closer to the center of Berkeley than the Hotel Claremont.... The North Grove Street car line, transferring to every section of the city at Berkeley Station, is built within a third of a mile of the park, and will be extended to the park entrance as soon as the town has purchased the property.[35]

UC Berkeley President Benjamin Ide Wheeler was passionate about the park as well. His words of support were included in this same pamphlet:

> I have been up on that noble North Berkeley hill a good many times in my life, and I must say that it is a beautiful natural park as it stands today, and I think that

To the left is a large rock called the Great Stone Face. It became a Berkeley city park of that name. This photo records the Thousand Oaks area in a more natural state when picnickers visited the remote site. By 1908, developers had began to sell the land, lot by lot.

nothing better could be done with the land than to give it to the public. It would be a shame and a disgrace if those splendid oak groves, those huge boulders, those sunny glades, and those slopes should be given over to private holdings. We should not allow that hillside, which was shaped by the hand of the Almighty, to go to waste and be devastated by the hand of man. It is a natural park, and we should keep it as a park. It is intended for the people, and should be enjoyed by the people. The University grounds can hardly be looked on as a city park, for it belongs to the State, and as time goes on it will be too crowded to be comfortable for the people. Against that time, Berkeley must secure a park of its own. We must look to the future. We must plan for many generations to come. Now is the time for the city to buy that land. If we let go that park-site on the hillside, we shall stand condemned in the eyes of the people of today and of all generations to come. This is going to be a very great city, and that park is going to be in the very center of it. It cannot be duplicated. There isn't another just like it. Who knows when an opportunity will ever come again to find a plot of land located as that is, so admirably suited to park purposes naturally, and an opportunity so good as far as price is concerned? I believe in reserving the best for the people and the children of the people. I say all this because I have implicit faith in the future of the community that is settling in these hills.

THIS IMAGE LOOKS SOUTHEAST FROM WHAT IS NOW STONE FACE PARK AT THOUSAND OAKS BOULEVARD AND SAN FERNANDO AVENUE. NOTE THE PICNICKERS TO THE RIGHT OF STONE FACE ROCK. THIS WAS ONE OF THE FAVORITE PLACES EARLY BERKELEYANS PICNICKED. WHEN A 1908 BOND MEASURE TO PRESERVE IT AS A NATURAL PARK FAILED, THE AREA WAS DEVELOPED AS A HIGH-END RESIDENTIAL NEIGHBORHOOD.

AN EARLY PHOTO OF THE COUNTY ROAD, NOW SPRUCE STREET.

On April 30, 1908, the votes on the park bond measure were tallied: 1,702 people voted for the bond and 1,143 voted against it. Since it needed a two-thirds majority to win, this meant that the park lost by 194 votes. What would Berkeley be like now if that park had been approved? It was rejected within a decade of the time when land barons like Nevada senator John Paul Jones, who had owned much of the ranch land north of the Berkeley town limits at Eunice Street, sold their vast land holdings to realty syndicates, which began to replace the land barons as the developers of the town. Horses and cows still trudged up the Berkeley Hills munching on the lush grasses where wooden bridges spanned the creeks.

Benjamin Boswell was quickly forgotten after he left Berkeley in 1896. His sprawling ranch lands would be gobbled up by development within a matter of decades. As the flood of 1906 San Francisco earthquake refugees covered Berkeley, this area was soon transformed from rugged ranch land, uniquely beautiful and used for picnics in the hills, to an area plotted with streets and train lines, and within a few years, neighborhoods named Thousand Oaks, Northbrae, Regents Park, Kensington, and much of the city of Albany.

A photo displaying the proposed parksite of Thousand Oaks in 1908.

The boulders used in a display to woo voters to vote for the bond measure for a park in the Thousand Oaks area.

LEFT: A 1908 PROMOTIONAL PHOTO SHOWING PICNICKERS LOOKING DOWN FROM THE OAK GROVES ONTO THE HUGE BARN AT BOSWELL'S RANCH. THE HILL IS THE ONE THAT RISES IN THE AREA OF ENSENADA AND SAN LORENZO AVENUES.

BOTTOM LEFT: A PICNIC IN THE PROPOSED PARK LAND. IT WAS OFTEN CALLED THE OLD INDIAN BURIAL GROUND.

BOTTOM RIGHT: ANOTHER NEWSPAPER PHOTO SHOWING PICNICKERS USING THE THOUSAND OAKS AREA. THE PHOTO WAS INTENDED TO PROMOTE PASSAGE OF A PARK BOND MEASURE IN 1908.

ABOVE: FROM A PAINTING BY THAD WELSH, PRE-
SERVING FOR US AN IMAGE OF THE NORTHBRAE
DISTRICT BEFORE MASON-MCDUFFIE BEGAN
DEVELOPMENT OF THE AREA.

LEFT: A CONSTRUCTION CAMP AT HOPKINS
STREET AND THE ALAMEDA CIRCA 1910. NOTE
THE WOODEN WAGON WITH WATER TANK. THIS
WAGON WAS USED TO SPRINKLE THE DRY UNPAVED
ROADS TO KEEP THE DUST DOWN. THAT FEATURE
CONFIRMS THAT THIS PHOTO WAS TAKEN DURING
THE DRY SEASON. ALSO NOTE THE WHITE CROSS,
PROBABLY AN EARLY STREET SIGN, AT THE MID-
RIGHT. BELOW THE LINE OF EUCALYPTUS TREES
IN THE UPPER MIDDLE AND LEFT OF THE PHOTO
THERE ARE LARGE LETTERS SPELLING OUT
"CRAGMONT," ONE OF THE NEW DEVELOPMENTS.

ABOVE: A PHOTO IN A 1904 PROMOTIONAL PAM-
PHLET ABOUT BERKELEY CAPTIONED, "AN ALL-
THE-YEAR SCENE ON THE BORDERS OF BERKELEY."
SINCE THIS PHOTO DISPLAYS A BUILDING CLUSTER
THAT RESEMBLES THOSE IN THE NEIGHBORHOOD
OF SOLANO AND PERALTA AVENUES AND THE
HILLS APPEAR TO BE THE HEIGHT ONE WOULD
SEE LOOKING EAST "ON THE BORDERS OF
BERKELEY," THIS COULD WELL BE A PHOTO OF
WHAT WAS ONCE BOSWELL'S RANCH.

LEFT: STANDING ON SOLANO AVENUE LOOKING
DOWN AT PERALTA AVENUE, AND SOME OF THE
REMAINING RANCH HOUSES OF BOSWELL'S RANCH
AFTER NEIGHBORHOOD ROADS WERE CONSTRUCT-
ED SOME TIME AROUND 1908.

ABOVE LEFT: THE LAYING OF RAIL TRACKS TO WHERE SOLANO AVENUE TUNNEL WAS ABOUT TO BE DUG. AS THE CREWS CARVED A TRENCH TO FORM THE CONCRETE TUNNEL, DIRT WAS HAULED AWAY ON THESE TRACKS. THE TRACKS LED TO THE AREA AROUND EUNICE AND BERRYMAN STREETS, WHERE A TRESTLE SPANNED A NATURAL CANYON THAT WAS PART OF THE CODORNICES CREEK DRAINAGE. DIRT HAULED ON RAILCARS TO THIS AREA ON THE TRESTLE WAS DUMPED TO FILL THE CANYON. THE TRESTLE WAS BURIED IN THE PROCESS. TODAY THERE IS A TWENTY-FOOT-HIGH RETAINING WALL AT THE SCHOOL OF THE MADELEINE WHERE IT ABUTS HENRY STREET, A TESTAMENT TO THE AREA'S FORGOTTEN LANDSCAPES.

ABOVE RIGHT: THE DIGGING OF THE TRENCH THAT WOULD FORM THE SOLANO TUNNEL BY THE SOUTHERN PACIFIC AROUND 1910.

THE TRESTLE BY HENRY STREET NEAR BERRYMAN STREET THAT WAS BUILT TO HAUL AND DUMP THE SPOILS OF THE EXCAVATION OF THE SOLANO TUNNEL. NOTE THAT ALL ALONG THE NEAR SIDE OF THE TRESTLE ONE CAN SEE DUMPED EARTH FROM THE RAILCARS ON THE TRACKS. EVENTUALLY THE TRESTLE WAS COVERED AND THE CREEK CHANNEL WAS FILLED IN TO MAKE A LEVEL STREET.

ABOVE: This incredible image details the area that is North Berkeley, Albany, and El Cerrito. Marin Avenue winds its way over Marin Creek on the left. Solano has streets laid out beside it, but they are still empty. The area by San Pablo Avenue is developed, probably by post-1906 earthquake refugees, many from the North Beach area in San Francisco. Oxford, Indian Rock, and Santa Barbara are noted on the photo. In the days of the Rancho Codornices of Domingo Peralta (he moved to the area in 1842), Albany Hill was known as "Cerrito de San Antonio" and "El Picacho," which is the Spanish name for a hill of that shape. In the days of the '49ers, Albany Hill was known as McKeevers Hill. It was known later as El Cerrito Hill. After the powder works were established there, it was known as DuPont Hill. Brooks Island can be seen in the Bay behind Albany Hill. The unfilled bayshore arcs north.

LEFT: A photograph taken from somewhere above Fairmont and Colusa avenues, looking southwest. Colusa is shown as an early road and the southwest orientation of the shot gives a view of the area that was Boswell's Ranch.

A VIEW UP THE COUNTY ROAD, NOW KNOWN AS SPRUCE STREET. ITS WAGON-RUTTED DIRT SURFACE UNDU-
LATED UP THE HILL TO GRIZZLY PEAK BOULEVARD. CAPTAIN BOSWELL GRADED THIS ROAD IN 1888.

11

THE WAGNER RANCH ROAD
AND BENJAMIN BOSWELL

IN 1881, GENERAL THEODORE WAGNER, A FORMER U.S. SURVEYOR general, purchased a ranch from the Duncan Cameron family, which had owned the remote but rich acreage for years. It was in open country by the wide and lively San Pablo Creek. Within a year, Wagner made significant improvements to the property—known as Orinda Park—amounting to about $140,000, including planting some of the best orchards in the state and building a fourteen-room house and other ranch buildings.[1]

In the spring of 1881, the *Berkeley Advocate* reported that a toll road was about to be built jointly by Alameda and Contra Costa counties through Berkeley to Wagner's ranch.[2] It would run from the east end of College Way (today renamed Hearst Street) out to the Wagner property. The toll was to be collected at Rose Street, and the road would run north through the Berryman and Shaw ranches of North Berkeley and continue north and east all the way to Martinez. The road would save Contra Costa farmers a twenty-mile ride around the hills to San Pablo and then south to Berkeley and Oakland to deliver their goods to markets in the more densely populated East Bay. (In days past, the Contra Costa farmers would take an old wagon road from Martinez that would have followed what is now Miner Road as far as the eastern slope of the Berkeley Hills. There was no road the farmers could safely and directly take over these hills with their heavy wagonloads. Instead, they took an old road north through San Pablo Creek canyon to the bay side of the hills and then turning south toward Berkeley and Oakland. The agricultural valleys of Contra Costa were considered to be almost inaccessible from Berkeley.) Private subscriptions and funding by Contra Costa County were not enough to cover expected costs, thus the proposed toll. A stock company was formed, and fencing and other preliminary work began in 1881.

THEODORE WAGNER CIRCA 1883.

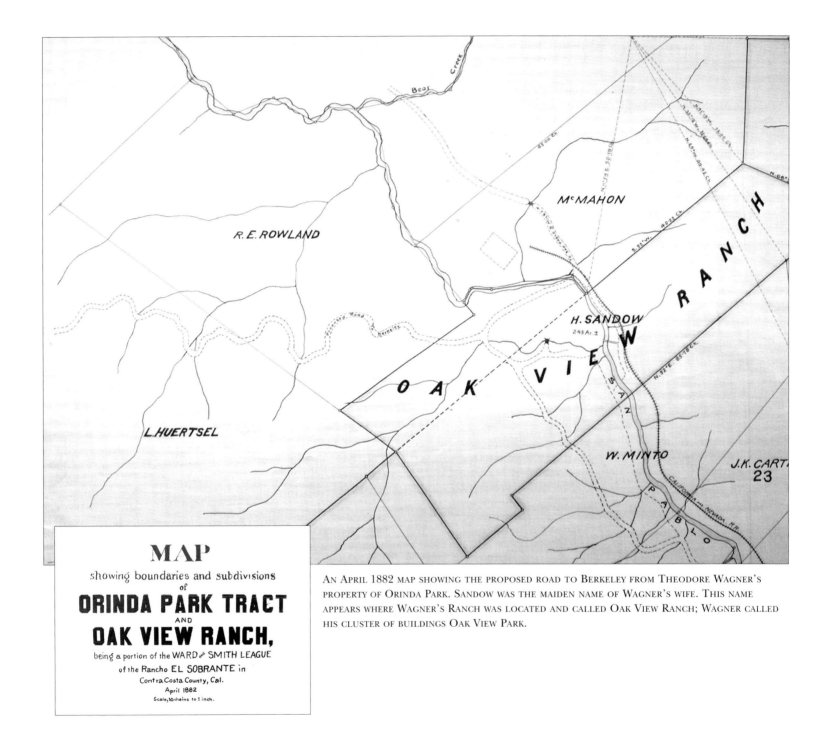

AN APRIL 1882 MAP SHOWING THE PROPOSED ROAD TO BERKELEY FROM THEODORE WAGNER'S PROPERTY OF ORINDA PARK. SANDOW WAS THE MAIDEN NAME OF WAGNER'S WIFE. THIS NAME APPEARS WHERE WAGNER'S RANCH WAS LOCATED AND CALLED OAK VIEW RANCH; WAGNER CALLED HIS CLUSTER OF BUILDINGS OAK VIEW PARK.

Wagner, speaking before the Alameda County Board of Supervisors in the fall of 1882, said that the project would cost about $20,000.³ Surveyors began their work in the winter of 1882, choosing a route over the two ranges of hills between Alameda and Contra Costa counties. An earlier primitive trail over the generally proposed route called the Cameron Road was named for the previous owners of Wagner's property. Cameron had wanted to build a road to Berkeley since 1875, when he had the road surveyed by Eugene Sullivan, brother of Wildcat Canyon rancher Patrick Sullivan. Cameron's lack of finances to construct the road beyond a rude trail prevented the fulfillment of his dream.

After a number of years of preparations, road construction began in the spring of 1888, led by Berkeley's Captain Benjamin Boswell. The road cut could be seen from North Berkeley, and residents were excited at the prospect of a new connection with neighboring farmers and orchardists in Contra Costa County as well as the communities growing there.⁴

Boswell started fencing the road's edge at the Jones tract in North Berkeley, on which he himself had leased a large section of ranch land (covering most of the neighborhoods now known as Thousand Oaks, Northbrae, Cragmont, and Albany) from Nevada senator John Paul Jones. Several of the wealthiest Californians also held land along the new proposed road, including Senator Leland Stanford and Charles Crocker, both railroad magnates, and Oakland Mayor Horace Carpentier. They gave a right-of-way for the road and agreed to fence their properties.

On May 7, 1888, Boswell spoke before the Berkeley Town Board, asking that the new road be declared public from Rose Street to Durant Street.⁵ (This Durant Street was where Harrison Street currently runs and, if extended to east Berkeley, would come out somewhere around Eunice. It was not the Durant Avenue by the campus that modern residents recognize.) Boswell estimated that the new road would be opened to the Shaw Line, the northern Berkeley boundary at Eunice Street, in one week, and that in two weeks the road would be open all the way to downtown Berkeley. This road would be known as the County Road (now Spruce Street).

By mid-1888, Contra Costa had appropriated $1,000, private subscriptions had raised $3,000, and Wagner had spent $1,600 of his own money on the road-building effort. Berkeleyans had raised $250 in subscriptions, realizing the importance of the road to their city. The money Berkeleyans raised would be paid when the project was complete. But there was a problem with the funding allotted by the Alameda County supervisors. One supervisor told Boswell, who had been the road overseer of the Ocean View district for more than five years, that he could use all the remaining $500 in the county's road fund for the Wagner Ranch Road, and

Road over the Hills to San Pablo Creek.

Mr. W. W. Cameron has projected a road from Berkeley over the hills into the valley of San Pablo creek. The object is to accommodate the present population of San Pablo creek and to bring into easy reach a large area of valley land with a view to opening it up to settlement. The projector is determined to get over the hills and down into our slope by an easy grade, and if he succeeds he will furnish the lover of mountain roads with as lovely a ride as could be desired. The road will come over the crest of our hills to the north of the University domain, and a little to the south of where the present steep road crosses over into San Pablo creek, thence it will meander southward by an easy grade along the brows of jutting points of hillside and in and out the canyons, crossing the University grounds on the round hillside above the trees, go back into the canyon of Strawberry creek, return out again on the south side of the canyon, pass down around the point south of the Palmer mansions, and reach the slope of Berkeley about the head of Channing way. The only trouble about this route is the traversing the University grounds, which as yet, we believe, the regents have not consented to. Not knowing the mysterious intentions of these authorities we are inclined to think they ought to let Mr. Cameron pass his road through the domain, for we believe it would be an improvement to the at present barren hillside.

Berkeley Advocate, February 2, 1878.

A BOULEVARD FOR BERKELEY.

A recent trip over the delightful Wagner road from North Berkeley to Orinda Park has caused one to wonder greatly why this most beautiful boulevard is not fully opened to Berkeley and Oakland. A more picturesque route could hardly be imagined. Ladies could enjoy driving upon such a road with no fears of trolley cars.

Do merchants and grocerymen realize what they are losing by not having this road fully opened? It would furnish an avenue for the oringing in of fresh produce from Contra Costa county. Now produce is shipped to San Francisco then re-shipped to Berkeley, and in what condition, and with what prices do we get it? If one wants anything fresh and nice they must send to Oakland for it. With this road open, we could have a good market of our own. All our merchants would reap an advantage from an enlarged trade.

The obstruction on Spruce street requires either the building of a culvert or the filling in of the road. Have we not sufficient public spirit in Berkeley to accomplish this? Must we always remain a little shut-in suburban town?

A CITIZEN.

BERKELEY ADVOCATE, MAY 15, 1897.

that the 1889 budget would contain the money for the road's completion.[6]

Troubles arose when a woman named Maria Hall complained about an unmet assurance of free fencing along a right-of-way through her property, which was to have been provided in return for an easement for the road.[7] Boswell, who was said to represent the interests of powerful landowners Hall and Horace Carpentier, advised the Alameda Country officials to pay for the promised fence. Alameda County officials balked at this, replying that they had been promised that they would incur no expenses in allowing the road to be built. Wagner was appointed to ask Boswell to persuade Hall to relinquish her demand. Work moved forward.

Alameda County supervisors personally examined the road site and had promised they would support the road project after Contra Costa County put up its money. By 1888, after Contra Costa had built more than six miles of the most expensive portion of the road to the county line, Alameda County was still not paying to complete the project on its side. Despite these setbacks, the road was finally completed and radically changed the region's commerce and transit patterns.

On July 10, 1888, Wagner took a wagon ride over the new road, listening to the harnesses jingle and the wagon frame creak. He was carrying his crop of one ton of apricots grown in his orchard—the first load of produce ever delivered by way of this road. He reported with satisfaction that the Wagner Ranch Road was in "fair condition." In spite of the heavy load of fruit, his horse team had "not turned a hair."[8]

In December 1888, Boswell told the *Advocate* that the Wagner Road was better than any previous road to Contra Costa and was in excellent condition.[9] On August 8, 1889, the *Berkeley Advocate* wrote of the road: "Any person wishing to take a fine drive and witness magnificent scenery should by all means travel over this grand highway." The 800- to 1,000-foot rise of the new road connecting Berkeley with the bountiful inland valleys afforded magnificent vistas of the San Francisco Bay, the cities that bordered it, and Marin and Contra Costa counties.

The road was to be improved every year. Finally, convenient travel was possible between the two counties; farmers would save time and have safer journeys, and Berkeley and Oakland residents would enjoy better market prices. Residents of the two counties would also feel the effects of easier travel and connections with people living on the other side of the hills. G. M. Waterbury of the Berkeley Livery Stables told of how thrilled his customers were when he took them for rides over this road—according to him, without doubt one of the finest rides in the two counties.[10]

A PHOTO OF AN UNNAMED ROAD CUTTING ACROSS THE BERKELEY HILLS. IT IS POSSIBLE THIS IS THE WAGNER RANCH ROAD BUILT BY BENJAMIN BOSWELL.

GENERAL THEODORE WAGNER OF WAGNER RANCH

Theodore Wagner was born on September 9, 1841, to a military family in Hesse-Cassel, in the Westphalia region of Germany. King Jerome, the brother of Napoleon, ruled this area, and the men of Hesse-Cassel fought in Napoleon's army. When Wagner's father led a battalion to take a mill site on top of a hill, almost the entire battalion was annihilated. Napoleon's adjutant told Wagner that Napoleon himself had witnessed his heroics and was going to award him the Cross of the Legion of Honor. Wagner replied that he wished he had it right then, since he did not expect to live through the next horrific assault. Napoleon heard the conversation, rode up on his horse, removed a medal from his own uniform, and handed it to the elder Wagner. This medal was supposedly kept by Theodore Wagner in a bank vault in the Berkeley area after he moved to California.[11]

A PARTY AT THE WAGNER HOUSE IN 1890.

Theodore's parents wanted him to learn the disciplined life, and when he was twelve years old put him on a German ship as part of the crew. Three years later, young Theodore responded to "the disciplined life" by jumping ship when it docked in New York City. Speaking no English, he decided to move to a German neighborhood in St. Louis, where he worked and studied law at night. When the Civil War began, Theodore joined the Union army and rose to the rank of captain.

After the war, he married and moved to Little Rock, Arkansas. There he served as deputy secretary of state before moving to Missouri, where he practiced law and surveying. He and his wife had two daughters, Louise and Carrie. Tragically, his wife passed away, and Wagner moved back to New York City. After hiring a woman to help raise his daughters and keep his house, he again opened a law practice, which quickly became successful. As fate would have it, he met Ida Sandow and fell in love again. The couple married in 1871, and the family came to California in 1872, first settling in Visalia. Ida raised her stepchildren as if they were her own, and Theodore opened yet another law office specializing in land cases, and also established a real estate firm.

Theodore became active in politics on a national level and, when Rutherford B. Hayes was elected, he appointed Wagner U.S. surveyor general. Many people thought he received the appointment because of his astute legal performance in prosecuting a series of desert land swindles. This is when

TOP: LOOKING EAST AT THE WAGNER ORCHARDS IN THE DAYS WHEN THEY PROVIDED MUCH FRUIT AND BEAUTY.

BOTTOM: A FOURTH OF JULY PARTY ON THE WAGNER RANCH IN 1891.

people stopped calling him Captain Wagner from his Civil War service and began calling him General Wagner. The title stuck for the rest of his life.

In the 1880s, the Wagners gave birth to a son, George, and moved to a wide-open valley where the town of Orinda is now established. They purchased 240 acres in the area, then called Orinda Park, located just southeast of the intersection of Wildcat Canyon and San Pablo Dam roads. The tall and blond-mustached Wagner was said to be friendly and well-liked. It is estimated that he spent about $140,000 on his ranch land, and the groves of fruit and nut trees were said to be some of California's best.[12] He built a mushroom cellar, a carbide gas facility, and a conservatory on his estate, which he called Oak View Park. The May 30, 1888, *Contra Costa Gazette* reported that the Wagners' orchard trees included "100 quinces, 100 nectarines, 2,500 apples, 2,000 pears, 800 peaches, 1,500 apricots, 800 prunes, 100 plums, 400 cherries, 1,000 olives, 200 almonds, 400 pecans, 100 walnuts, forty Japanese persimmons, twenty-five oranges and twenty acres of grapevines."[13]

When Wagner constructed his high-ceilinged fourteen-room house, he conducted an elaborate cornerstone-setting ceremony. He placed three packages of seeds and a note in a bottle, sealed it, and placed a bottle of wine next to it.[14] The bricks used in the building of the house came from kilns that

A VIEW OF THE LARGE ACREAGE OF FRUIT ORCHARDS ON THE WAGNER RANCH BEFORE THEY WERE DESTROYED FOR DEVELOPMENT.

Wagner built on his property.

The homestead grounds still exist in a protected area on the Orinda School District grounds. Wagner had the area's first telephone installed with a line running all the way to Berkeley. He donated some of his land for the Orinda Park School, a common thing for wealthy Americans to do in those days. Domingo Peralta had done the same for West Berkeley.

When the California and Nevada Railroad was built, it ran up San Pablo Canyon by San Pablo Creek. Wagner's Ranch was an early terminus. Later the railroad was extended to

Bryant Corners, now downtown Orinda.

Wagner was known for throwing huge parties on holidays like the Fourth of July or Admissions Day.[15] Chinese cooks prepared food for days ahead of the big events. Picnic tables were set up on the front lawn, and barrels containing lemonade and ginger beer were iced next to gallons of homemade vanilla, chocolate, and strawberry ice cream. Fine wines were opened inside the house. After the old-time sport and entertainment of oration, which would on these occasions include lengthy patriotic speeches, live bands would inspire singing among the partygoers. When

the sky was dark enough, there were all kinds of fireworks, from rockets to pinwheels. Roman candles were beautifully reflected in the tall windows of the Wagner house. After the noise of the fireworks ceased, the guests would often hear loud, eerie cries of the mountain lions for which nearby Wildcat Canyon was named.

Tragically, Wagner's house burned to the ground when a flue fire ignited in the kitchen. He then rebuilt a smaller house. In spite of the fire, General Wagner felt so successful that in 1887 he built the Orinda Park Hotel on his grounds, but his inexperience proved fatal to that endeavor.[16] Because no bar was built in the hotel, every prospective operator turned down the opportunity. Wagner excluded a bar from his plans because the building was next to the Orinda Park one-room schoolhouse, and he felt a bar would be inappropriate in that location. Mr. and Mrs. George Keener finally leased the hotel and accepted boarders in harvest season and had locals in on Saturdays for dances. Diners from Berkeley and Oakland visited the establishment and delighted in the change of scenery in rural Contra Costa County. The general eventually sold his Orinda Park Ranch to Moses Hopkins, brother of San Francisco railroad tycoon Mark Hopkins.

In 1895, Wagner built a beautiful home at the northeast corner of Milvia Street and Bancroft Way. After a number of incarnations, the house was razed prior to World War II and the Berkeley Motel was erected on the site. The Wagners moved to Glen Ellen, naming their new home Casa Wagner. There they were neighbors of Jack London and his Valley of the Moon estate.

TOP: LOUIS STEIN (ON THE RIGHT WITHOUT A HAT), THE PREMIER HISTORIAN OF HIS ERA AND THE MAN WHO IS RESPONSIBLE FOR MORE PHOTOS OF EARLY BERKELEY AND CONTRA COSTA COUNTY BEING SAVED THAN ANYONE ELSE. HERE HE LOOKS OVER THE WAGNER RANCH IN THE MID-TWENTIETH CENTURY.

BOTTOM: A BENCH BUILT BY THEODORE WAGNER THAT STILL EXISTS ON THE OLD WAGNER RANCH, NOW ORINDA SCHOOL DISTRICT PROPERTY.

TOP: UNEARTHING THE CORNERSTONE CEREMO-
NY ITEMS LEFT BY THEODORE WAGNER IN THE
WALL OF HIS NEW HOUSE.

BOTTOM: A LIVELY SAN PABLO CREEK AS IT
WINDS ITS WAY THROUGH THE WAGNER RANCH.

A VIEW OF THE FERNDALE RANCH COMPOUND.

12

THE BOUNDARY DISPUTE OF PAT SULLIVAN AND ROBERT LYLE, WILDCAT CANYON

IN THE WILD DAYS OF THE MID- TO LATE NINETEENTH CENTURY, owning property in the East Bay was not always a certain proposition. It was common for property titles to be disputed, and people knowingly sold property to which they did not hold clear title. Every scheme that could be used to make money by selling land was employed. The appreciation rates were as high as the interest rates of the time. Boundaries were another oft-disputed issue. Court battles could last decades and sometimes did not settle the disagreements. There were many incidents of violence.

One such long-running dispute involved Pat Sullivan, who settled in Wildcat Canyon in the late 1860s. He and his wife, Johanna, both recent immigrants from Ireland, met in Jersey City, New Jersey, and came west around 1860, joining the flood of pioneers seeking opportunity on the shores of the Pacific. Pat spent some time as a hired hand on the canyon's Atlee Ranch, and then in the 1870s acquired his own Wildcat Canyon land where he raised cattle and grew wheat and oats. The big Sullivan brood included five sons and three daughters. Sullivan's ranch was known around the East Bay as Ferndale. For a time, the name was painted in large letters on his barn so those on the ridges could recognize the ranch far down below in the canyon.[1] When it was time to sell cattle, Sullivan drove the animals toward the west, up and out of Wildcat Canyon, then down a steep, dusty trail (now Regal Road) heading to the bay and the slaughterhouses of southwest Berkeley and Emeryville.

Sullivan often quarreled with Robert Lyle, a neighboring rancher who believed Sullivan was running cattle over his land. The Contra Costa County Court in Martinez tried to settle the boundary dispute, but failed. Dark words were hurled across the pastures. Lyle showed his anger by killing Sullivan's horse,

WILDCAT CANYON CIRCA 1888.

PART OF THE SULLIVAN RANCH COMPOUND AT THE BOTTOM OF WILDCAT CANYON, NORTH OF WHERE JEWEL LAKE IS TODAY. NOTE THAT ON THE SIDE OF THE BARN IS PAINTED FERNDALE RANCH, THE NAME PATRICK SULLIVAN GAVE TO HIS PROPERTY.

one of his cows, and a number of pigs. He destroyed $4,000 worth of Sullivan's hay and grain with phosphorus in 1876, and burned his crops again in 1877. Lyle repeatedly threatened to kill Sullivan, even "if I hang for it." One of Sullivan's sons heard Lyle threaten to kill his father.[2]

On a Saturday afternoon, March 28, 1881, Pat Sullivan hitched up his carriage to get supplies in Berkeley. Johanna wasn't surprised when her husband didn't show up for dinner, since ranchers often missed meals when they were busy in the fields. She lay down alone that night, or perhaps spent the night in a chair. Fog engulfed the ranch, blurring all its features. The chilly air was biting, even in the house. A sporadic wind disturbed her thoughts.[3]

Shortly after sunrise, two neighboring ranchers hurried to Mrs. Sullivan's door. They didn't tell her that they had found her husband dead in a pool of blood, shot at close range. Instead they told her that Sullivan had been badly hurt and that they needed a blanket. They used it to cover his body and waited for the coroner.[4]

The *Contra Costa Gazette* of April 2, 1881, reported details of the murder scene:

A VIEW DOWN WILDCAT CANYON FROM THE FERNDALE RANCH. NOTE WHAT APPEARS TO BE THE FAMILY HOUSE ON THE MID-LEFT OF THE PHOTO.

> *His dead body was found riddled with buckshot and one arm around the axletree of the wagon several hundred yards below the road near the creek-side. From appearances, it was concluded that after being shot he fell forward over the front of the wagon, and grasped the axletree in an unconscious dying effort, the horses breaking from the road and running (dragging the body) to the place near the creek where the wagon was found. Firing had been heard by some of the people living in the vicinity the previous evening . . . suspicion led to the arrest of a neighbor named Robert Lyle, in whose house was found a double-barreled shotgun that had the appearance of having been recently fired and several buckshot of the size of those with which Sullivan was shot.*

Sullivan's horses were still hitched to his rig—from the wheel marks in the dirt, they must have circled Sullivan all night. The neighbors who found him were wide-eyed and aghast. One had said that he heard Mrs. Lyle shout, "Don't do it, Bob. Don't!"

All evidence pointed to Lyle, and his trial caused such a sensation that even the San Francisco papers covered it.

One document submitted to the California Supreme Court referred to the crime as "the most deliberate, cold-blooded assassination ever perpetrated in Contra Costa County."[5]

Police took Lyle's boots from him after his arrest. The imprints matched identically the

> *tracks which were made by some person crossing Wildcat Creek, the banks of which were soft and a full impression left. A torn fragment of the* Call *newspaper of February 4th was found on the shelf where defendant kept his ammunition, which fitted a piece of newspaper wadding found near where the deceased was shot. . . . The tracks led both up and down the hill in the direction from and to defendant's house, and the defendant was seen about 9 o'clock on the evening of the murder going towards his house and coming from the direction of the scene of the murder.*
>
> *... The theory is also that defendant, after hearing deceased pass his house between 8 and 9 o'clock on the evening of April 28th, 1881, took his shotgun, and by going over the hill by a shortcut, got upon a secluded place by the road behind a bush; that deceased soon after came along unconscious of harm and after passing the bush and when within half a mile of his home the deceased was shot in his back with buckshot, one shot going through his heart, from which he must have almost instantly died.*[6]

The district attorney said that Sullivan had no enemies except Lyle and that they had been arguing for ten or twelve years.

Lyle was tried for Sullivan's murder three times. The first trial, in April 1881, ended in an acquittal because one juror, a Mr. Wells, refused to convict. Some accused Lyle's attorney—the famous W. W. Foote of San Francisco—of paying Wells fifty dollars for his vote of acquittal.[7] Others believed that Foote bribed Wells with whiskey. A letter to the governor some years later noted that when Wells was trapped in the jury room where no one was allowed to drink, he would drop a string out the window as a signal for Foote. Some claimed that Foote and his associates would tie a whiskey bottle to the string and Wells would hoist the beautiful bottle up and secretly quench his deep thirst.[8]

Lyle was again represented by Foote in his second trial in October and November of 1881. Nine jurors voted for acquittal, three for conviction. Prosecutors believed that Foote used "chicanery" to suppress all the prosecution's evidence against Lyle. Lyle was released on bail on January 15, 1882.

His third and final trial began on December 10, 1883, and was completed by

January 11, 1884. The jury, carefully chosen of varied ethnic backgrounds so as not to favor the prosecution or defense, had thirty-two days to consider the testimony and evidence. Foote had not been paid for his previous services and declined to represent Lyle in this trial.

In this third trial the jurors were unanimous. On February 21, 1884, Lyle was convicted of murder in the second degree and sentenced to twenty years in prison. Friends of Lyle approached Foote and perhaps paid for him to rejoin the defense, since Foote then represented Lyle in appeals that went all the way to the state Supreme Court.[9] Foote argued the odd defense that Lyle should either be guilty of murder in the first degree and hanged, or released as not guilty. The court disagreed and the judgment was confirmed. Government documents show that it cost the county $80,000 to convict him.[10] A number of local people still expressed doubt about the proceedings and Lyle's guilt.[11]

Lyle developed tuberculosis in prison and applied for a pardon in 1890. When the appeal was published in the *Contra Costa Gazette*, it inspired letters urging the governor to deny the pardon. One was signed by the arresting sheriff, prosecuting attorney, the current district attorney, and seven of the jurors who convicted Lyle. They called the crime "very atrocious," as the murder was unprovoked and the victim shot from behind.[12] They also pointed out that the evidence of the shotgun wadding was convincing. General Theodore Wagner wrote to the governor about Lyle's behavior and reasoned that Lyle's family had already been shown mercy by sparing Lyle the death penalty.[13] Those who favored the conviction also requested to be informed prior to Lyle's release if that should occur.

The pardon was denied.

In 1894, after Lyle had spent ten years in San Quentin and was in failing health, he again applied for a pardon in order to spend his last days with his family. His daughters begged Foote to help them get their father released. In early 1895, Foote wrote a letter to Governor James Budd. Many people still believed that there was evidence that Lyle had been with his wife the night of the murder. There was vague talk that more evidence of Lyle's innocence had been discovered since the trial, but no new evidence was ever presented in a letter to the governor.[14] Many people appealed to then Governor Budd in a letter, requesting that he release Lyle due to the doubt about his conviction and to ease the suffering of his family. Seventy people signed this letter, among them many of Berkeley's prominent citizens, including the well-respected rancher Benjamin D. Boswell, Berkeley liveryman John Brennan, and Berkeley merchants Joseph McClain and D. H. Bruns. A number of jurors who had served at Lyle's first trial also wrote the governor asking for Lyle's release.

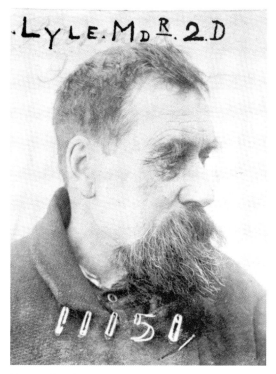

ROBERT LYLE'S PRISON MUG SHOT.

—Robert Lyle who had three trials for the murder of Patrick Sullivan in 1881, was sentenced on Thursday by Judge Brown, of the Superior Court of Contra Costa County to twenty years imprisonment in San Quentin.

BERKELEY ADVOCATE, FEBRUARY 23, 1884.

Top: San Quentin State Prison circa 1888.

Bottom: An urgent 1890 telegram by Dr. Mansfield, a prison doctor, to the State Capitol informing officials that Robert Lyle was gravely ill after contracting tuberculosis.

THE WESTERN UNION TELEGRAPH COMPANY.
21,000 OFFICES IN AMERICA.   CABLE SERVICE TO ALL THE WORLD.

Form No. 1.

This Company TRANSMITS and DELIVERS messages only on conditions limiting its liability, which have been assented to by the sender of the following message. Errors can be guarded against only by repeating a message back to the sending station for comparison, and the Company will not hold itself liable for errors or delays in transmission or delivery of Unrepeated Messages, beyond the amount of tolls paid thereon, nor in any case where the claim is not presented in writing within sixty days after the message is filed with the Company for transmission.
This is an UNREPEATED MESSAGE, and is delivered by request of the sender, under the conditions named above.

THOS. T. ECKERT, General Manager.   NORVIN GREEN, President.

NUMBER	SENT BY	REC'D BY	CHECK
5	W So	15 Collect	944a

RECEIVED at STATE CAPITOL OFFICE. "C" SACRAMENTO, Cal.   M. Standard Time.   Nov 3 rd 189 X

Dated San Quentin Prison Cal 3

To T. M. Eby

Private Sec'y

Robert Lyle in very bad condition cough weakness age against him chances recovery doubtful

Dr. Mansfield

Robert Lyle was discharged from San Quentin on July 22, 1896, looking much older than his fifty-nine years and still professing his innocence. He died a short time after his release, ending a very sad chapter in Bay Area history.

THE OLD WOMAN AND THE SULLIVAN RANCH

In 1960, an old woman who called herself Miss Sullivan walked into the Tilden Park Nature Area. Noticing the unaccompanied elderly woman slowly wandering around with an intense gaze, a naturalist quietly spoke to her.[15] Miss Sullivan said that she had grown up on her father's 300-acre farm, which encompassed an area north of and including Jewel Lake. She was Pat Sullivan's daughter. She recalled that when she was young, only bay, live oak, buckeye, and madrone trees grew in the hills, and only along the creeks. Fields of grain covered the hillsides and were harvested with horse-drawn mowers.

HARVESTING HAY ON THE SULLIVAN RANCH IN THE EARLY TWENTIETH CENTURY.

Miss Sullivan relished her time revisiting her childhood home and reminisced about life before the turn of the century. Branded cattle roamed the area around what is now the Nature Area. She said that she remembered how the taste of milk varied depending on what the cows ate in the surrounding hills.

She recalled how Wildcat Creek ran all summer and how the kids caught large trout from it with bent-pin hooks. Everyone gathered wild nuts and berries to eat: hazelnuts, blackberries, thimble berries, and countless others. She remembered that mothers made tea of "the aromatic creeping vine," *yerba buena,* when their children were sick. Men hunted deer on the western slope of Wildcat Canyon, while the women stood on the eastern slopes, signaling to the hunters which way the deer had run.

Coyotes fought with dogs and chased rabbits; quail made meals for all. Miss Sullivan said that there were lots of beechy ground squirrels when her family arrived in the area, but that the farmers poisoned them for eating their grain. The ranchers considered red-tailed hawks as pests to be shot for preying on the ranch chickens.

The Sullivan children would make dams in the creeks to create swimming holes. They used cow parsnip stems as blowguns and snow berries for ammunition. The kids would smear their faces with blackberry juice to feel more "savage."

Johanna Sullivan eventually sold the ranch to the water company, which created the Jewel Lake reservoir.

Old Miss Sullivan slowly shuffled away from the Nature Area. She stared at the ground as she walked and then scanned the hills to the east and west, perhaps still musing about her childhood home.

Some of the naturalists listening to Miss Sullivan's tales believe that the squirrel problem had been caused by the ranchers' killing of hawks. It is the author's speculation that many of the remaining hawks, crows, ravens, and other scavengers were killed when they ate poisoned squirrel carcasses. That may be the reason ravens disappeared from the East Bay around that time, not reappearing until recently.

East Bay Regional Parks Naturalist Dave Zuckermann standing by an old fruit tree that was planted in the old Curran Ranch orchard.

The Squirrel Nuisance.—Resident farmers and land owners very generally throughout the county are vigorously at work poisoning off the squirrels on their lands, and there are likely to be but few who will leave any for the official operations of the Inspectors. It is due, however, to those who clear their own lands that the Inspectors should see that they are not overrun again from the lands of negligent neighbors. We hear it said that some of the large non-resident land owners are disposed to contract with the Inspectors of the Districts in which they are situate, for killing the squirrels ; and this would be a mutually advantageous and satisfactory way of insuring a thorough clearing out of the pests without involving any controversies or any public expense.

Contra Costa Gazette, October 24, 1874.

Contra Costa Gazette, 1874.

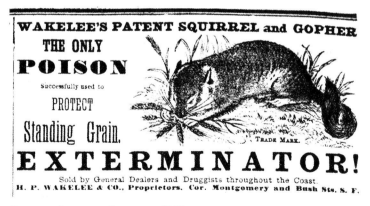
Berkeley Advocate, December 1879.

MARY THOMPSON'S HOTEL AND SALOON, ESTABLISHED IN MAY OF 1883. AFTER THE 1906 EARTHQUAKE, BERKELEY'S SCHOOLS WERE OVERFLOWING WITH NEW RESIDENTS AND THOMPSON'S HOTEL WAS CONVERTED INTO A SCHOOL HOUSE. THE VERANDAS AND PORCH WERE REMOVED BY THIS TIME AND MARY HAD ALREADY PASSED ON IN 1905.

13

MARY THOMPSON, BERKELEY'S NOTORIOUS, WONDERFUL WORKING WIDOW

WHEN MARY THOMPSON AND HER NINE CHILDREN MOVED FROM SAN Francisco to Berkeley in 1885, her new East Bay neighbors expressed a broad range of opinions about her and her entrepreneurial endeavors.[1] Some Berkeley residents thought of Mary Thompson, sole proprietor of a popular hotel and saloon, as a working-class hero. She was a widow who supported herself and her large family by investing in real estate and running a successful business. Others condemned her as a blot upon the neighborhood and a supporter of disgraceful activities like drinking and gambling. Whatever Mary Thompson's contemporaries thought of her, it was rare indeed that a woman, widowed and with children to raise, would appear on the scene, buy a number of houses, open up a boardinghouse and saloon, and operate them herself. Those things alone gave people reason to wonder about her—even if they didn't know about the "curse" she had carried with her from San Francisco.

In 1850, ten-year-old Mary emigrated to the United States from County Mayo, Ireland. She met a Norwegian sailor named William "Hog" Thompson in 1859, and they married one week later and began a large family.[2] According to the 1880 San Francisco census, the Thompsons had nine children: Mary A., Kate, William, Dominick, Peter, Sarah, Rose, Bridget, and Joseph. Together Hog and Mary Thompson opened a sailors' boardinghouse and saloon at 820 Battery Street in San Francisco. The establishment moved a number of times and was located at 10 Broadway in 1880. Rumor had it that many an overnight guest awoke at sea, having been "shanghaied" after drinking an alcoholic beverage spiked with a "mickey" at the Thompsons' saloon the night before.[3]

One night, Mary had a heated quarrel over money with a windjammer captain from Nova Scotia. He cursed her, shouting, "May you live to bury your

—Mrs. Mary Thompson has opened a liquor saloon just above Berryman's station. She and her sons have displayed much taste in fitting it up. This lady has recently purchased four houses in that part of town.

BERKELEY ADVOCATE, MAY 2, 1885.

A VIEW OF THE LITTLE ENCLAVE OF NORTH BERKELEY
WHERE MARY THOMPSON SET UP HER BOARDING
HOUSE. THE HUGE BUILDING WEST OF THIS LITTLE
VILLAGE IS THE MONUMENTAL PERALTA PARK HOTEL,
COMPLETED BY 1889.

———————————

—Last evening the northern heavens
were flushed with the beautiful Aurora
Borealis. At times its color was blood
red and the streaks of orange would shoot
up towards the zenith from the horizon.
The color and its form was ever changing,
the phenomenon lasting an hour or more.
The news comes from the East that all
day yesterday a violent electric storm
was raging in the United States and Canada as evinced by the condition of the
telegraph wires which for most of the
time were out of working order.

BERKELEY ADVOCATE, NOVEMBER 18, 1882.

husband and your whole litter."[4] As he spoke, he pointed one finger toward the sky and shifted his wad of chewing tobacco, or mouth cargo, as sailors called it. Hog Thompson died soon after the curse was uttered.

Mary had had enough of the men of the sea and their crude manners. To distance herself from them, she moved with her nine children to the open fields and sparsely settled enclave of North Berkeley. She immediately purchased four houses there with the proceeds from closing up her business in San Francisco.

She opened a hotel and saloon at the northwest corner of Shattuck Avenue and Rose Street in May of 1885. The big white building had shaded verandas facing both streets, and out front Thompson raised a green flag with a golden harp, a symbol of Ireland from the 1640s.[5] Horses would drink at the wooden trough on the Shattuck Avenue side of the hotel. From the porch, visitors could relax staring at the wild oat fields and boulders of the north Berkeley Hills, or look just down-hill toward the old Wilson Hotel, a large yellow building right below San Pablo Avenue that had been used as a roadhouse during the gold rush. As the sun set, one could see the shimmering on the bay and Codornices Lagoon near Albany Hill with the smokestacks of the far-off chemical plant at Fleming Point poking up against the sky. Even the smokestacks seemed serene. Mt. Tamalpais stood majestic in the distance.

There were no streetlights back then, and it got so dark in Berkeley that many locals reported seeing the aurora borealis in the night sky.[6] People carried kerosene lanterns to find their way in the dark streets. As night settled and stars began to twinkle in the sky over Thompson's establishment, little lights could be seen weaving in the distance—someone walking home from the train after work, someone going out for a beer and a newspaper, another walking to a friend's house for a game of cards or to visit his girlfriend.

Visitors might approach the hotel from several directions. Vine Street, rolling downhill from the site, had been one of the early dirt trails pioneers followed on foot in the 1850s. San Pablo Avenue was still a dirt country road, but broad enough for wagon traffic. Dust would rise following the horse-drawn farm wagons. As the wagons passed, flocks of blackbirds fled from the tall mustard plants that draped over the edges of the road, and crows and many other birds swooped around the fields.[7]

The neighborhood was a pleasant wooded enclave of modest, but fine, Victorian houses sitting above the local ranches in the open flats below. The Thompson hotel was nestled in between two branches of Schoolhouse Creek. Mary's younger boys would spend some of their free time away from chores running out to the remote Boswell Ranch, north of town, where they likely climbed and crawled through old Indian caves—as boys in those times were known to do—and stained their fingers and shirts with wild blackberries.[8]

The Thompson family must have been very close, for the children were always there to lend a hand. Mary's sons helped her with "fitting up" when she opened the hotel.[9] Her daughters were known as sweet girls who never got into trouble. One daughter, Rosie, married a San Francisco boxing promoter named Tommy Chandler, who trained his boxers at the hotel so they could strengthen their legs running up the trails in the grass-covered North Berkeley Hills.[10]

Mary Thompson was well liked by the many townsfolk who patronized her establishment, and her saloon earned a reputation for serving excellent, ample meals. Card games in the saloon would go on late into the night, and Mary was often heard shushing the laughter of the players, trying to protect the sleep of her teamsters upstairs.[11]

Mary did get into trouble once for flying the green flag with the golden harp above the Stars and Stripes, a mistake in the little patriot hamlet of Berkeley with its many Civil War veterans.[12]

Thompson House had its share of regulars, many of whom were colorful characters. Bob Barrett, a long-term resident of the Thompson House who hailed originally from Australia, concocted a steak sauce made of black walnut oil, shallots, tamarind, and spices from the Far East, and Mary Thompson decided to add it to the menu.[13] It was so delicious that it attracted diners to the hotel, the only place where it was available. With all the positive response, Barrett began to arrange for distribution of the sauce, but he never followed through with the plan. Berkeley might have earned its reputation for culinary innovation much

—A daughter of Mrs. Thompson's of North Berkeley, who was stricken dumb suddenly last week has recovered her speech. The cause of such a serious deprivation could not be accounted for. The girl says."—I was deaf for over four years, and was stricken speechless as above stated. I was recommended to call on Dr. Geo. M. Baronidis. On the 15 inst. I called on the doctor at his office, No 254 Ellis street, San Francisco, and by his treatment recovered my hearing and speech in ten minutes. Any one doubting this fact can be convinced by calling —or address Miss Sarah Thompson, cor Shattuck avenue and Rose streets Berkeley.

Berkeley Advocate, May, 1885.

Mrs. Mary Thompson Entertains.

Mrs. Mary Thompson of North Berkeley handsomely entertained a large number of her friends at her residence, yesterday afternoon. Tempting refreshments were served in a most artistic manner and social diversions indulged in. Those present were Mrs. Winnie C. Allen, Miss Mattie L. Allen, Mrs. W. M. Sanford, Mrs. and Hellen Springer, Irene Thompson, Mr. and Mrs. P. Thompson, and others.

Oakland Tribune, August 15, 1898.

A CHILD'S CARE.

Hearing of the Application in the Driscoll Appeal.

earlier had Barrett been able to shake his haunting and overwhelming grief and concentrate on his business. No one was sure what caused it. Rumor was that he had left a sweetheart behind in Australia; some said he was a "ticket of leave" man (an ex-con) from Down Under.[14] Whatever the source of the feelings, he could not outrun his despair and much of his time was spent drinking. Patrons and friends were accustomed to Bob Barrett's drunken antics, but one night he stumbled up the hotel's stone steps with a more ominous stagger. He collapsed on Thompson's wooden floor and moaned, "I'm dying. Goodbye to you all." He had drunk carbolic acid, hoping to escape his grief for good. He died right there with Mary by his side.[15]

Mary had other troubles as well, but she was a tough businesswoman and considered most of them minor inconveniences. The town officials were pressured to arrest Mary a number of times for breaking the liquor laws of Berkeley (though they were ever changing). So often was she arrested and called to appear at hearings that she was used to the drill: she was nonchalant about being called to court, paid her fines, and was on her way back to her saloon to restock and begin all over again. She considered it all just a part of the cost of doing business in Berkeley. It did not seem to hurt her business. It was hard to tie up your horse in front some afternoons and almost always on Sunday.[16]

In the 1890s, Mary, though retaining Thompson as her last name, married a man named John Bradley, who had been a Civil War bugler.[17] Bradley often spoke to the guests about General Grant and his big, black cigars. Mary and John had a few happy years working the hotel together, and Mary Thompson was listed in the Berkeley city directories until 1905. When she died, John Bradley inherited everything.[18] Sadly, the curse of the angry sea captain proved true. Mary Thompson had lived to bury her first husband and all nine of her children.

Looking north on Shattuck Avenue. The large white house on the hill is Mary Thompson's boarding house.

BILL HENDERSON CIRCA 1906 PUTTING TOGETHER ONE OF HIS FAMOUS "DOG SANDWICHES."
THIS TYPE OF HUMOR WAS BILL'S TRADEMARK, AND HE PROBABLY THOUGHT OF THIS POSE
HIMSELF. HE WAS KNOWN TO WAIL LIKE A DOG WHEN HE RAN HIS MEAT GRINDER.

14

BILL "HOT DOG" HENDERSON

"EAT HERE; DIE AT HOME!" THOSE WORDS GRACED THE SIGN THAT hung for years at Berkeley's favorite hot dog stand, the city's first outdoor lunch cart. When the stand opened around the turn of the twentieth century, Berkeley residents were quickly fascinated by the new establishment and its boisterous and eccentric chef, William "Bill the Hot Dog Man" Henderson.

Bill opened the dog wagon with his wife, Louise, and together they ran the business, working long hours, day and night, for many years. Business was good, but it wasn't always easy. When Bill first arrived in Berkeley, he stored his dog wagon in a barn on Addison Street below Shattuck Avenue. On January 18, 1902, someone broke into the barn and took Bill's wagon for a joyride along Louisa Street (now Bonita Street) and up University Avenue.[1] Finally, the troublemaker dumped the rig at Shattuck Avenue. The cart was a mess: its awning was torn, the stove was broken, and food was scattered everywhere. The next day, as word spread about the destructive prank, a group of locals expressed outrage and quickly took up a collection for Bill. But when the perpetrator was caught and confessed to the crime, kindhearted Bill would not take revenge. He said, "Oh no, he couldn't have done it," and refused to prosecute the man.

By 1903, Bill the Hot Dog Man was regularly setting up his stand across from the new Key Route train station. The newly bustling downtown Berkeley now sported two train lines—the Key Route and the Southern Pacific. At the Key Route station, customers would find Bill singing, smiling, and chopping vegetables as the smells from his outdoor grill wafted among the local pedestrians and San Francisco commuters. Bill, who sported a huge handlebar mustache, was a natural at drawing attention to his business. Before opening his cart, Henderson had worked as a cook for a circus called Rawson's Performing Animals, where he mastered the art of imitating the animal calls he heard while preparing food for humans. Now in Berkeley, he used his roars and growls to turn heads and sell hot dogs.[2]

THE NEW

OWL CAFE AND OYSTER GROTOT

BILL HENDERSON   PROPRIETOR

IN NEW QUARTERS, Opp. Key ROUTE.. Special attention to Banquets and Private Parties

ONE OF BILL'S MANY CAFÉ INCARNATIONS IN BERKELEY, WHICH HE ADVERTISED IN JOHN E. BOYD'S 1907 BOOK, *ANCIENT POETRY*.

A VERSION OF THE FAMOUS OUTDOOR DOG CARTS OPERATED AT VARIOUS LOCATIONS AROUND BERKELEY. NOTE THAT BILL'S NEIGHBOR IS THE REALTOR J. P. HALE, WHO CHANGED FROM BEING A CABINETMAKER TO A REALTOR AND BICYCLE SALESMAN IN 1902, KEEPING HIS SAME ADDRESS OF 1504 SHATTUCK AVENUE (AROUND SHATTUCK AVENUE AND VINE). THIS POSTCARD IS DATED 1906, AND BY THEN HALE HAD AN OFFICE AT 1511 SHATTUCK AVENUE AND A BRANCH AT 2515 SHATTUCK AVENUE, NEAR DWIGHT WAY. THE 1907 CITY DIRECTORY PLACES HALE AT THE NORTHWEST CORNER OF UNIVERSITY AND SHATTUCK AVENUES. IT IS KNOWN THAT BILL THE HOT DOG MAN DID HAVE A CART AT THIS LOCATION.

The best thing about operating a portable lunch wagon was that Bill could move his business as he saw fit. Bill served his fare and entertainment for about twenty-five years at locations around Berkeley. Occasionally, he set up shop indoors. From his early locations at the southwest and northeast corners of Shattuck Avenue and Center Street, he moved inside to a second-floor restaurant on Shattuck. When he moved out of that location, it was back to the famous dog wagon, this time stationed at Shattuck and University. His most popular stand, Millionaire's Lunch, was on Allston Way near Shattuck Avenue. He also operated the much-loved Dog House, and the UC Pup. By 1912, Bill was rolling his cart every day to his new location by Sather Gate, at the entrance to the UC Berkeley campus.

William Henderson often disappeared to go "rambling" up and down the California coast. If someone mentioned a nice town while sitting at the counter, Bill would close up shop and leave to visit this new place. Sometimes he would

even open a hot dog stand or restaurant there. Over the years, he temporarily relocated to Sacramento (1909), Stockton, and Oakland (1917), among other places. But he always came back, and his return to Berkeley was always so celebrated by residents, especially Berkeley High and UC students and alumni, that it inevitably made the newspapers, even in Oakland. Here's what he told the *Oakland Tribune* when he returned from one of his trips in 1917:

> *Yep. I'm comin' back. I needed the university influence. I missed the old "Oski Wow" and "give 'em the ax" and the rest of the yells. I was in Oakland for several years but it ain't the same. Out here is different. I've got to get back on the faculty. The university needs me. Besides, Hoover has wired me that Berkeley is eating too much and to help the government cut down the consumption. I'm the boy that can do it. Give me a handful of sawdust and a bad egg and I'll feed an army. Besides, I want to get my degree in the university. Sure, I'm after a degree—L. L. B. is it— Long Line of Bull! Gosh! It's good to get back again.*[3]

But Bill couldn't sit still, even in his beloved Berkeley. In 1919 he traveled to Oxnard, California, where he planned to relocate his roving cafe. He looked around and immediately decided that he had to go home and reopen his Berkeley dog house in the familiar shade of the UC oaks. Wherever Bill traveled, he would eventually return to Berkeley and set up shop again at a new locale, replete with his distinctive and unnerving signs hanging behind the counter:

A TRIBUTE AND PEN AND INK DRAWING OF BILL THE
HOT DOG MAN FROM THE STUDENTS AT UC BERKELEY
IN THEIR BLUE AND GOLD YEARBOOK OF 1902.

Don't tease the butter for you may be old yourself some day.
Bring your own napkin if you can't keep your food in your face.
If an egg crows the price goes up.
Soup must be eaten in the telephone booth.
Ice water is free—That's why we don't have it.

From the signs to the service, everything was just so "Bill" at his dog wagon.
Along with the signature hot dogs, the wagon menu included items such as liberty
steak patties with onions, and the "Romeo," a kind of grand hamburger sandwich.
Orders were tossed across the counter, and coffee was referred to as "mud." Regular
customers learned to speak Bill's lingo. Even the pies—raisin, apple, berry, and
custard—were known as "San Quentin," "Honest to God," "Appendicitis," and
"Salvation." When things got busy, it wasn't unusual for customers to wait on themselves. Bill cooked, and that was all he guaranteed he'd do. People learned not to

confront the hot dog man, especially when he was waving a big butcher knife.

Bill served up entertainment as well as hot dogs. He might pretend to pull cockroaches from food, swat imaginary bugs, or make the sound of an anguished dog while turning his meat grinder. He loved playing with his customers. He would say, "You want coffee? Coffee? In here? Why, all we have is mud!" Then he would present the cup using sleight-of-hand so it appeared his thumb was immersed in the liquid. To the shocked customer, he would say, "Oh, it isn't hot enough to burn me." When someone was within earshot, Bill might turn to Louise and say, "Ma, how can they stand eating here? I couldn't."

But people really did love Bill's food. According to a 1919 article in the *Oakland Tribune,* "thousands upon thousands of people around Berkeley and throughout the state know him," and recognized the preeminence of his culinary skills—at least when it came to hot dogs: "No man knows like William Henderson the low-down, ground-floor, rock-bottom secrets of the hot dog."[4]

The local high school and college students loved to visit Bill's stand between classes. The university students were so charmed by his antics and felt he was such an integral part of their Berkeley experience that in 1902 they included a portrait and a poem about him in the college yearbook. Those who stayed in the area would keep coming back; years after graduation they could be found snuggling

ABOVE: BILL HENDERSON AS AN OLDER MAN. BILL WAS A FAMOUS ENOUGH FIGURE TO BE KEPT IN THE COLLECTION OF THE VOLUNTEER FIREMAN'S HISTORICAL COLLECTIONS.

LEFT: BILL AT HIS STAND THE UC PUP. NOTE THE EARLY PEDESTAL PHONE ON THE LEFT OF THE COUNTER. ONE SIGN READS, "TRY OUR CHILI EXPERIENCE."

THE FAMOUS VAUDEVILLE TEAM OF KOLB AND DILL.
THEY WERE THE INSPIRATION FOR AN IMITATION OF
ONE OF THEIR PLAYS BY BERKELEY TALENT, INCLUDING
THEIR MANAGER, BILL HENDERSON.

onto their old lunch counter stools.

In the summer of 1917, during World War I, Bill was taking his only child, Nellie, to a women's college in the Pacific Northwest and decided to stop at an army basic training camp, Camp Lewis, in Washington. He knew that many of the boys he had served hot dogs to in their college or high school days were stationed there, and as soon as Bill the Hot Dog Man arrived at Camp Lewis he caused a riot of excitement among the Berkeley and Oakland recruits. They started clamoring about munching hot dogs and Romeos from Bill's dog wagon in the old days. A crowd quickly formed around this well-loved Berkeleyan. Two ex-Cal football players lifted Hot Dog Henderson on their shoulders and carried him around the camp like a hero. The exuberant young army men happily screamed "Oski-wow-wow" (an old Cal cry) and "Speech! speech!" Bill, in classic form, did not disappoint them:

> Boys don't tease me. Remember that butter you used to eat in my place
> and have respect for the aged. I just dropped by to see if the government
> was feeding you right. President Wilson said to me, "Bill—look 'em over.
> If the commisary department isn't up to standard, come back to
> Washington, and tell me about it and I'll fire the whole crowd." Boys, I'm
> going back and tell Woodrow it's all right—the cooks can keep their jobs.[5]

Before the men let Bill and Nellie continue on their way, they commanded Bill to cook up some of his Romeo sandwiches, as always, using his secret ingredients. After the meal, they introduced their hero to their commanding officers, and Bill then left to a cheering sea of green uniforms. Bill was touched by their enthusiasm. "Gosh," he said. "It makes me want to go to war just to keep up with the boys I used to know." Bill could not have known what awaited these men in the trenches on the western front.

Bill was a bit of an entertainer, and a part of him pined to be a star on a bigger stage. When he was at work, Bill always sang in a low baritone as he chopped onions, using his knife to tap out a beat on the chopping block. His quick-witted creative mind, his habit of singing while he worked, and his love of attention led Bill to long for more of an audience than could be seated at the stools of his cart or restaurant. He hungered for the glare of the lights, the glamour, and the applause of the theater. This new passion at midlife, just when he and Louise had made a nice nest egg, did not come without a price.

In early 1909, Charles H. White, a Berkeley journalist, short story writer, and

"Have You Seen Myah?"

A Three-Act Comedy with Music.

The Dog Man's Farewell

MACDONOUGH THEATER

Friday Evening

April 30, '09

TICKETS:
50 and 75 Cents.

Reserve at the Boxoffice or at Bill's Cafe, Berkeley.

AN AD FOR BILL'S PLAY THE DAY BEFORE IT OPENED. NOTE THAT TICKETS COULD BE PURCHASED AT BILL'S RESTAURANT, WHICH AT THAT TIME WAS AT 2125 CENTER STREET. *BERKELEY DAILY GAZETTE*, APRIL 29, 1909.

playwright, stopped at Bill's stand.[6] White told tales of the excitement of the stage and plied Bill with his ideas for farcical musical comedies. Farce? Comedies? Bill was hooked. White built up the allure and promised riches. White knew that Bill's dog wagon and restaurant had showered nickels upon the Hendersons for many years. White laughed as he told Bill about his new play, *Have You Seen Myah?*, describing it as a sure hit. It was a parody of a popular comic vaudeville skit about two recent German emigrants called *Have You Seen Meyer?*, performed by the then-famous vaudeville team of Kolb and Dill. In White's play, the "Myah" would refer to Oscar Meyer, the brand of hot dogs. White was setting Bill up, and Bill could not resist. He accepted White's offer to become the manager of the production. As part of the arrangement, Bill would also put up all of the money. White told Bill that the play was booked at downtown Oakland's renowned Macdonough Theatre, located at the northwest corner of Fourteenth Street and Broadway. The Macdonough showcased national talent, but in between the big-name acts local talent was hired to fill out the calendar. In fact, Kolb and Dill, the performers of the original *Have You Seen Meyer?*, were to appear at the Macdonough Theatre in *Lonesome Town* the week before the opening of Henderson and White's *Have You Seen Myah?*

Two Berkeley High School students are the lead actors, imitating the famous vaudeville team of Kolb and Dill in the local play *Have You Seen Myah?*

The cast of *Have You Seen Myah?* included twenty-five female students from UC Berkeley and Berkeley High School as the chorus; the UC Cadet Band accompanied the troupe. The production was assembled quickly with only eleven days of rehearsals. Bill drummed up interest for his three-act comedy and built suspense by offering teasers that were picked up by the local press:

> *Because of a certain feature in the third act Henderson requests that opera glasses be brought to the show so that no one will miss seeing it. Considerable curiosity has been attached to his strange request but up to the present the reason for it has not been divulged.*[7]

Advance ticket sales were good, and UC fraternity houses had reserved entire rows of seats. Bill was prepared for a big hit and is said to have negotiated with the Oakland Traction Company to arrange for several theater cars to transport the band and Berkeley patrons from the corner of Shattuck and University avenues directly to the Macdonough in Oakland.

Despite all the attention leading into the production, local papers did not seem to publish any follow-up articles about *Have You Seen Myah?*, and details of the special third-act feature remain a mystery.

Have You Seen Myah? was a flop. Still, White kept after Bill to back his plays, and Bill continued to be drawn in by the hustler's charm. This relationship deeply troubled Louise Henderson. She had worked side by side with Bill for many years. They had built a very comfortable life together, which included real estate investments said to be worth $40,000, and a Berkeley home at 1818 Delaware Street. She did not want to see their savings thrown away on risky theater productions. She neither liked nor trusted this Mr. White, who was hounding her husband for more money. But Bill would not listen to his wife. In April 1909, he sold his restaurant to fund more theatrical productions.

Louise spoke publicly about her troubles in the May 9, 1909, Sunday morning edition of the *Oakland Tribune*:

> *He wanted to back a play that White was anxious to produce in the Macdonough Theater in Oakland. I objected it would cost money and my husband knows nothing of the theatrical business.*
>
> *My husband backed a recent farce comedy in the Macdonough theater and lost money as I predicted. Anyway, he made nothing that I had heard of. We have divided the property we owned and Mr. Henderson*

is, as I understand, going to Sacramento. I will make my home in Berkeley.[8]

THIS BEAUTIFUL YOUNG WOMAN, BONNIE BROWNING, WAS THE LEAD ACTRESS IN THE PLAY *HAVE YOU SEEN MYAH?* IT IS LIKELY THAT THIS IS THE WOMAN BILL'S WIFE THOUGHT HE WAS HAVING AN AFFAIR WITH.

Louise and their daughter Nellie moved to a cottage at 1602 Edith Street, where the family had lived in previous years. (She and Bill first lived there in 1902.) Louise denied the rumors going around that Bill was smitten with a young actress who appeared in *Have You Seen Myah?*, and that the hot dog man had an affair with her or was going to be her sugar daddy.

Soon rumors were flying in both directions. Bill accused his wife of having an affair with one of his former employees, and the newspapers closely followed the whole incident. Bill and Louise separated, divided their property and real estate, and divorced. Bill received custody of their daughter, Nellie.

Bill, then forty-eight years old, moved to Sacramento in May of 1909 and opened a new restaurant. In July, he became paralyzed while trying to move a large boiler.[9] The doctors thought the situation grave and telegraphed Mrs. Henderson in Berkeley. She rushed to his bedside. Their friends in Berkeley thought that if Bill lived, the couple would get back together. Bill did make a remarkable recovery and by the end of July was released from the Hayward sanitarium where he'd been recovering. But Bill would return to Sacramento after settling his affairs in Berkeley. The Hendersons did not rekindle their marriage.

Bill came back to Berkeley the following year and opened a restaurant with his brother Edwin, also a professional cook, at 2238 Telegraph Avenue. Over the next fifteen years, Bill would operate a series of restaurants in Berkeley and Oakland; when he was between locations, he usually returned to selling his famous street cart fare.

In the spring of 1912, after four years of single life, Bill was secretly wed in San Rafael to his new sweetheart, Julia Talbot, a Jamaican-born nurse. She had been working in the Bay Area for seven years. At some point they divorced, and Bill married a woman named Melinda, who is listed as his wife in Berkeley directories beginning in 1925.

In the 1930s, Bill left Berkeley for the last time. Everyone believed he had died, but in 1940 some Berkeley folks found him living in Monterey.[10] He was seventy-nine years old and his huge mustache was pure white. A stroke had robbed him of some of his agility, but he startled his visitors and reminded them of his former virtuosity by barking like a vicious dog.

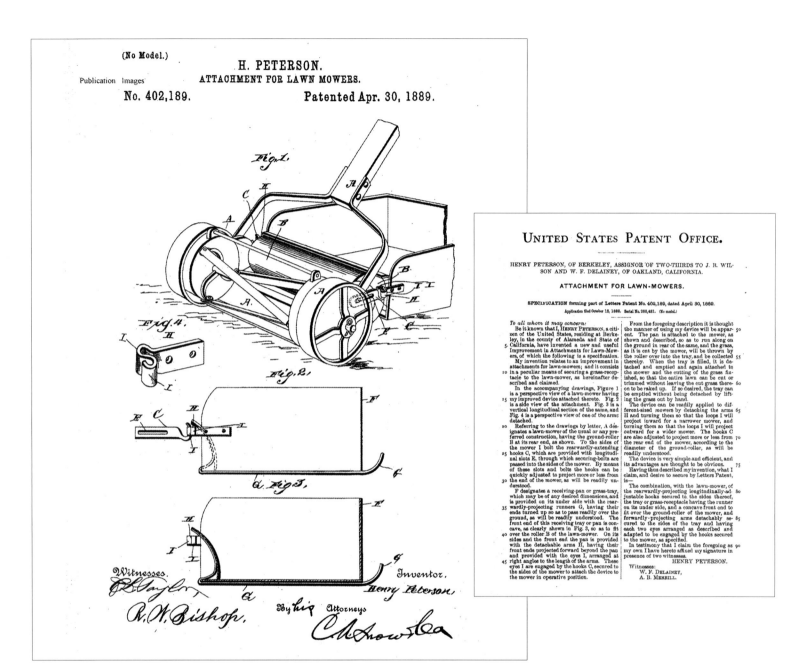

LEFT: THE PATENT ILLUSTRATION SUBMITTED BY HENRY PETERSON FOR HIS LAWNMOWER BAG, WITH AN OFFICIAL NOTE THAT THE PATENT WAS GRANTED ON APRIL 30, 1889. NOTE THE ACTUAL SIGNATURE OF HENRY PETERSON ON THE LOWER RIGHT OF THE DOCUMENT.

RIGHT: THE TEXT OF PATENT NO. 402,189 OF HENRY PETERSON FOR HIS LAWNMOWER BAG INVENTION, USED TO THIS DAY. PETERSON INVENTED IT WHILE LIVING IN BERKELEY. NOTE THAT THE SIGNING WITNESSES ON THE PATENT WERE THE SAME TWO MEN WHO PURCHASED INTERESTS IN THE INVENTION, MAKING HENRY PETERSON A WEALTHY MAN. THE AUTHOR OF THIS BOOK USED PETERSON'S INVENTION THROUGHOUT HIS CHILDHOOD IN THE 1950s AND 1960s, NEVER DREAMING HE WOULD DISCOVER THE FORGOTTEN INVENTOR MANY DECADES LATER.

15

HENRY S. PETERSON AND THE
BERKELEY LAWN MOWER INVENTION

THE LEGACY OF AFRICAN-AMERICAN INVENTOR HENRY PETERSON HAS largely been lost save for this brief 1889 article from the *Berkeley Advocate*, the records of the United States Patent Office, and his obituary in the *Berkeley Daily Gazette:*

> *Mr. Peterson, who lives on Dwight way, has been offered $15,000 for his patent appliance for a lawn mower. The invention consists of a pan which is attached to the lawn-mower so as not to leave any grass on the lawn after it has been cut. Mr. Peterson perfected his invention and obtained a patent on it some two or three years ago. He has disposed of a two-thirds interest in the invention.*[1]

THE FIRST CONGREGATIONAL CHURCH, BERKELEY.

But one might imagine the magnitude of his invention: The $15,000 he was offered for the final one-third interest in his lawn mower tray could have purchased five nice houses in those days. But even before they had access to such money, Henry S. and Caroline Peterson had already made a lasting contribution to the city of Berkeley.

Henry S. Peterson and his wife, Caroline, arrived in Berkeley by 1872, in time to witness the laying of the cornerstone of the first building of the University of California, which was erected that year.[2] Only about 600 people were living in all of Oakland Township at the time.

Four years before Berkeley was incorporated, Henry Peterson and two others founded the First Congregational Church, according to the *Berkeley Daily Gazette.*[3] The best known of the three founders was Dr. Samuel Willey, also a founder of UC Berkeley. On June 24, 1874, a Congregational church service was conducted by Reverend E. S. Lacy in a room at the Berkeley Hotel at the corner of Choate

The C. T. Wilkinson residence, neighbors of the Petersons on Dwight Way, just below College Avenue. C. T. Wilkinson was the head of the nearby Deaf, Dumb and Blind Asylum.

Street (now Telegraph Avenue) and Bancroft Way. Henry and Caroline Peterson were undoubtedly in attendance.

On March 22, 1875, Reverend Edward B. Payne held the first service in the Congregational Chapel at Dwight Way and Choate Avenue in the first church building in Berkeley. Later the congregation constructed a new building at Dana and Durant streets. Peterson is first listed in the Berkeley directories as early as 1876, two years before Berkeley incorporated as a city, and is listed continuously until 1899. According to the city directories, he worked variously as a gardener, laborer, and dairyman, all very typical trades in early Berkeley. His residence is listed on Dwight Way between Fulton and Ellsworth streets from 1887 to 1890. He had previously lived in the same neighborhood on Channing Way near Bowditch for at least five years. The area was composed of small farms and ranches, and was near Berkeley's first commercial center at Shattuck Avenue and Dwight Way.

Henry Peterson was born in New York in 1841. The 1880 Census indicated that thirty-nine-year-old Henry lived with his forty-two-year-old wife, Caroline, and his sister, E. E. Phelps, a forty-four-year-old widow.

When Peterson applied for his patent on October 18, 1888, his invention was a secret. Two Oakland investors, J. R. Wilson and W. F. Delainey, saw the potential of Henry's grass catcher and offered him a huge sum for a two-thirds interest in

TOP: LOOKING EAST ON THE UPPER END OF DWIGHT WAY.

BOTTOM: A SCENE OF THE DWIGHT WAY AREA LOOKING NORTHWEST.

HENRY AND CAROLINE PETERSON'S HOME AT 2222 DWIGHT WAY.

THE House erected by John Spencer on Dwight Way near Fulton St. will be occupied by Mr. Petersen and family. It is the model cottage of Berkeley.

BERKELEY HERALD, NOVEMBER 24, 1886.

the invention. These two men maintained a close relationship with the inventor and acted as witnesses on the patent application. Henry S. Peterson was issued patent number 402,189 from the United States Patent Office on February 30, 1889. According to the patent, Wilson and Delainey held a two-thirds interest, and one can assume it was in exchange for a previous payment to Henry Peterson. Just what Henry and Caroline did with their well-earned financial reward is unknown, save for the fact that they moved to a house at 2222 Dwight Way, appraised at three times the value of their previous home. But as Berkeley directories show, they lived for many more years in the comforts of the same east Berkeley neighborhood where they had resided for decades prior to Henry's success.

In 1896, the *Berkeley Advocate* published a piece recalling all of the 302 pioneers of the town of about 1,500 souls who had voted in the election of May of 1878 to form the city of Berkeley. They checked the Great Register to see how many of those famous voters were still residents who would still be eligible to vote almost twenty years later. Stalwart Henry Peterson was among those 105 names. The article provides proof that Henry Peterson, by his voting, was a founding father of the city of Berkeley.

The aging Henry and Caroline Peterson survived the April 18, 1906, earthquake and witnessed the flood of refugees into Berkeley. It could not have been easy for them since Caroline had been an invalid for some time. On September 22, 1906, sixty-three-year-old Henry Peterson died suddenly of heart failure while coming in the rear door of his home. He had been in declining health for a number of years, but his death was totally unexpected, and his wife was devastated by his loss. The couple had been Berkeley residents for more than thirty-three years. Henry's obituary in the *Berkeley Daily Gazette* called him "one of the best known and pioneer residents of Berkeley."[4]

Caroline Peterson lived only a few months longer than her husband. On January 22, 1907, four months after Henry's passing, the following appeared in the *Berkeley Daily Gazette:*

> *Mrs. Caroline Peterson, a resident of Berkeley for thirty years, died Sunday at her home, 2222 Dwight Way, after a prolonged illness. Mrs. Peterson was widely known throughout her home town, and enjoyed the respect and good will of a host of friends.*
>
> *She was a charter member of the First Congregational Church of Berkeley. The funeral was held at 1:30 this afternoon from the Peterson home.*[5]

A PEN AND INK DRAWING OF THE FIRST CONGREGATIONAL CHURCH, WHICH HENRY AND CAROLINE PETERSON HELPED FOUND.

THIS 1908 IMAGE OF AN UNDEVELOPED AREA IN BERKELEY'S THOUSAND OAKS NEIGHBORHOOD REVEALS A ROCK WITH INDIAN MORTARS. THERE WERE MANY SCORES OF INDIAN SITES ALL OVER BERKELEY, MORE THAN ANYONE, INCLUDING ARCHEOLOGISTS, ANTICIPATED, MOST HAVING BEEN RECORDED ONLY IN THE PAST DECADE OR SO. THERE IS EVIDENCE OF INDIAN OCCUPATION FROM AT LEAST 5,900 YEARS AGO IN BERKELEY. WHEN THE SPANISH ARRIVED WITH THE MISSION SYSTEM IN 1769, THE INDIANS OF THE EAST BAY WERE ESSENTIALLY DRIVEN FROM THEIR HOMES BY THE FORCES OF THE CHURCH AND THE SPANISH MILITARY. WHEN THE AMERICANS ARRIVED, THE TREATMENT OF INDIANS IN CALIFORNIA REACHED A NEW LOW. THERE WERE MANY INCIDENTS OF SLAVERY, INCLUDING CHILD SLAVERY IN THE AREA AROUND BERKELEY. RAIDS WERE MADE TO THE NORTH AND INDIANS, MANY WOMEN AND CHILDREN, WERE BROUGHT TO THE AREA AGAINST THEIR WILL TO WORK ON LOCAL RANCHES. BY THE LATE 1800S THE PRACTICE HAD BEEN MODIFIED TO THE USE OF INDIAN CHILDREN AS DOMESTICS IN HOUSES IN THE AREA, INCLUDING BERKELEY.

16

"Indian Girl Was Homesick"

The old-fashioned complaint of home-sickness, emphasized by a common case of quarrel, inspired little Lizzie McCarey, a full-blooded Indian maiden, to leave the home of her guardians in this town Wednesday night and begin a long tramp back to the reservation.

Mr. and Mrs. M. Johnson, living at Dana and Derby streets, asked the police today to assist in recovering the little Indian maiden. Marshal Kerns received a description of the girl and wired the details to the police of Oakland and San Francisco, where search will be made for Miss McCarey. She is about 12 years old, slender, black-haired, wearing short skirts and revealing in her features her racial origin.

Those acquainted with the "child of the forest," however, say that the police of the big cities may as well spare their efforts in searching for her along the brick or stone pavements for they believe that Lizzy McCarey has been moved by a strong feeling of home-sickness to pick up her belongings and start on a trip back to the spot from which she was taken a little more than a year ago by the Berkeley family in whose home she recently lived.

Lizzie McCarey, of course, is not the Indian maiden's original name. She was called "Artmah" when with her people in Modoc County, and received the name savoring of Hibernian origin when she was brought to the university town and domiciled at Dana and Derby streets. Her home life there was happy enough apparently, until recently, when she evinced a distaste for its confining character. This led to friction in the family, resulting in her disappearance.[1]

AN OFFICIAL 1896 ALAMEDA COUNTY DOCUMENT PROHIBITING PAUPERS, INSANE PEOPLE, AND INDIANS FROM PAYING THE POLL TAX—THEREFORE PROHIBITING THEM FROM VOTING. THE PAYMENT OF TAX WAS TO BE MADE TO PHILO MILLS, DEPUTY ASSESSOR, AT 2033 HASTE STREET, BERKELEY. THIS DOCUMENT OF THE COUNTY POLITICAL CODE CLEARLY ILLUSTRATES THE STATUS AND HATRED OF INDIAN PEOPLE IN LOCAL SOCIETY.

This article from the February 17, 1905, edition of the *Berkeley Daily Gazette* gives but a momentary glimpse into the life of a Modoc Indian girl on the threshold of womanhood. Sadly, there were many Artmahs in California at the turn of

An artist's depiction of a California Indian mother and child, though styled on images of the plains Indians rather than local tribes.

the twentieth century. Indian children were taken from reservation schools or their families for "training" as domestics in California households. At the time it was considered to be a good future for them, a proper use of their abilities. Very few townsfolk, even into the twentieth century, questioned keeping them away from their families and their culture.

How many of these child-domestics were there in Berkeley? No one knows, but it was clear that domestics were in demand during that era. There were large numbers of young Indian children in such situations all over the state. It is not known if Artmah was paid for her services, and it does not appear that this twelve-year-old was in school. One can only hope the brave young child, named Artmah by her own people and Lizzie McCarey by her Berkeley "guardians," safely survived her long trek home.

Artmah's Modoc People

Berkeley's Artmah was a Modoc. Her people had lived in northeastern California and southern Oregon. In the 1850s, settlers began to take root on the Lost River in Modoc country, and soon petitioned the U.S. government to remove the Modocs from their land to help the settlers feel safe.[2] The Modocs were removed to the Klamath Reservation between 1867 and 1869, and this created a new set of problems, not the least of which was that the Klamath people and the Modocs were traditional adversaries. All the while, the Modocs were demanding their own reservation back in their Lost River homeland. The settlers made sure this did not happen. When the conflict at the reservation proved too much for the Modoc, they returned home. The settlers again convinced authorities that Modoc presence was unacceptable and, in spite of Modoc protests, once again authorities moved them to the Klamath Reservation.

In April of 1869, nearly 400 Modoc left the reservation, refusing to negotiate further with U.S. authorities. By the end of 1872, settlers pressured U.S. troops to forcibly remove the Modoc yet again. The troops burned a Modoc village, which the Modoc considered an act of war. After a group of Modocs killed fourteen male settlers to avenge the burning of their village, the Modoc were forced to flee with their families into the Lava Beds area. This is where, in early 1873, Captain Jack, a Modoc leader, and fifty Modoc men sent more than 300 troops and volunteers into retreat with heavy casualties. Captain Jack's band was then reinforced by other Modocs.

President Grant hoped to halt the violence and formed a peace commission to negotiate an end to the fighting. After many meetings, the government representatives told the Modoc again that they could not have their own reservation. The Modoc felt bitter and betrayed. They retaliated and killed two of the four U.S. representatives sent to meet with them. U.S. reinforcements arrived, cut the Modocs off from their water, and soon stormed the lava bed fortress. They found it empty.

But this small band of Indians, now 160 strong, was no match for the U.S. Army. The Modoc suffered a devastating loss after an attack on the U.S. encampment. One of their most beloved men, "Ellen's Man George," was killed, leaving the Modoc thoroughly demoralized. They also took these setbacks as a sign that their shaman's "ghost dance" spell, protecting them from harm, had failed. Captain Jack surrendered on June 1, 1873, ending the conflict. He and other Modoc leaders were hanged.

I have been told that I must give up my young men and have them hang and not cry, but I should cry if my men were hung. I never asked you to give up to us the men who shot my people when they were asleep. I don't think my men were so much to blame about it and I can't give them up.[3]

—*Captain Jack, 1873*

When history records the cruel fact that a United States army deliberately slaughtered every man, woman and child of a small but bold and brave tribe of Indians, because five of their chief men treacherously murdered two of our Peace Commissioners, history should also be invoked to show the real causes which led the savages to that fatal act of treachery. . . . We are much in error if the verdict of history shall not be more against the white Christian than the dusky heathen.[4]

—Sacramento Union, *1873*

A TURN-OF-THE-CENTURY POSTCARD DEPICTING THE "OLD INDIAN BURIAL GROUND" ON THE UC BERKELEY CAMPUS. MANY BURIALS HAVE BEEN FOUND IN DIFFERENT LOCATIONS ON AND NEAR THE CAMPUS. THIS POSTCARD CONFIRMS TRADITIONS FROM AN EARLIER TIME WHEN INDIAN REMAINS WERE BEING DISCOVERED.

17

Professor Joseph Voyle's Buried Ancient City under UC Berkeley

The members of the Berkeley Society for Psychical Research were sure. Their president, Professor Joseph Voyle, and other officers were very sure. On June 21, 1908, the society announced that Voyle had discovered a huge prehistoric ceremonial site buried on the UC Berkeley campus. The members of the society were confident in their conclusions.[1] It seemed perfectly logical to them that ancient people would have chosen to honor this place where Strawberry Creek was cloaked by bay, alder, sycamore, and oak trees, its lower banks shrouded in strawberry and watercress plants, and where the ancient coast live oaks extended their gnarled limbs over the campus beneath the sheltering hills. Here they would have enjoyed the commanding view of the Bay and Golden Gate, the mild weather, and the abundance of all forms of food. Indeed, many artifacts were found and graves uncovered during the construction of buildings in the nineteenth and twentieth centuries; it is certain that Native Americans lived on and around the UC Berkeley campus.

Most UC Berkeley professors considered the society's claims to be a little too fanciful—and totally unsubstantiated. Voyle said that he had discovered a buried grid of an ancient habitation or ceremonial site, claiming that he and his students had used psychic magnetic compasses, or divining rods, to probe the invisible force fields of attractive matter underground. He claimed that this grid, measuring 1,200 feet in each direction, was one of a system of grids established around Berkeley. The grid under the UC campus, he said, was the only one that was subdivided into 120-foot square plots, making it, according to his thinking, a ceremonial site used during a certain time of year. He believed the smaller grids were privately owned by members of the ancient society. Voyle claimed to have seen similar markings all across the American continent, from Oregon to Florida.

PSYCHIC SEES PREHISTORIC CITY BENEATH BERKELEY

University on Top of Mysterious Village

BERKELEY, May 25.—Joseph Voyle, a member of the Berkeley Psychical Society, has, according to Z. W. Lothrop, local realty broker, discovered that underneath the town site of Berkeley lies the remains and ruins of a prehistoric city.

Voyle has made his discovery, it is claimed, partly through pshysic information and partly by examination of the excavations being made on the university campus for the Doe library.

The city, Lothrop says, Voyle believes he has discovered. was of rectangular form. The heart of this mysterious city was located near the spot where the Bacon library now stands. Voyle makes its corner boundries at Harmon gymnasium, Hearst Hall, Greek Theater and mining building. It was laid out in squares or sections after the manner of the modern city, blocks.

How far back in the history of time the city flourished or how deep in the earth its remains now lie buried or what class of people inhabited or built it, Voyle has not said. He is reserving these details for a report to be made to the Berkeley Psychical Society.

Oakland Times, May 25, 1908.

SAYS ANCIENT CITY
UNDERLIES BERKELEY

That this city and the university are built over a prehistoric city is the opinion of Joseph Voyle, president of the society for physical research. Voyle has made his discovery by means of a peculiarly delicate instruments, with an "aura" susceptible to various elements and compounds.

The society for physical research numbers in its membership many well-known men and women. Yesterday Mrs. R. C. Shaw, wife of Professor Shaw of the university, Mrs. Rebecca Johnson and other prominent members went over the ground covered by Voyle in his experiments and are said to have confirmed his theories by finding the outlines of the boundaries of the

BERKELEY GAZETTE, 1903.

Voyle's claims were wild. According to the *Berkeley Daily Gazette:*

The ambition of the collectors of antiquities seemed to have been attained when a row of ordinary everyday rocks was reached and made by the fertile brains of the searchers to resemble the walls of a prehistoric North Hall.

Towards the close of the day Voyle led his disciples back to the univer-
sity grounds, where he proceeded to make a test that he said proved con-
clusively that the seat of learning of California today was the prized resort
of sun worshipers ages ago. The test consisted of sticking up a pole in the
ground at sundown and following the shadow as a base line for observa-
tions. In explanation of this, Voyle said:

"From Arab and Oriental mystics versed in Egyptian lore, I have
learned that it was an ancient custom to stick a rod in the ground at
sundown of June 21st, the day on which the sun reaches its northernmost
point, and that the shadow cast was used as a base line for the observa-
tions of the ancient engineers. My compass responds to certain markings
I am convinced lie beneath these grounds." [2]

Despite the outrageousness of his claims, there was something about this charis-
matic man Voyle that led a considerable number of people to accept his theories.

Joseph Voyle was born in England in 1839, the son of a minister. As a boy of
nine, he taught himself Latin. He spoke Hebrew, French, Spanish, Liaboe, Indian
dialects, and Hindu dialects, among others. As an adult he wandered over much
of the world. He was once shipwrecked and yet made his way to New Orleans,
where he lived in the French Quarter. Joseph Voyle enlisted in the Confederate
army on April 9, 1862, and served as a private until May 18, 1865, in the First
Louisiana Heavy Artillery. He was wounded at the battle at Yorktown, Virginia,
some time between April and May of 1862 and served in the battles of New
Orleans, Vicksburg, Grand Gulf, and Mobile Bay.[3] For a time, Joseph Voyle
became a prisoner of war.

In wandering around the United States after the war, Voyle studied with a
Cherokee man versed in American Indian mystic lore. Voyle also studied with
learned men from "the Orient." The *Oakland Tribune* reported that he was "legally
dead, having been declared so in a long and tangled suit which involved his family's and his own finances."[4] He listed himself as a photograph artist in 1870 while
living in Tuscaloosa, Alabama.[5] In 1880, he lived in Gainesville, Florida, working
as a civil engineer, and moved to Berkeley later that year.[6] In the Bay Area, he
earned a reputation as "a well known chemist and physicist."[7] This led the papers
and others to give him the title of "professor," one that stayed with him for the
rest of his life.

Voyle arrived in Berkeley in its pioneer days. At some point during his time in
California he made a considerable fortune from mining operations in California

and Nevada. In 1880, after arriving from Florida, Voyle lived at Berkeley's Pacific Theological Seminary and later in a rented room at 2223 Atherton Street.

Prior to his public declarations about the Berkeley grid, Voyle spent much time in 1903 studying the effects of radium. From his room at the New Western Hotel in San Francisco, Voyle ran tests on the properties of radium.[8] He found that the element had what he called "directive properties," or "radio sympathetic action," making it useful, he thought, in tracing locations. Voyle began to use his hotel room as a base for his studies, believing that there was a radium source beneath San Francisco. He told reporters that he first placed some radium in an electric vortex of high voltage in which its properties of emitting light were destroyed and its qualities of burning the hand if held were reduced.[9] He felt the burning sensation was reduced enough that he tested it by putting the radium in his mouth, where he found it took a minute or two before he noticed a burning sensation. He became so comfortable with it that he carried it around in his vest pocket. He then marched around the San Francisco streets carrying the radium in his hand, following where the tip of it led him. He claimed that it led him to a radium source under the U.S. Customs House. There he held the radium and reported that his hand burned, then the pain moved up his wrist and arm, his heart became distressed, and he was forced to let go of it. He complained of being dizzy and weak for hours. Voyle also began searching for radium sources in Berkeley later in 1903.

In the spring of 1905, Voyle was part of an effort by citizens to open a practical college, trade school, and lecture center for the general public. The People's College of South Berkeley was to include a manual training school for boys, a polytechnic school for young men, a school of domestic science for young women, and a school of science and general improvement for older citizens and the general public. The school was intended to help mainly working-class people and those who could not attend regular high schools or colleges.[10] By 1907, a People's College is listed in the city directory at 1886 Alcatraz Avenue. The following year it is absent from the listings, never to appear again.

Voyle lost his fortune and San Francisco work studio, as well as most of his possessions, in the fires following the 1906 San Francisco earthquake.

By 1908 he had turned his focus to the Berkeley grid. Voyle contended that the center of the grid was located near UC Berkeley's Bacon Hall, built in 1881, which stood (until it was demolished in 1961) just east of Sather Tower. Voyle claimed that the corners of this buried site were the Harmon Gym, Hearst Hall, the Greek Theatre, and the Hearst Mining Building. He believed that the first two campus buildings, North and South Halls, were right within the area of this buried prehistoric square-shaped city. Voyle claimed that the grid was made of some kind of matter laid down by the ancients. He further maintained that disturbances of the "attractive matter" of this prehistoric work were noted in the recent 1908 construction work on the Doe Library and the southwest corner of the Hearst Mining Building. He was sure that the founders of the university were subliminally affected by the buried site.[11]

According to Voyle, everything in the site was laid out with mathematical accuracy, though its orientation was not in a north–south direction. Rather, the orientation was the same as the one the Egyptian pyramid builders used—along the line created by the shadow of a pole when the sun set on the summer and winter solstices, when the sun sets at its northernmost point on the western horizon. Voyle believed, though he did not yet have exact proof, that these lines ran about thirty degrees north of west. If a pole was placed at the southwest corner of this ancient square on UC campus, which was west of South Hall, the shadow cast by the pole on June 21 would run directly on or very near to the edge of this buried ancient grid.

While the professor did not claim to have solved the entire mystery of the site, he believed that his speculations could be supported by the location's incontrovertible beauty:

> *What the object of this particular subdivision of this prehistoric square*
> *was, I know of no way of deciding: that is purely a matter of speculation,*
> *but the natural beauty of the position, the grandeur of the view on all*
> *sides, but especially the view of the Golden Gate, the entrance to San*
> *Francisco bay, where from this well marked prehistoric spot, at certain*
> *well known times of the year, the setting sun sinks to rest beyond the*
> *Pacific ocean, often in a grand halo of misty golden glory, that would*
> *thrill the soul of a sun worshipper to enthusiastic ecstasy, and make the*
> *spot, where now stands the university of California, a sacred spot for*
> *semi-annual pilgrimages where each family had its own abiding place on*
> *the national ceremonial site is probably as near truth as we can get, until*
> *further facts may be discovered.*[12]

While it was fairly easy to poke holes in Voyle's theories, his ideas about ceremonies occurring near that spot were not entirely unsupported. In fact, early European explorers observed sun ceremonies enacted by Bay Area Indians with

On the left, Professor Voyle's psychic compass is about to drop on a special point. On the right, Professor Voyle shows a woman the psychic compass indicating a point of significance.

much feeling and adoration. According to one explorer's account of an event he witnessed in the Bay Area, a sun ceremony was performed every day by an entire village, during which the members would gather and hold hands at sunrise to assist the sun in rising. This participation was part of the Indians' belief in their ability and duty to partake and assist in balancing the forces of their world. To them, waking up together, joining hands, and singing as the sun rose to help it in its daily ascent was their duty and their concern. Indian solstice ceremonies were also recorded at local Spanish missions. The Indians, still performing the duties of their own culture after joining the church, would try to convince the sun to reverse its path northward and keep the world from going dark. Voyle's speculations show at least some small degree of awareness of these cultural references.

No University of California professor wanted to address the merits of Voyle's theories. Voyle claimed to understand their keeping professional distance from him. He said that classical truth always laughed at what it did not understand, but that one day they would understand the true nature of this site on UC Berkeley's campus, and at that point they would give it another name.[13]

The *Sacramento Bee* had a field day with this story, poking fun at the students who believed Voyle's claims.[14] The students, armed with divining rods, repeated the demonstration—supposedly finding the same energy lines in the same places,

without prodding or instruction. To Voyle, his detractors were simply misguided; he believed they would come around to his way of thinking. The *Sacramento Bee* commented, "Still the doubters have one comfort. When Isaac Newton discovered the law of gravitation the people wouldn't believe him, even when he showed them the apple."[15]

To prove his case, on Monday, June 20, 1908, Voyle took one hundred fifty people up into the hills four miles from the UC campus where he showed them the lines of two long, low rock walls. Like a preacher, Voyle boomed: "There lies before you the remnants of the building of a city of the ancients."[16] The crowd gasped. He then announced that the walls, according to his survey, showed "regularity." The crowd gasped again, right on cue. The next day, Voyle met two hundred people at the north side of the Greek Theatre. The *San Francisco Call* mocked

Voyle and his followers, saying that they were there to be led "away from the conventional archeology, away from the bondage of modern geology to the promised land pointed out by divining rod and psychical compass."[17] Indeed, Voyle led them with the vigor of a mountain goat and the conviction of Moses, losing some of the less devout in the climb. One newspaper noted the division of labor that must have existed in the ancient civilization, as the women on Voyle's trek were carrying the divining rods and the men the lunch baskets.[18]

Afterwards, the *San Francisco Call* satirized the event:

> *The scientific world stands agape and palpitates with subdued expectation while Professor Voyle and the psychical society of Berkeley conduct their learned post mortem of the buried cities that underlie the University of California and its classic environs. . . . The* Call *rejoices in the learned labors of Professor Voyle and his band of psychics. He has found not one defunct metropolis, but a whole covey of buried cities. With the eye of faith he finds them, scorning the vulgar pickax. It is a triumph of mind over matter. The plodding paleontologers and anthropologers of the university, their kitchen middens and their stuffy piles of undisturbed bones, are put to shame by the easy process of psychical divination.*[19]

By the spring of 1909, Voyle was making national news on yet another "science" front:

> *Prepare, O reader, to fall upon the neck of Prof. E. J. Voyle, the Berkeley chemist, and weep tears of joy. For Prof. Voyle says he has made one of the greatest discoveries of the age, a method of removing the "drunk" from whisky, without diminishing that fluid's exhilarating power.*
>
> *Voyle's receipt takes the kick out of whatever alcohol you may imbibe, leaving all the food and recuperative powers to bear you up and sustain you. In other words, you shall live to spend the night with the boys and have no headache the morning after.*
>
> *Prof. Voyle says that the thing in whisky which causes all our woe is not alcohol, but "cynamide." Extract this and you may drink to your fill.*[20]

Voyle received national attention for his alcohol "studies" and even met with a congressman who was a temperance campaigner.

In 1910, Voyle, the "well known chemist and physicist,"[21] was no longer the president of the Berkeley Society for Psychical Research. But he had announced that, after losing his prized invention, a delicate earthquake predicting machine, in the 1906 earthquake and fire in San Francisco, he was able to finish his project anew. He claimed that this new instrument recorded tiny changes in "lines of forces" on earthquake faults two or three days before a quake.[22]

> *The sensitive needles which he has prepared readily respond to the action along these lines of force, and hence detect the coming quake days in advance, when cosmic forces are beginning to operate.*[23]

Although Voyle pursued many "scientific" projects, the buried city below the UC Berkeley campus grounds remained his favorite research project. He was a well-known character around Berkeley, and was often seen pacing with rapt countenance, looking down at his psychic magnetic compass and dutifully following wherever it guided him, around town or into the hills. If someone asked him why he seemed to go this way, then that, he would respond that previous earthquakes had disturbed the lines left by the ancients.[24]

In 1914, Voyle was interviewed in the *Oakland Tribune*. Still excited and further advancing his hypothesis about UC's buried ancient city based on his radium research, Voyle was convinced that the Indians had a knowledge of attractive power. From his early studies with a Cherokee Indian, he knew that Indians often hid their sacred things underground and that they marked special places, he said, so that only the "initiated" could locate them by the very techniques Voyle employed.[25]

In the 1914 interview, Voyle explained how in 1908 he had hiked up in the Berkeley Hills and found some loose rock north of Grizzly Peak. He ground it up and ran it through a fine sieve. He repeated this process a few times and believed he had seen tiny balls of gold that he subsequently ground flat in a mortar. He then wrote about his findings:

> *Finely divided gold has a very strong activity on the compass. So a small quantity of that finely ground and washed ore was probably used for special markings, for identifications and guidance to certain positions by those prehistoric scientists.*[26]

Voyle was now convinced that the Indians had marked the boundaries of the ancient UC Berkeley site, which he now called Campania, with radium packets, and his experiments proved this fact to him.[27]

Voyle even hired a boat to take him and his equipment beyond the Golden Gate, returning with "evidence" that the prehistoric peoples used certain gold-containing markers and their psychic compass to guide them into the Bay; he speculated that they would have taken in harbor and guide fees from ancient visiting ships. Voyle believed that they used concrete blocks on the ocean floor with radium markers in them just like the ones that he claimed were found in the waters off Tampa, Florida. He reasoned that these methods were more durable and less expensive than the methods used to guide ships into San Francisco Bay in 1914.[28]

During this period, the professor also talked about the condition of the lines laid by ancients in other parts of Berkeley. He told the *Oakland Tribune* that in the Claremont area the lines the ancients laid down were very disturbed and confused. He believed this was evidence that the prehistoric people occupied the region before the hills were lifted by seismic activity. The ancient lines in the flatlands, he claimed, were continuous and in excellent condition.[29]

Voyle's final address was 2226 Chapel Street in Berkeley. Following an operation at Berkeley's Roosevelt Hospital in the spring of 1915, people concerned with Voyle's health placed him in the Berkeley county infirmary. He had no relatives to help take care of him.

Though Joseph Voyle never earned the recognition of the university or academic community, he was still acknowledged and sometimes touted highly by the greater public. The *Oakland Tribune* described him thus: "Never a recognized man among the recognized scientists, yet an original investigator of untiring industry, Professor Voyle continued his studies to the day when his illness bade him halt."[30]

Berkeley Pioneer James B. Woolsey, tallest man in the center, visiting Yosemite Valley in the 1850s. Woolsey had come to Berkeley by horseback. When the new city of Berkeley told him it would put a public street through his property but that he could name it, he chose to name it after the horse that brought him to California. The horse was named Prince, and Prince Street is his legacy, the only street in town named after an animal.

ACKNOWLEDGMENTS

IN WRITING THIS BOOK, I HAD INVALUABLE HELP FROM MANY GENEROUS people and institutions. I thank the following associates and friends:

The Berkeley Civic Arts Commission made generous grants toward the production of this book. My special thanks to Mary Ann Merker and Charlotte Fredricksen of the commission and the Berkeley Architectural Heritage Associa-tion for acting as my fiscal agent; and to ex-Berkeley Mayor Jeffery Shattuck Leiter and Sylvia McLaughlin for their support and underwriting a portion of the printing of this book.

I acknowledge my heartfelt gratitude to Thomas A. Smart, Esq., Robert Barnes, Esq., and Victoria Haje, Esq., of the firm Kaye Scholer LLP, whose brilliant work in the copyright field resolved crucial issues regarding my use of historical material.

Penny Hearn Adams for sharing her family's history and images with me; Albany Fire Chief Marc McGinn and the Albany Fire Department; Alameda County Library, Albany Branch, Richard Russo and staff; the Baxter family for their generous donation of Berkeley images; the Berkeley Architectural Heritage Association and Wendy Markel, Leslie Emmington, Anthony Bruce, Carrie Olson, Susan Cernie, Stephanie Manning, Austene Hall, Sally Sachs, Daniella Thompson, and Janice Thomas; the University of California Bancroft Library, especially Susan Snyder, Erica Nordmeier, David Farrell, Peter Hanff, David Kessler, Dean Smith, and Iris Donovan; the Berkeley Firefighters Association and Michael Flynn, for his crucial help with my history endeavors, and Randy Olsen; the Berkeley Public Library History Room and Tom Fortin, Jane Scantlebury, Robert Saunderson, Alan Bern, and staff; the South Berkeley Branch Library and Jerri Ewart, Kay Finny, and staff; Sergeant Michael J. Holland, retired, head of the Historical Preservation Society of the Berkeley Police Department; the staff of the Blue and Gold Yearbook of UC Berkeley; the staff at Black Oak Books, Don Pretari, Nick Setka, Jeremy Vela, Herb Bivins, Sara Glickstien, and Kim Neilson for their support and thinking enough of my books to schedule book talks and good store space; John Bosko of Bosko's Framing Gallery on College Avenue, who always shares his unique finds with the joy of a believer; Dr. Gray Brechin, geographer and author of *Imperial San Francisco: Urban Power, Earthly Ruin*, for his willingness to donate his time and talents in support of my historical research; John Brennan, for sharing his pioneer family history and his willingness to listen; to Elizebeth Brennan for sharing her photos and for running Berkeley's best, Brennan's Tavern; Anthony Bruce, who generously shared Berkeley images from his personal collections for this book; Builders Booksource, especially George and Sally

---

DOG ARRESTED FOR STEALING DOUGHNUTS

Policeman Barff today arrested a foxhound on a charge of petit larceny. The dog was a hound pup which was caught stealing doughnuts from the Capital lunch counter on University avenue, near Shattuck and was taken by the officer to the police station.

Later it was learned that the dog belonged to Gladstone Morris, residing at 2229 Vine street, and when notified of the trouble into which his dog had gotten himself, Morris agreed to pay for the doughnuts if the dog were turned loose.

The dog was permitted to go home.

BERKELEY DAILY GAZETTE, MARCH 1, 1908.

—James Edgar hasn't slept a wink in a week because he dreamed that someone was going to steal his dog Logan.

BERKELEY ADVOCATE, SEPTEMBER, 30, 1882.

—We notice that quite a number of our Berkeley people have been lopping off their whiskers and moustachoes. Some call it the "Presbyterian Cut," as it seems mostly to prevail with members of that denomination. The ladies talk of the change as "horrid," and will not countenance it. One wife went even so far as to say that she would get a divorce if her husband "presisted" in his unnatural conduct.

BERKELEY ADVOCATE, DECEMBER, 23, 1882.

Kiskaddon; the California Alumni Association for their contributions; The California Historical Society for being so inspirational and the special help of David Crosson, who kindly wrote a profound forward for this book, and the truly talented help of Joe Evans, Darlene Plumtree, and Sy Russell; Laurel Collins for sharing her significant photo archive with me; the California State Library and Dawn L. Rodriques for their archives and assistance; the California State Archives for their Robert Lyle information; James Chanin, Esq., for the loan of his collections; the East Bay Regional Parks and Brenda Montano and Carol R. Victor for their prompt assistance; to the late Walter Crinnion, whose ancestors help build Berkeley and Virginia Crinnion for their support, friendship, and love of history; Allen Cohen for sharing a bit of his wide-ranging research on Berkeley history; Ray Colvig for his kind donation of historical images; the Contra Costa Historical Society for its inspiring facilities and collections, its love of history and especially the friendship and help of Betti Maffei (whose kindness, enthusiasm, and love of animals and history is always with me) and Mary-Ellen Jones, who has what it takes to make a difference; to the staff at Copy Central at 1553 Solano Avenue, who were always there to help a little more with a smile, especially manager Greg Tomeoni, Greg Schmalz, Lynn McBride, and Del Elliott; the staff at Cody's Books for kindly thinking enough of my books to have always given me a window to display historic photos from them; Charles Denson, Coney Island historian and author of *Coney Island: Lost and Found,* for his ideas and support and for suggesting the missing word in the title of the book; the Doe Library of UC Berkeley and Victoria Jourdan and staff at the Newspapers and Periodicals Room; to Judith Dunham, for her professional vision and her gifts of time and friendship; to Pamela Edelstein, whose careful copyediting contributed to the book's polish; Dr. Stephen Edwards, who I am sure is only posing as a modern man and really exists as a professor in the 1890s, for his friendship and for reading my manuscripts and offering such knowledgeable suggestions; the El Cerrito Historical Society and Tom Pannas for their support and donations to further my investigations into local history; Lisa Elliot of Elysium Design, for making *Berkeley 1900, Earthquake Exodus, 1906,* and this book the wonderful visual feasts they became through her skills; Dennis Evanosky for his friendship, his love of history, and his sharing of all that he finds without ever using notes; Kevin Fagan of the *San Francisco Chronicle,* whose writing, vision, and help were inspirational; Gary Fong of the *San Francisco Chronicle* for his able and kind help in procuring photos; the Douglas County Museum of Oregon and the kind efforts of Jena K. Mitchel for archiving and sharing information on Benjamin D. Boswell; Barbara Gamba, for sharing her treasured family photos, for editing an earlier version of this book, and for her friendship throughout; Gale

Garcia, who brought me a number of articles on topics I was writing on and edited an earlier version of this book; Berkeley's W. R. Gorman family for their generous donation of family photos; Dr. Elmer and Pam Grossman for their donation of historical images to my history endeavors; *Harper's* magazine and Irene M. Castagliola for use of their images; to Professor William E. Halpin of St. Mary's College whose friendship and wisdom have offered me guidance for a quarter-century; to Steven Hiatt, whose final editing and formatting prepared us to go to press with confidence; Sonoma County Library and Genealogy and Archives Librarian Anthony Hoskins, who helped track down what happened to Mary Townsend; Pat Jansen for generously sharing her family photos; Lila LaHood, who edited my manuscript and made it flow so well; Dr. Kent Lightfoot of the Anthropology Department and the Phoebe Hearst Museum of Anthropology at UC Berkeley, who defines the terms "a gentleman and a scholar"; Stephanie and Kurt Manning, for photo contributions and their decades of work in preserving West Berkeley; Malcolm Margolin, whose works in the fields of history and publishing have made such a huge impact that they are truly inspirational and for his taking time to write his comments on this book; Betty Marvin for her assistance and years of preservation work; Jeffrey Neidleman for sharing photos of old Berkeley; to Maggie Newsom, my friend, for reading every manuscript and offering valuable feedback; the North Point Gallery and Jessie Dunn-Gilbert for their in-depth and kind help with my research; the Oakland Fire Department, especially Chief Daniel Farrell for his time and kindness, and Captain Jeff Hunt, and Captain Dave Hector for sharing their photos; the *Oakland Tribune* and Theresa Martinez and Mario Dianda for their help; the Oakland Public Library History Room and Steve Lavoie, Simone Klugman, Kathleen Di Giovanni, and Lynn Culter for being such great people and operating such a unique place; the Oakland Public Library Newspaper and Magazine Room and Paul Schiesser, Terry Egan, George Celli, Ricardo Antoni, Siegfried Kutin, Joan Garvin, Nadina Wilson, and staff, for their professionalism and making my research much easier; the Pacific School of Religion and Ellen M. Weston and Russell Schock, for sharing their history and collections; Prudential California Realty and Ginny Cain for happily helping me gather material and kindly opening their photo collections to me; to Sue Rosenthal for reading my manuscripts and offering valuable advice; the San Francisco Public Library History Room staff, for always offering able assistance; San Pablo Historical Society for sharing its images and kindness; Marge Saarni for her donations of photos to my historical efforts; Sandra Sher, for sharing reference data and for her decades of being a friend of preservation; Melissa Schwarz, for reading my manuscripts and giving insightful feedback; to my second set of parents, Ben and Shirley Serota for their donation of their

A Sensible Girl.

A quiet, lady-like, neatly dressed young girl was passing along Shattuck avenue the other day enjoying the bright sunshine and intent on her own thoughts. There was nothing remarkable or noticeable about the young lady except that her right hand was bound in linen (she had a felon on one of her fingers) and her hair was cut short. A young fellow who earns an honest living by loafing around the streets and smoking cigarrettes noticed her as she passed by and began to sing "Chippie get your hair cut," and quick as a flash the young girl turned around and with her left hand gave the young hoodlum a blow in the face and passed quietly away, remarking to some bystanders, I won't allow anybody to call me "chippie" or insult me.

BERKELEY GAZETTE, FEBRUARY 29, 1888.

family photos and for being so amazing; ex-Berkeley Mayor Jeffery Shattuck Leiter, who opened his family's grand and important history to me; John Sobrero for keeping my Macintosh computer running and for his great help in setting up my website, www.richardschwartz.info; Pat Keats and the California Society of Pioneers Library for their help; St. Joseph The Worker Church for sharing its history collections; John Strohmeier of North Bay Books for sharing his always sage advice and enthusiasm on many aspects of publishing; Jerry Sulliger, for discussing Berkeley history with me so often and for his love of early Berkeley history, his constant dedication, years of work, and depth of knowledge in the field—his sharing of his work has been a source of constant support and an inspiration to my history endeavors, and many stories in this book came from his collections and able research assistance; *Sunset* magazine and Lorraine Reno for their use permissions for images; the great pioneer Teague family: Gary and Joan Herbertson, Gail Ramsey, Beverley Hansen, and Jim Herbertson and their families for being so open and excited over sharing their ancestors' history and making me a member of their special family; the late Madelyn "Mika" Wright, whose memories of ninety years in Berkeley will always be treasured; to Ten Speed Press, Phil Wood, and Hal Hershey who have been so uncommonly knowledgeable and kind in offering their time, resources, and experience to aid my efforts; Allen Kaplan (now retired) and Dave Zuckermann of the Tilden Park Nature Center, who have maintained a mutually sharing relationship with me; the United States Military Museum for its records and images; the United States Patent Office for posting patents online for all to utilize; Tara Weaver, whose suggestions in her conceptual edit were most helpful in shaping this book; the Western Train Museum for maintaining such a great place and Bart Nadeau and Harry Aitken for their able assistance; Richard Wessel, for his untiring search for lost Berkeley history and for sharing what he finds; Sarah Wickander, for being such an invaluable resource to many in the Berkeley history community; the Woolsey family, especially the late Dorthy Prouty for sharing her family's history with me; Steve Zerbe, a true professional researcher of history on the Civil War and many other subjects for his assistance; a special thanks to the late Hal Johnson of the *Berkeley Daily Gazette* and the late Louie Stein of Kensington, who together made the job of sharing history in the twenty-first century so much more rewarding through their monumental efforts of recording history and their love of this town.

And to my family for their support and caring: my parents, Milton and Mildred Schwartz; my brother-in-law Tom Smart and nephews Cody and Zach; my cousins Roberta, Merrideth, Dylan, and Rachael; my Aunt Blanche and Uncle Al; and my cousins Stevie, Andrea, Marcie, Candy, David, Sydney, Marlyn, and Herbie. To my sister Maxeen Smart, now departed: I remember you every day.

NOTES

CHAPTER 1

1. J. N. Bowen, "The Birthdays of Urban Communities," *California Historical Society Quarterly*, 31, no. 4 (December 1952): 328.
2. Alameda County Recorder's Office, Book of Deeds, Book E, pp. 468–493, July 1, 1856.
3. Natlee Kenoyer, *The Firehorses of San Francisco* (Los Angeles: Westernlore Press, 1970), 27.
4. Ibid., 52.
5. Ibid., 83.
6. Ibid., 32, 33.
7. Ibid., 65–67.
8. Hal Johnson, "Last of the Dunns," So We're Told, *Berkeley Daily Gazette*, March 18, 1954.
9. Ibid.
10. *Berkeley Daily Gazette*, May 4, 1914, Jerry Sulliger Collection.

CHAPTER 2

1. *Berkeley Daily Gazette*, July 14, 1941.
2. *Berkeley Daily Gazette*, January 11, 1908.

CHAPTER 3

1. William Warren Ferrier, *Berkeley, California: The Story of the Evolution of a Hamlet into a City of Culture and Commerce* (Berkeley: William Ferrier, 1933), 37.
2. Ibid., 284.
3. Federal Writers' Project, Works Projects Administration, *Berkeley: The First Seventy-Five Years* (Berkeley: Gillick Press, 1941), 32.
4. Ibid., 33.
5. Kevin Starr, "Has Religious Life Shaped the City? Intersections of Faith and Public Life," speech, October 6, 2004, San Francisco.
6. WPA, *Berkeley*, 34.
7. Ferrier, *Berkeley, California*, 45, 46.
8. Ibid., 81.
9. Ibid., 55.
10. Ferrier, *Berkeley, California*, 77; WPA, *Berkeley*, 40, 41.
11. Ferrier, *Berkeley, California*, 59, 60.
12. Ibid., 316.
13. *Berkeley Daily Gazette*, July 20, 1940.
14. Ibid., 56.
15. Ferrier, *Berkeley, California*, 315.
16. Ibid., 285.
17. Ibid.

CHAPTER 4

1. Hal Johnson, "Oldest Oldtimer," So We're Told, *Berkeley Daily Gazette*, October 14, 1952.
2. Hal Johnson, "Wildcat Canyon Farmer," So We're Told, *Berkeley Daily Gazette*, January 29, 1948.
3. Ibid.
4. J. P. Munro-Fraser, *History of Contra Costa County, California* (San Francisco: W. A. Slocum, 1882), 367.
5. Johnson, "Wildcat Canyon Farmer."
6. Hal Johnson, "45th Wedding Anniversary," So We're Told, *Berkeley Daily Gazette*, January 28, 1948.

CHAPTER 5

1. *Oakland Daily News*, February 20, 1871; M. W. Wood, *History of Alameda County, California* (Oakland: M. W. Wood, 1883), 356, 357.
2. *Oakland Daily News*, February 22, 1871.
3. *Oakland Daily News*, February 21, 1871.
4. *Oakland Daily News*, February 20, 1871.
5. *Oakland Daily Transcript*, February 18, 1871.
6. *Oakland Daily News*, February 20, 1871.
7. Wood, *History of Alameda County*, 358.

CHAPTER 6

1. *Berkeley Herald*, March 18, 1886.
2. Hal Johnson, "Oldtime Milk Boy Talks," So We're Told, *Berkeley Daily Gazette*, January 10, 1951.
3. Phil Teague/Herbertson family.
4. *Oakland Evening Tribune*, June 5, 1876.
5. Mary Bennett Ritter, *More Than Gold in California 1849–1933* (Berkeley: Professional Press, 1933), 189.
6. *Berkeley Daily Gazette*, March 24, 1913.
7. George A. Pettitt, *Berkeley: The Town and Gown of It* (Berkeley: Howell-North Books, 1973), 64.
8. *Berkeley Advocate*, November 10, 1877.
9. Pettitt, *Berkeley: The Town and Gown*, 63, 64.
10. *Berkeley Advocate*, October 11, 1877.
11. *San Francisco Call*, November 6, 1896.
12. *Berkeley Daily Advocate*, November 6, 1896.
13. Ferrier, *Berkeley, California*, 216.
14. Pettitt, *Berkeley: The Town and Gown*, 64.
15. *Berkeley Daily Advocate*, November 6, 1896.
16. *San Francisco Call*, November 6, 1896.
17. *Berkeley Daily Advocate*, November 6, 1896.
18. Ibid.; *San Francisco Call*, November 6, 1896.
19. *Berkeley Daily Advocate*, November 6, 1896.
20. Ibid.
21. Ibid.
22. *San Francisco Chronicle*, November 8, 1896.
23. *Berkeley Daily Advocate*, November 24, 25, 1896.

24. *Berkeley Gazette,* November 25, 1896.

25. *Berkeley Gazette,* December 1, 1896; *Berkeley Daily Advocate,* December 1, 1896.

26. *Berkeley Daily Advocate,* December 2, 1896.

27. *Berkeley Daily Gazette,* July 24, 1901.

28. Alameda County, Book of Deeds, Book 923, 319–21.

29. *Berkeley Daily Gazette,* March 24, 1913, from the Jerry Sulliger Collection; personal conversation with Jerry Sulliger.

30. *San Francisco Chronicle,* July 29, 1901.

CHAPTER 7

1. Declaration for an Original Invalid Pension, John E. Boyd, July 18, 1890. *General Index to Pension Files, 1861–1934,* T288, Reel 4J, Bowles, Daniel–Boyd, William H., National Archives, Washington, D.C.

2. John E. Boyd, *The Berkeley Heroine and Other Stories by Boyd, the Boss Baggage Buster of Beautiful Berkeley* (Berkeley: Berkeley Printing Company, 1899).

3. U.S. Naval History Division, *Dictionary of American Naval Fighting Ships, Volume 6, R–S* (Washington, D.C.: Department of the Navy, 1976).

4. Pettitt, *Berkeley: The Town and Gown,* 133.

5. *Berkeley Advocate,* March 17, 1877.

6. Hal Johnson, "Berkeley Baggage Smasher," So We're Told, *Berkeley Daily Gazette,* May 20, 1954.

7. *Berkeley Advocate,* September 25, 1880.

8. *Berkeley Advocate,* October 23, 1880.

9. *Berkeley Advocate,* November 27, 1890.

10. *Berkeley Advocate,* January 22, 1891.

11. *Berkeley Herald,* November 5, 1891.

12. *Berkeley Advocate,* November 5, 1891.

13. *Berkeley Advocate,* October 1, 1891; *San Francisco Call,* August 26, 1893.

14. Johnson, "Baggage Smasher."

15. Ibid.; *Berkeley Independent,* January 24, 1908; *Berkeley Daily Gazette,* June 29, 1901.

16. Pettitt, *Berkeley: The Town and Gown,* 133, 134.

17. Surgeon's Certificate, Pension Claim 598,363, John E. Boyd, *General Index to Pension Files, 1861–1934,* T288, Reel 45, National Archives, Washington, D.C.

18. Pension Declaration, John E. Boyd, July 18, 1890.

19. Surgeon's Certificate, Pension Claim 32,326, John E. Boyd, February 19, 1904, *General Index to Pension Files, 1861–1934,* T288, Reel 45, National Archives, Washington, D.C.

20. *Berkeley Daily Gazette,* May 8, 1906.

21. *Berkeley Daily Gazette,* November 14, 1907.

22. *Berkeley Daily Gazette,* January 29, 1912.

CHAPTER 8

1. *Overland Monthly* 19 (2nd series), no. 13 (May 1892): 450.

2. *Calcoin News* 15, no. 3 (Summer 1961): 91.

3. Andrew G. Jameson, "San Francisco's Emperor Norton I," *Bohemian Club Library Notes,* no. 119 (Summer 2002): 2.

4. Ibid.; William Drury, *Norton I, Emperor of the United States* (New York: Dodd, Mead & Company, 1986), 31.

5. *Calcoin News* 15, no. 3 (Summer 1961): 92.

6. Drury, *Norton I,* 32.

7. *Calcoin News* 15, no. 3 (Summer 1961): 93; Drury, *Norton I,* 41

8. *Calcoin News* 15, no. 3 (Summer 1961): 93.

9. Ibid., 94.

10. Drury, *Norton I,* 7.

11. *Overland Monthly* 19 (2nd series), no. 13 (May 1892): 452.

12. Drury, *Norton I,* 138; and http://www.ffic-heritageserver.com/storbank/sfhist/sfh5.htm.

13. See http://www.ffic-heritageserver.com/storbank/sfhist/sfh5.htm.

14. Drury, *Norton I,* 13.

15. David Warren Ryder, *San Francisco's Emperor Norton: The Story of Norton I, Emperor of America and Protector of Mexico* (San Francisco: Dulfer Printing, 1939).

16. Drury, *Norton I,* 107; Jameson, "San Francisco's Emperor Norton I," 13.

17. Ibid., 216.

18. Drury, *Norton I,* 220.

19. Jameson, "San Francisco's Emperor Norton I," 13.

20. Allen Stanley Lane, *Emperor Norton, the Mad Monarch of America* (Caldwell, Idaho: Caxton Printers, 1939), 187.

21. *Berkeley Advocate,* August 7, 1879.

22. *Berkeley Advocate,* July 31, 1879.

23. Lane, *Emperor Norton,* 187.

24. Ibid., 187.

25. Ibid., 187, 188.

26. *Berkeley Advocate,* March 5, 1879.

27. *Oakland Times,* January 12, 1880.

28. *San Francisco Call,* January 9, 1880.

29. *Overland Monthly* 19 (2nd series), no. 13 (May 1892).

CHAPTER 9

1. Richard Parks Thomas, et al. "Commercial History and Progress of California: Notes and Letters, 1881–1887." Bancroft Library, University of California, Berkeley (CD 794, pp. 1, 2, handwritten portion).

2. Ibid., pages 2, 3, handwritten portion.

3. Ibid., page 4, handwritten portion.

4. Ibid., page 5, handwritten portion.

5. Hal Johnson, "Garrison on Hilltop," *Berkeley Daily Gazette,* May 5, 1949.

6. Thomas, "Commercial History and Progress," pages 8, 9, handwritten portion.

7. Ibid., pages 10–12, handwritten portion.

8. Ibid., page 13, typed portion.

9. Thomas, "Commercial History and Progress," pages 6, 7, handwritten portion.

10. Ibid., page 7, handwritten portion; J. H. Stevenson, *Boots and Saddles: A History of the First Volunteer Cavalry of the War, Known as the First New York (Lincoln) Cavalry, and Also as the Sebre Regiment* (Harrisburg, Penn.: Patriot Publishing, 1879), 28.

11. United States et al., *The War of the Rebellion: A Compilation of Official Records of the Union and Confederate Armies*, Series 1, Vol. 5 (Serial #5) (Washington, D.C.: U.S. Government Printing Office, 1882), 449.

12. Thomas, "Commercial History and Progress," pages 8, handwritten portion; page 10, typed portion.

13. Thomas, "Commercial History and Progress," page 8, handwritten portion.

14. Stevenson, *Boots and Saddles*, 102.

15. Johnson, "Garrison on Hilltop."

16. Thomas, "Commercial History and Progress," page 13, handwritten portion, and page 2, typed portion.

17. Ibid., pages 2, 4, typed portion.

18. Ibid., page 7, typed portion.

19. George A. Pettitt, *History of Berkeley* (Berkeley: Alameda County Historical Society, 1976), 24.

20. *Berkeley Gazette*, September 19, 1896; *San Francisco Call*, September 15, 1895.

21. *Nevada State Journal*, March 30,1895.

22. Ibid.

23. Ibid.

24. *The Democratic Standard* (Coshocton, Ohio), March 22, 1895.

25. *Berkeley Advocate*, March, 1880.

26. Wilhelmine Cianciarullo, *Berkeley as I Knew It in the Early Days* (Berkeley: Berkeley Unified School District, n.d.).

27. Thomas, "Commercial History and Progress," page 11, handwritten.

28. *San Francisco Call*, May 29, 1900; United States Patent and Trademark Office,http://patimg1.uspto.gov/.piw?Docid=00138712&homeurl= http%3A%2F%2Fpatft.uspto.gov%2Fnetacgi%2Fnph-Parser%3FSect1 %3DPTO1%2526Sect2%3DHITOFF%2526d%3DPALL%2526p%3D1 %2526u%3D%25252Fnetahtml%25252FPTO%25252Fsrchnum.htm %2526r%3D1%2526f%3DG%2526l%3D50%2526s1%3D0138,712.PN. %2526OS%3DPN%2F0138,712%2526RS%3DPN%2F0138,712&Page Num=&Rtype=&SectionNum=&idkey=NONE&Input=View+first+page.

29. *Berkeley Daily Gazette*, April 11, 1908.

30. *Berkeley Advocate*, July 11, 1885; *San Francisco Examiner*, July 5, 1887; and *Berkeley Advocate*, June 27, 1888.

31. *Berkeley Advocate*, June 23, 1883.

32. *Berkeley Advocate*, July 11, 1885; "The Annual Entertainment Given to the Employees of the Standard Soap Company, La Loma Park, Monday, July 5, 1886," Berkeley Volunteer Firefighters Association; *Berkeley Advocate*, July 5, 1887; Thomas, "Commercial History and Progress," page 11, typed portion; *Berkeley Advocate*, June 27, 1888 and July 18, 1888; *Berkeley Advocate*, July 10, 1890.

33. Complete Pension File Records of 1st Lieutenant/Adjutant Richard Parks Thomas, Company F, 1st New York Cavalry Regiment, claim 298475, January 15, 1898, Department of the Interior, Bureau of Pensions, *General Index to Pension Files, 1861–1934*, T288, Reel 469, Thomas, George–Thomas, William.

34. *Berkeley Daily Gazette*, April 3, 1901; *Berkeley Daily Gazette*, August 31, 1901.

35. *Berkeley Advocate*, March 16, 1897.

36. Ibid.

37. *Berkeley Daily Gazette*, June 2, 1900.

38. Ibid.

39. Ibid.

CHAPTER 10

1. Cornelius Beach Bradley, "Walks about Berkeley," pp. 44–47 in Eva V. Carlin, ed., *A Berkeley Year* (Berkeley: Women's Auxiliary of the First Unitarian Church, 1898).

2. Kenneth Munford and Harriet Moore, "The Boswells of Boswell Springs," *Oregon Historical Quarterly* 83, no. 4, (1892): 363; and Complete Pension File Records of Major Benjamin D. Boswell, 4th West Virginia Regiment, 2nd West Virginia Veteran Infantry Regiment, *General Index to Pension Files, 1861–1924*, T288, Reel 43, Boreman, Thomas–Boulson, Kennett; *Sunday Oregonian* (Portland), June 1907.

3. Benjamin D. Boswell Pension Records.

4. Ibid.; Letter to Commissioner of Pensions by E. E. Boswell, September 27, 1908.

5. Munford and Moore, "The Boswells of Boswell Springs," 348.

6. Benjamin D. Boswell Pension Records, deposition of Emma E. Boswell, case no. 686, 130, June 18, 1910.

7. Ibid.

8. *Sunday Oregonian* (Portland), June 29, 1907.

9. Munford and Moore, "The Boswells of Boswell Springs," 349.

10. Ibid., 351.

11. Ibid., 355.

12. Ibid.

13. Ibid.

14. Hal Johnson, "Boswell's Ranch," So We're Told, *Berkeley Daily Gazette*, May 11, 1944.

15. *Oakland Daily Evening Tribune*, April 7, 1890.

16. *Berkeley Advocate*, June 13, 1888.

17. *Berkeley Advocate*, January 12, 1884.

18. *Berkeley Advocate*, March 13, 1890, June 26, 1890, and June 25, 1891.

19. *Berkeley Advocate*, June 5, 1890.

20. Munford and Moore, "The Boswells of Boswell Springs," 342.

21. Ibid., 365.

22. Ibid., 365–67.

23. Ibid., 366.

24. Ibid., 367.

25. State of California Archives, Robert Lyle File (Letter to Governor, undated, signed by many).

26. Munford and Moore, "The Boswells of Boswell Springs," 366.

27. Ibid.

28. Benjamin D. Boswell Pension Records, letter by G. H. Hursh, special examiner to commissioner of pensions, December 30, 1910, page 3.

29. *Berkeley Daily Gazette*, December 26, 1903; Ferrier, *Berkeley, California*, 307.

30. Munford and Moore, "The Boswells of Boswell Springs," 367.

31. *Oakland Tribune*, August 6, 1907.

32. Munford and Moore, "The Boswells of Boswell Springs," 368, 369.

33. Ibid., 368–70.

34. "Park and Playground Bonds," Berkeley Chamber of Commerce Campaign Committee, Election Wednesday, April 29, 1908.

35. Ibid.

CHAPTER 11

1. Hal Johnson, "Memento of Orinda," So We're Told, *Berkeley Daily Gazette*, March 7, 1950.

2. *Berkeley Advocate*, March 26, 1881, and June 24, 1882.

3. *Berkeley Advocate*, September 9, 1882.

4. *Berkeley Advocate*, April 4, 1888.

5. *Berkeley Advocate*, May 16, 1888.

6. Ibid.

7. *Berkeley Advocate*, October 1, 1887.

8. *Berkeley Advocate*, July 11, 1888.

9. *Berkeley Advocate*, December 18, 1889.

10. *Berkeley Advocate*, June 12, 1889.

11. Hal Johnson, "The Wagners of Orinda Park," So We're Told, *Berkeley Daily Gazette*, March 8, 1950.

12. Johnson, "Momento of Orinda."

13. *Contra Costa Gazette*, May 30, 1888.

14. Johnson, "Momento of Orinda."

15. Johnson, "The Wagners of Orinda Park."

16. Johnson, "Momento of Orinda."

CHAPTER 12

1. Photograph, Contra Costa Historical Society.

2. *Berkeley Advocate*, April 2, 1881.

3. Hal Johnson, "Wildcat Canyon Murder," So We're Told, *Berkeley Daily Gazette*, May 4, 1948.

4. Ibid.

5. State of California Archives, Supreme Court, Points and Authorities by Respondant, *People v. Robert Lyle*, 6.

6. Ibid., 5–7.

7. Dennis McCarthy to Governor Waterman, December 12, 1890, State of California Archives, Robert Lyle File, page 2.

8. Ibid.

9. W. W. Foote to Gov. James Budd, February 4, 1895, State of California Archives, Robert Lyle File.

10. Dennis McCarthy to Governor Waterman, December 12, 1890, page 1.

11. Letter to Governor Waterman, undated, signed by many, State of California Archives, Robert Lyle File.

12. Letter to Governor Waterman, December 8, 1890, signed by many, State of California Archives, Robert Lyle File, page 1.

13. Ibid., page 2.

14. Letter to Governor Waterman, undated, signed by many, State of California Archives, Robert Lyle File, page 2; Letter to Governor Waterman, December 8, 1890, signed by many, State of California Archives, Robert Lyle File, page 2.

15. *Tilden Nature News* 12, no. 8 (May–June 1960): 3.

CHAPTER 13

1. *Berkeley Advocate*, May 2, 1885 and April 4, 1885; and Hal Johnson, "Thompson's Hotel," So We're Told, *Berkeley Daily Gazette*, April 13, 1944.

2. Hal Johnson, "North Berkeley Tintype," So We're Told, *Berkeley Daily Gazette*, May 12, 1954.

3. Johnson, "Thompson's Hotel."

4. Ibid.

5. Ibid.

6. *Berkeley Advocate*, November 18, 1882.

7. C. C. Emslie, "City's History—Local Pioneer Tells of Trek to West Berkeley for Swim," *Berkeley Daily Gazette*, April 18, 1941.

8. C. C. Emslie, "City's History—Local Pioneer Tells of Fire That Razed Deaf, Blind Home," *Berkeley Daily Gazette*, April 17, 1941; Emslie, "City's History—Local Pioneer Tells of Trek to West Berkeley for Swim."

9. *Berkeley Advocate*, May 2, 1885.

10. Johnson, "Thompson's Hotel."

11. Ibid.

12. Johnson, "North Berkeley Tintype."

13. Johnson, "Thompson's Hotel."

14. Ibid.

15. Ibid.

16. Johnson, "'Ma' Thompson's Hotel." So We're Told, *Berkeley Daily Gazette*, June 3, 1948.

17. Johnson, "North Berkeley Tintype."

18. Johnson, "Thompson's Hotel."

CHAPTER 14

1. *Berkeley Daily Gazette*, January 18, 1902; and Hal Johnson, "Berkeley's Old Bill," So We're Told, *Berkeley Daily Gazette*, May 7, 1940.

2. Johnson, "Berkeley's Old Bill."

3. *Oakland Tribune*, September 12, 1917.

4. *Oakland Tribune*, July 11, 1919.

5. *Oakland Tribune*, October 6, 1917.

6. *Oakland Tribune*, May 9, 1909.

7. *Oakland Tribune*, April 29, 1909.

8. *Oakland Tribune*, May 9, 1909.

9. *Oakland Tribune*, July 7, 1909.

10. Johnson, "Berkeley's Old Bill."

CHAPTER 15

1. *Berkeley Advocate*, June, 1888.

2. *Berkeley Daily Gazette*, September 22, 1906.

3. Ibid.

4. Ibid.

5.   *Berkeley Daily Gazette*, January 22, 1907.

CHAPTER 16
1.   *Berkeley Daily Gazette*, February 17, 1905.
2.   See http://maxpages.com/modocwar.
3.   Ibid.
4.   Ibid.

CHAPTER 17
1.   *Oakland Tribune*, May 25, 1908.
2.   *Berkeley Daily Gazette*, June 22, 1908.
3.   *Oakland Tribune*, September 27, 1914; Andrew B. Booth, compiler,
     *Records of Louisiana Confederate Soldiers and Louisiana Confederate
     Commands* (Spartanburg, S.C.: Reprint Company Publishers 1984),
     948; and Stewart Sifakis, *Compendium of the Confederate Armies,
     Louisiana* (New York: Facts on File, 1992), 6, 7.
4.   *Oakland Tribune*, September 27, 1914.
5.   United States Census, 1870.
6.   United States Census, 1880.
7.   *San Francisco Call*, May, 27, 1910.
8.   *Oakland Tribune*, September 26, 1903.
9.   Ibid.
10. *Oakland Tribune*, May 30, 1906.
11. *Oakland Tribune*, September 27, 1914.
12. *Berkeley Daily Gazette*, May 30, 1908.
13. *Oakland Tribune*, September 27, 1914.
14. *Sacramento Bee*, "That Buried City Hoax."
15. Ibid.
16. *San Francisco Call*, June 22, 1908.
17. Ibid.
18. Ibid., and *San Francisco Call*, June 24, 1908.
19. *San Francisco Call*, June 24, 1908.
20. *Evening Times* (Cumberland, Md.), June 25, 1909.
21. *San Francisco Call*, May 27, 1910.
22. Ibid.
23. Ibid.
24. *Oakland Tribune*, September 27, 1914.
25. Ibid.
26. Ibid.
27. Ibid.
28. Ibid.
29. Ibid.
30. *Oakland Tribune*, March 29, 1915.

BIBLIOGRAPHY

MANUSCRIPTS AND DOCUMENTS COLLECTIONS
Jerry Sulliger Collection, Berkeley, California.

INTERVIEWS AND CORRESPONDENCE
Cohen, Allen. Personal conversations, 2000.
Garcia, Gale. Personal conversations, November 2003–August 2004.
Hoskins, Anthony, History, Genealogy and Archives Librarian, Sonoma County Library. Correspondence, October, 2006.
Kaplan, Allen. Personal conversations, 2000–2007.
Keats, Pat, California Society of Pioneers Library. Correspondence, January–September 2006.
Sulliger, Jerry. Personal conversations and correspondence, June 2003–present.
Zerbe, Steve, research archivist. Correspondence, July 2002–March 2007.

NEWSPAPERS
Berkeley Advocate
Berkeley Daily Advocate
Berkeley Gazette
Berkeley Daily Gazette
Berkeley Evening Standard
Berkeley Herald
Berkeley Independent
Berkeley Independent and Gazette
Berkeley Sun
Berkeley Voice
Berkeley World-Gazette
Contra Costa Gazette
Coshocton (Ohio) Democratic Standard
Cumberland (Maryland) Evening Times
Nevada State Journal (Reno)
Oakland Daily Evening Tribune
Oakland Daily News
Oakland Daily Transcript
Oakland Evening Tribune
Oakland Times
Oakland Tribune
Portland Sunday Oregonian
Roseburg (Oregon) Review
Sacramento Bee
San Francisco Call
San Francisco Chronicle
San Francisco Examiner

BOOKS AND OTHER MATERIALS
Appointment, Commission, and Personal Branch, Letters Received, 64 ACP 1872, Lt. Benjamin Boswell. Record Group 94: Records of the Adjutant General's Office, 1783–1917. U.S. National Archives microfilm.
Beach, William, A. M. *The First New York (Lincoln) Calvary from April 19, 1861 to July 7, 1865*. New York: The Lincoln Cavalry Association, 1902.
Beck, Warren A., and Ynez D. Hasse. "California and the Indian Wars: The Modoc War, 1872–1873," in *Historical Atlas of California*. Norman: Oklahoma State Univesity Press, 1974. Available at www.militarymuseum.org/Modoc1.html.
Berkeley Chamber of Commerce. "Park and Playground Bonds." Berkeley: Berkeley Chamber of Commerce Campaign Committee, 1908.
Berkeley Volunteer Firefighters Association. "The Annual Entertainment Given to the Employees of the Standard Soap Company, La Loma Park, Monday, July 5, 1886."
Blue and Gold Yearbook. University of California, Berkeley (1877, 1902).
Booth, Andrew B., compiler. *Records of Louisiana Confederate Soldiers and Louisiana Confederate Commands*. Spartanburg, S.C.: Reprint Company Publishers, 1984.
Boyd, John. *The Berkeley Heroine and Other Stories by Boyd, the Boss Baggage Buster of Beautiful Berkeley*. Berkeley: Berkeley Printing Company, 1899.
Bowen, J. N. "The Birthdays of Urban Communities." *California Historical Society Quarterly* 31, no. 4 (December 1952).
———. *California Historical Society Newsletter*, December 1952.
Calcoin News 15, no. 3 (Summer 1961).
Carlin, Eva V. *A Berkeley Year*. Berkeley: Women's Auxiliary of the First Unitarian Church, 1898.
Colquhoun, Jos. Alex. *Illustrated Album of Alameda County, California; Its Early History and Progress—Agriculture, Viticulture and Horticulture—Educational, Manufacturing and Railroad Advantages—Oakland and Environs—Interior Townships—Statistics, etc., etc.* Oakland: Pacific Press, 1893.
Cianciarullo, Wilhelmine. *Berkeley as I Knew It in the Early Days*. Berkeley: Berkeley Unified School District, n.d.
D. M. Bishop & Co. *Bishop's Oakland Directory*. San Francisco: B. C. Vandall (1876–1882).
Drury, William. *Norton I, Emperor of the United States*. New York: Dodd, Mead & Company, 1986.
Dyer, Frederick H. *A Compendium of the War of Rebellion*. 3 vols. New York: Thomas Yoseloff, 1959 [1908].
Faust, Patricia L., ed. *Historical Times Illustrated Encyclopedia of the Civil War*. New York: Harper and Row, 1991.
Federal Writers' Project, Works Projects Administration. *Berkeley, the First Seventy-Five Years*. Berkeley: Gillick Press, 1941.
Ferrier, William Warren. *Berkeley, California: The Story of the Evolution of a*

Hamlet into a City of Culture and Commerce. Berkeley: William Ferrier, 1933.

Gove, Otis M. *A Trip to Berkeley, Cal.* American Mutascope & Biograph Company, 1906; 3 min, 5 sec.

Hewett, Janet. *The Roster of Union Soldiers, 1861–1865. Vol. 13, Ohio (S–Z), West Virginia, Virginia.* Wilmington, N.C.: Broadfoot Pub. Co., 1997.

Husted, F. M. *Husted's Oakland, Alameda, Berkeley and Alameda County Directory.* Oakland: Enquirer Publishing Co. (1898–1910).

Jameson, Andrew G. "San Francisco's Emperor Norton I," *Bohemian Club Library Notes,* no. 119 (Summer 2002).

Johnson, Hal. "Baggage Smasher." So We're Told. *Berkeley Daily Gazette,* May 4, 1940.

———. "Berkeley's Old Bill." So We're Told. *Berkeley Daily Gazette,* May 7, 1940.

———. "Thompson's Hotel." So We're Told, *Berkeley Daily Gazette,* April 13, 1944.

———. "Boswell's Ranch." So We're Told." *Berkeley Daily Gazette,* May 11, 1944.

———. "Long Wedded Life." So We're Told. *Berkeley Daily Gazette,* November 9, 1945.

———. "45th Wedding Anniversary." So We're Told. *Berkeley Daily Gazette,* January 28, 1948.

———. "Wildcat Canyon Farmer." So We're Told. *Berkeley Daily Gazette,* January 29, 1948.

———. "Pioneer Is Laid at Rest." So We're Told. *Berkeley Daily Gazette,* May 3, 1948.

———. "Wildcat Canyon Murder." So We're Told. *Berkeley Daily Gazette,* May 4, 1948.

———. "Garrison On Hilltop." So We're Told. *Berkeley Daily Gazette,* May 5, 1949.

———. "Momento of Orinda." So We're Told. *Berkeley Daily Gazette,* March 7, 1950.

———. "The Wagners of Orinda Park." So We're Told. *Berkeley Daily Gazette,* March 8, 1950

———. "Old Time Milk Boy Talks." So We're Told. *Berkeley Daily Gazette,* January 10, 1951.

———. "Oldest Oldtimer." So We're Told. *Berkeley Daily Gazette,* October 14, 1952.

———. "Last of the Dunns." So We're Told. *Berkeley Daily Gazette,* March 18, 1954.

———. "North Berkeley Tintype," So We're Told, *Berkeley Daily Gazette,* May 12, 1954.

———. "Berkeley Baggage Smasher." So We're Told. *Berkeley Daily Gazette,* May 20, 1954.

Johnson, Mary. *The City of Berkeley: A History, From the First American Settlers to the Present Date.* Berkeley: Mary Johnson, 1924.

Kenoyer, Natlee. *The Firehorses of San Francisco.* Los Angeles: Westernlore Press, 1970.

Lane, Allen Stanley. *Emperor Norton, the Mad Monarch of America.* Caldwell, Idaho: Caxton Printers, 1939.

Lang, Theodore F. *Loyal West Virginia from 1861 to 1865.* Huntingdon, W.

Va.: Blue Acorn Press, 1998 [1895].

Langley, Henry G. *A Directory of the City of Oakland and the Town of Alameda for the Year Ending September 1, 1876, Embracing a General Directory of Residents and a Directory of Streets, Public Offices, etc.* Oakland: H. G. Langley (1874, 1876).

Munford, Kenneth, and Harriet Moore. "The Boswells of Boswell Springs." *Oregon Historical Quarterly* 83, no. 4 (1982): 341–70.

Oakland, Alameda and Berkeley City Directory Giving Name, Occupation and Residence of All Adult Persons, Together with a Street Directory. Oakland: L. M. McKenney & Co. (1883, 1884, 1886–1889).

Overland Monthly 19 (2nd ser.), no. 113 (May 1892).

Panorama of the Battle of Chattanooga. San Francisco Public Library, San Francisco History Center, 917461PM37.

Pettitt, George A. *Berkeley: The Town and Gown of It.* Berkeley: Howell-North Books, 1973.

———. *History of Berkeley.* Berkeley: Alameda County Historical Society, 1976.

Polk-Husted Directory Co. *Polk-Husted Directory Co.'s Oakland, Berkeley and Alameda Directory: Comprising an Alphabetically Arranged List of Business and Professional Men, Firms, Corporations and Private Citizens.* Oakland: Polk-Husted Directory Co, 1911–1918.

Powell, William H. *Powell's Records of Living Officers of the United States Army.* Philadelphia: L. R. Hamersly, 1890.

Ritter, Bennett Mary. *More Than Gold in California 1849–1933.* Berkeley: Professional Press, 1933.

R. L. Polk & Co. *Polk-Husted's Oakland (California) City Directory, Including Alameda, Berkeley, Emeryville and Piedmont.* Oakland: R. L. Polk & Co., 1921.

R. L. Polk & Co. *Polk's Oakland, Berkeley, Alameda City Directory.* Oakland: R. L. Polk & Co. (1925–1927).

R. L. Polk & Co. *Polk's Oakland (California) City Directory.* Oakland: R. L. Polk & Co. (1928, 1930, 1933).

Robert Lyle File. State of California Archives, Sacramento, California.

Roger D. Hunt Collection. U.S. Army Military History Institute, Carlisle, Penn.

Ryder, David Warren. *San Francisco's Emperor Norton: The Story of Norton I, Emperor of America and Protector of Mexico.* San Francisco: Dulfer Printing, 1939.

San Francisco Fire Department. "Order No. 1, as Amended, January 1895, Relative to Attending Horses of the Dept." Journal entry, San Francisco Fire Department Museum, www.sffiremuseum.org/journal.html.

Schwartz, Richard. *Berkeley 1900: Daily Life at the Turn of the Century.* Berkeley: RSB Books, 2000.

———. *Earthquake Exodus, 1906: Berkeley Responds to the San Francisco Refugees.* Berkeley: RSB Books, 2005.

Shuck, Oscar Tully, ed. *Sketches of Leading Representative Men of San Francisco: Being Original Sketches of the Lives of the Prominent Politicians, Lawyers, Divines, Pioneers, Merchants, Orators, Etc., Etc., of San Francisco.* New York: London and New York Publishing Company, 1875.

Sifakis, Stewart. *Compendium of the Confederate Armies, Louisiana*. New York: Facts on File, 1992.

Slocum, W. A. *History of Contra Costa County, California*. San Francisco, 1882.

Starr, Dr. Kevin. "Has Religious Life Shaped the City? Intersections of Faith and Public Life." Speech, Calvary Presbyterian Church, San Francisco, October 6, 2004; www.calvarypresbyterian.org/history/KevinStarrSpeech.php.

Stevenson, J. H. *Boots and Saddles: A History of the First Volunteer Cavalry of the War, Known as the First New York (Lincoln) Cavalry, and Also as the Sebre Regiment*. Harrisburg, Penn.: Patriot Publishing, 1879.

Stilwell, B. F. *Directory of the Township and City of Oakland Together with the Townships of Brooklyn and Alameda, for the Year 1869; Containing a Comprehensive List of their Inhabitants, with Their Places of Residence and Business; Also, Its Public Officers and Their Offices; Also, a Complete List of All Public Societies and Organizations, with Their Officers … Also, a Review of the History of the City of Oakland*. Oakland: B. F. Stilwell, 1869.

Thomas, Richard Parks. "Improvement in the Manufacture of Soap." United States Patent and Trademark Office, Patent 138,712, May 6, 1873.

Thomas, Richard Parks, et al. "Commercial History and Progress of California: Notes and Letters, 1881–1887." Bancroft Library, University of California, Berkeley (CD 794).

Tilden Nature News 12, no. 8 (May–June 1960).

United States. Complete Military Service Records of 1st Sergeant/Captain Benjamin D. Boswell. *Compiled Service Records of Volunteer Union Soldiers Who Served in Organizations from the State of West Virginia*. National Archives microfilm M508, Reel 114, Bo–Ce, Companies I, H, 4th West Virginia Regiment. Washington, D.C.: National Archives and Records Service, 1964.

———. Complete Military Service Records of 1st Lieutenant, Company F and Adjuant, 2nd Battalion, Richard Parks Thomas, 1st New York Cavalry Regiment. *Compiled Service Records of Volunteer Union Soldiers Who Served in Organizations from the State of New York*. National Archives microfilm M551, Reel 139, Te–Thomas. Washington, D.C.: National Archives and Records Service, 1960.

———. *Official Army Register of the Volunteer Force of U.S. Army for Years 1861–1865*. Washington, D.C.: Government Printing Office, 1865.

United States et al. *The War of the Rebellion: A Compilation of Official Records of the Union and Confederate Armies*, Series 1, Vol. 5 (Serial #5). Washington, D.C.: U.S. Government Printing Office, 1882.

U.S. Bureau of the Census. Ninth Census of the United States, Population, June 1870. Jerry Sulliger Collection, Berkeley, California.

———. Tenth Census of the United States, Population, June 1880. Jerry Sulliger Collection, Berkeley, California.

———. Twelfth Census of the United States, Schedule No. 1–Population, June 1900. Jerry Sulliger Collection, Berkeley, California.

U.S. Department of the Interior, Bureau of Pensions. Complete Pension File Records of 1st Lieutenant/Adjutant Richard Parks Thomas, Company F, 1st New York Cavalry Regiment, Claim 298,475, January 15, 1898. *General Index to Pension Files, 1861–1934*. National Archives microfilm, T288, Reel 469, Thomas, George–Thomas, William.

———. Complete Pension File Records of Major Benjamin D. Boswell, 4th West Virginia Regiment, 2nd West Virginia Veteran Infantry Regiment. *General Index to Pension Files, 1861–1934*. National Archives microfilm T288, Reel 43, Boreman, Thomas–Boulson, Kennett.

———. John E. Boyd, Declaration for an Original Invalid Pension. *General Index to Pension Files, 1861–1934*. National Archives, T288, Reel 4J, Bowles, Daniel–Boyd, William H.

———. John E. Boyd, Surgeon's Certificate, Pension Claim 32,326, February 19, 1904. *General Index to Pension Files, 1861–1934*. National Archives microfilm, T288, Reel 45, Bowles, Daniel–Boyd, William H.

———. John E. Boyd, Surgeon's Certificate, Pension Claim 598,363. *General Index to Pension Files, 1861–1934*. National Archives microfilm, T288, Reel 45, Bowles, Daniel–Boyd, William H.

U.S. Naval History Division. *Dictionary of American Naval Fighting Ships, Volume 6, R–S*. Washington, D.C.: Department of the Navy, 1976.

Wilson, Carl. "Berkeley Historical Society: Nut Hill." *Berkeley Voice*, May 23, 1984.

Wood, M. W. *History of Alameda County, California*. Oakland: M. W. Wood, 1883.

FRONT MATTER

Page ii: Private collection. / Page vi: Private collection. / Page vii: Teague/Herbertson Family. / Page x: Bosko's Framing Gallery. / Page xii: California Historical Society.

CHAPTER 1

Page 1: Oakland History Room, Oakland Public Library. / Page 2: Private collection. / Page 3: Bancroft Library, UC Berkeley, 1905.17147:68-PIC. / Page 4: Oakland Fire Department. / Page 5: *Harper's Weekly.* / Page 6: Private collection. / Page 8: Ben and Shirley Serota. / Page 9: Berkeley History Room, Berkeley Public Library. / Page 10: Contra Costa Historical Society. / Page 12: *Top,* Berkeley Firefighters Association; *bottom,* Oakland Fire Department. / Page 13: Private collection.

CHAPTER 2

Page 14: Berkeley Firefighters Association. / Page 15: *1892 Blue and Gold of the University of California.* / Page 17: Berkeley Firefighters Association.

CHAPTER 3

Page 20: Bancroft Library, UC Berkeley, Willey, samuel-PORZ. / Page 21: Bancroft Library, UC Berkeley. / Page 24: Bancroft Library, UC Berkeley, 1976.039:BB-AX. / Page 25: Bancroft Library, UC Berkeley, 1905.17039-PIC. / Page 26: *Top, San Francisco Chronicle,* April 29, 1928; *bottom, Illustrated History of the University of California,* p. 72. / Page 28: *Top,* private collection; *bottom,* Earth Sciences Map Room, UC Berkeley. / Page 29: Oakland History Room, Oakland Public Library. / Page 30: *Top,* Bancroft Library, UC Berkeley, UARC PIC 3:74; *bottom,* Bancroft Library, UC Berkeley, 1905.17125:33-PIC. / Page 31: *Left,* Bancroft Library, UC Berkeley, UARC PIC 3:221; top right, *Illustrated History of the University of California,* p. 26; right bottom, *The Golden Book of California,* California Alumni Association.

CHAPTER 4

Page 32: Private collection. / Page 33: *Top,* St. Joseph the Worker Church; *Bottom, History of Berkeley,* George Pettitt. / Page 34: History Room, Berkeley Public Library. / Page 35: Private collection. / Page 36: Berkeley Architectural Heritage Association. / Page 37: Private collection. / Page 38: Berkeley Firefighters Association. / Page 39: Contra Costa Historical Society. / Page 41: *Left,* Berkeley Historical Society, #RS227; *right,* Berkeley Historical Society. / Page 42: Contra Costa Historical Society. / Page 43: Private collection.

CHAPTER 5

Page 44: Bancroft Library, UC Berkeley. / Page 46: Private collection. / Page 47: Jerry Sulliger collection. / Page 48: Private collection. / Page 55: Penny Hearn Adams.

CHAPTER 6

Page 56: Collection of the Teague/Herbertson Family. / Page 58: *Top,* Berkeley History Room, Berkeley Public Library; *bottom,* private collection. / Page 59: Bancroft Library, UC Berkeley. / Page 60: Jeffery Shattuck Leiter. / Page 61: *Berkeley: The Town and Gown of It,* George Pettitt. / Page 62: Berkeley Firefighters Association. / Page 64: Private collection. / Page 65: Bancroft Library, UC Berkeley, 1905.17125:29-PIC. / Page 66: Berkeley Firefighters Association.

CHAPTER 7

Page 72: Prudential Realty. / Page 75: Private collection. / Page 76: Berkeley Firefighters Association. / Page 77: Berkeley Historical Society, #113.188.3177 / Page 82: Private collection. / Page 83: Pat Jansen. / Page 84: *Oakland Tribune,* July 29, 1905. / Page 85: Library of Congress Broadcasting and Recorded Sound Division, lcp003m3a29754. / Page 87: Private collection. / Page 88: Private collection.

CHAPTER 8

Page 94: *San Francisco Chronicle.* / Page 95: *Overland Monthly,* May 1892. / Page 98: *Overland Monthly,* May 1892. / Page 99: *Overland Monthly,* May 1892. / Page 100: Private collection. / Page 101: Berkeley Firefighters Association.

CHAPTER 9

Page 104: Private collection. / Page 105: Private collection. / Page 108: San Francisco History Center, San Francisco Public Library. / Page 109: San Francisco History Center, San Francisco Public Library. / Page 110: California Historical Society. / Page 111: Bancroft Library, UC Berkeley, 1905.17500 V.3:5-ALB. / Page 112: Private collection. / Page 113: *Top,* Berkeley History Room, Berkeley Public Library; *bottom,* private collection. / page 114: *Top right, 1884 Blue and Gold of the University of California; bottom right,* Jerry Sulliger collection; *all others,* private collection. / Page 115: Private collection. / Page 116: Bancroft Library, UC Berkeley, 1981.056:7-PIC. / Page 117: Broadside, *World's Fair Exhibition at New Orleans, Compliments of Standard Soap Co. San Francisco,* c. 1887, collection of the Oakland Museum of California. / Page 121: Sarah Wickander Collection. / Page 123: Bancroft Library, UC Berkeley, 1905.17055-PIC. / Page 124: *Top,* Prudential Realty; *bottom, Birdseye View of Berkeley, Cal. 1891,* Irwin and Johnson. / Page 125: Berkeley Historical Society. / Page 126: Berkeley Firefighters Association. / Page 127: Private collection. / Page 128: *Berkeley Daily Gazette,* 1925. / Page 129: Prudential Realty. / Page 130: *Top,* San Francisco History Center, San Francisco Public Library; *bottom,* California Historical Society. / Page 132: Collection of Anthony Bruce. / Page 133: Berkeley Historical Society, #147189xxx.

CHAPTER 10
Page 134: US Army Military History Institute, Roger D. Hunt Collection. / Page 136: Society of California Pioneers. / Page 137: *Left*, private collection; *right*, Illustrated History of the University of California. / Page 138: Bancroft Library, UC Berkeley, 1957.024:1-PIC. / Page 139: Prudential Realty. / Page 140: Private collection. / Page 142: Douglas County Museum. / Page 143: Collection of Penny Hearn Adams. / Page 147: Douglas County Museum. / Page 147: Douglas County Museum. / Page 149: Private collection. / Page 150: Private collection. / Page 151: Private collection. / Page 152: *Left*, private collection; *right*, Berkeley Architectural Heritage Association. / Page 153: Private collection. / Page 154: *Top*, private collection; *Bottom left, Berkeley Daily Gazette,* April 29, 1908; *bottom right, Berkeley Reporter,* April 28, 1908. / Page 155: *Top*, California History Section, California State Library; *bottom*, Berkeley Historical Society. / page 156: *Top, Beautiful Berkeley*, Youngs and Barry, 2nd edn., Berkeley, 1904; *bottom*, Albany Fire Department. / Page 157: *Top left*, private collection; *top right and bottom*, Berkeley Historical Society. / Page 159: Jeffrey Neidleman Collection.

CHAPTER 11
Page 160: Berkeley Historical Society, #1502. / Page 161: *History of Alameda County, California*, M. W. Wood. / Page 162: Oakland Public Library. / Page 165: Berkeley Historical Society. / Page 166: Contra Costa Historical Society. / Page 167: Contra Costa Historical Society. / Page 168: Contra Costa Historical Society. / Page 169: Contra Costa Historical Society. / Page 170: *Top*, Contra Costa Historical Society; *bottom*, private collection. / Page 171: *Top*, Contra Costa Historical Society; *bottom*, private collection.

CHAPTER 12
Page 172: Berkeley Historical Society, #RS229. / Page 173: Private collection. / Page 174: Contra Costa Historical Society. / Page 175: East Bay Regional Parks and Laurel Collins Collection. / Page 177: California State Archive. / Page 178: *Top*, private collection; *bottom*, California State Archive. / Page 179: California State Archive. / Page 180: Contra Costa Historical Society. / Page 181: Private collection.

CHAPTER 13
Page 182: Berkeley Historical Society, #3165. / Page 184: Prudential Realty. / Page 187: Berkeley Historical Society, #3164.

CHAPTER 14
Page 188: Berkeley Firefighters Association. / Page 189: *Ancient Poetry*, John E. Boyd, B. B. B., Eagle Press, Berkeley 1907. / Page 190: Sarah Wickander Collection. / Page 191: *Left*, California Historical Society; *right, The Berkeley Heroine*, John E. Boyd. / Page 192: *1902 Blue and Gold of the University of California*. / Page 193: *Left*, Anthony Bruce Collection; *right*, Berkeley Firefighters Association. / Page 194: San Francisco History Center, San Francisco Public Library. / Page 195: Oakland History Room, Oakland Public Library. / Page 196: *Berkeley Daily Gazette*, April 20, 1909. / Page 197: *Berkeley Daily Gazette*, April 1909.

CHAPTER 15
Page 198: US Patent Office. / Page 199: Berkeley Firefighters Association. / Page 200: Bancroft Library, UC Berkeley, 1905.17053-PIC. / Page 201: *Top*, History of University of California; *bottom*, Berkeley Firefighters Association. / Page 202: Berkeley Architectural Heritage Association. / Page 203: Private collection.

CHAPTER 16
Page 204: Private collection. / Page 205: Private collection. / Page 206: Private collection.

CHAPTER 17
Page 208: Private collection. / Page 210: *Oakland Tribune*, September 27, 1914. / Page 214: *Oakland Tribune*, September 27, 1914. / Page 215: *San Francisco Call*, June 22, 1908.

BACKMATTER
Page 220: Private collection.

INDEX